The Tokyo Trials:

A Functional Index to the Proceedings of the International Military Tribunal for the Far East

Paul S. Dull and Michael Takaaki Umemura

Ann Arbor: The University of Michigan Press

Center for Japanese Studies · Occasional Papers No. 6

Paperback ISBN: 978-0-472-75113-6

Second printing 1962

Occasional Papers is published by the University of Michigan, Center for Japanese Studies. Director and Editor: Richard K. Beardsley. All correspondence should be directed to the University Press, Ann Arbor, Michigan, U.S.A.

PHOTOLITHOPRINTED BY CUSHING - MALLOY, INC.
ANN ARBOR, MICHIGAN, UNITED STATES OF AMERICA
1962

EDITORS' NOTE

The Proceedings of the Military Tribunal for the Far East have long been recognized as a major source for scholars working in the field of recent Japanese history and politics. At great expense of time and energy Professor Dull and Mr. Umemura have provided an index to the nearly fifty thousand pages of the Proceedings of the Tribunal. The Center for Japanese Studies is happy to be able to publish what it considers a most valuable research tool.

In addition to the compilors the editors wish to thank Donald Shore who aided in the preparation of the manuscript for publication.

PREFACE

The authors have compiled this functional index of the *Proceedings of the International Military Tribunal for the Far East* to enable the serious researcher to find his way through the some fifty thousand pages of subject material. Our own experience in trying to utilize the *Proceedings* without an index showed that this material could be categorized and systematized for the researcher in a number of equally useful ways. The decisions reached arbitrarily thus reflect our own particular attitudes in our approach to the problem. To use this index seriously will require, as any index does, study of the techniques used by the authors. We should like to emphasize that we are not professional constructors of indexes, but rather researchers who saw the necessity for an index and who could no longer wait for a professional to undertake the task. We hope nevertheless that our work will help others whose research leads them to these *Proceedings*.

The index covers all the material included in the *Proceedings of the Military Tribunal for the Far East* but nothing more. If an exhibit was made part of the record it was included. Rejected documents, and documents not read into the record, the judgments, and *Proceedings in Chamber* were not included. However, all defense exhibits rejected by the tribunal were noted under the category, "Tribunal Ruling, Document, Rejection of defense document."

Since there already exists an adequate name index of the *Proceedings*, names of counsel and witnesses other than defendants were not included.[1] The researcher will find it helpful to use the name index along with this functional index. The *Proceedings* available to the authors had, in a few instances, pages missing (pp. 41916-42110). Attempts to secure those missing pages from other sources were unsuccessful, and in a very few cases, we have had to use the notation "(unable to include in index)" to indicate this deficiency. However, because of the very small amount of material involved, it is felt that this lack will not seriously hamper the user of the index.

The basic model upon which this index was patterned was the *Subject Index to the Nuremberg Military Tribunal*. However, the authors tried to expand the number of subjects included and to subdivide them in greater detail. Moreover, the peculiar circumstances of the International Military Tribunal for the Far East made modifications of the original model necessary. Three major modifications were:

1. Within a subject category, any testimony, affidavit or interrogation of a defendant or defendants bearing upon this subject was included and notations of testimony, affidavit, or interrogation were made. Thus, it is possible to examine, beyond a defendant's general case, his relationship with any particular event from his standpoint. The authors felt the necessity, in such a broad criminal trial where twenty-eight defendants were tried, to link the defendant with each of the acts for which he was accused of criminal action. This would be particularly true when a researcher studying a particular defendant must weigh all the evidence for and against the accused.

2. The authors have established categories of the countries against which Japan was charged to have prepared, initiated and waged an aggressive war and have included the evidence presented by both the prosecution and defense relative to these categories. We have further made the notation for each of the countries of the prosecution and defense cases and the prosecution and defense summations. The problem which we constantly faced was the inconsistency on the part of both the prosecution and defense in presenting their cases. The prosecution separated its case into fourteen divisions. The defense, while meeting the prosecution in each of the major points, separated its presentation into five long divisions. As a result, defense evidence often related to two or more of the prosecution's divisions. The authors wish to emphasize that, therefore, despite the citation of each division of the prosecution and defense cases, a division may contain evidence which

---

[1] General Index of the Record of the Defense Case (International prosecution section document No. 0008), 1947; General Index of the Record of the Prosecution's Case (International prosecution section document No. 0005), 1947.

logically belongs elsewhere or which bears upon more than one division. The following illustrations indicate this difficulty:

- (a) Prosecution case: *Atrocities against civilians and others and the use of opium and other drugs in China.* Under this division, the prosecution presented evidence related not only to China but also to Manchuria and other Far Eastern areas, including Formosa and Korea. The defense presented evidence related to the use of opium in its China and Manchurian divisions. Thus there was no clear-cut dividing line drawn.

- (b) Prosecution case: *Individual responsibility*. The prosecution submitted much evidence without designating against which defendants it was directed. The defense handled its individual responsibility case on a strictly individual basis.

- (c) For the defense, there was neither a *French* division nor a *Netherlands* division to meet such prosecution divisions. Rather, the defense placed these two countries into its *Pacific War* division on the grounds that Japan never considered her actions against these two countries as aggression.

- (d) The defense met the prosecution's division: *Atrocities*, with its subdivision: *Prisoners of War*.

- (e) The defense in its *Russian* division dealt with both Russo-Japanese relations and collaboration among Germany, Italy and Japan. The latter category was presented as a separate division by the prosecution.

3. Subjects of law and courtroom procedure were expanded under the main headings of *Defense, Prosecution, President of Tribunal, Tribunal Law and Tribunal Ruling* so that a study of these subjects, hitherto a neglected field of inquiry, may now be made.

The names of Matsuoka Yosuke, Nagano Osami and Okawa Shumei were stricken from the indictment during the trials, and hence we have disregarded these men as defendants. However, their names were included, for the sake of consistency, under the category of defendants.

We wish to extend our sincere appreciation for the help we received in making this index. The project was initially made possible by grants given by the University of Oregon Graduate School. We are particularly indebted to Martin Schmitt and Inez Fortt of the Oregon Special Collection Division, and P. D. Morrison and R. D. Marshall of the Social Science Division of the University of Oregon Library for their valuable suggestions, and to Frances Pickett and Shirley Mikkelsen for their work in preparing the manuscript. An apology and a special thanks must be given to the wife of one of the authors, Ruth Dull, for her patience and her energy in proofreading the entire manuscript. Our gratitude goes also to many others who have helped in various ways, but who must go unmentioned. The authors, of course, assume full responsibility alone for the final manuscript.

Paul S. Dull
Michael Takaaki Umemura

May 11, 1956

The Tokyo Trials:

A Functional Index to the Proceedings of the International Military Tribunal for the Far East

INDEX TO MILITARY TRIBUNAL PROCEEDINGS

A

Accounts Bureau, Ministry of Finance ... 606

Accounts Section (*See:* Ministry of Foreign Affairs, Secretariat)

"Address to Young Men," Article by Hashimoto (Defendant) ... 11689-94; 15700-04

Aggressions (*See also:* China, Collaboration among Germany, Italy and Japan; Great Britain; France; Manchuria; Netherlands; Preparation for War; US; USSR):

  China:
    Economic aggression against:
      Pros. ... 4999-5847; Def. ... 20485-22399; Pros. summation 39326-517; Def. summation ... 42854-938
    Military aggression against:
      Pros. ... 3239-885; Def. ... 20485-22399; Pros. summation ... 39191-325; Def. summation ... 42854-938

  France and French Indo-China (FIC):
    Military aggression against:
      Pros. ... 6700-7195; Def. ... 26829-947; Pros. summation ... 39326-517; 39519-735; Def. summation ... 43050-175

  Great Britain:
    Military aggression against:
      Pros. ... 9263-11628; Def. ... 24763-27116; 36964-78; Pros. summation ... 39519-735; Def. summation ... 43050-222

  Manchuria:
    Economic aggression against:
      Pros. ... 4999-5847; Def. ... 18630-20485; Pros. summation ... 39061-190; Def. summation ... 42515-616
    Military aggression against:
      Pros. ... 1678-3238; Def. ... 18630-20485; Pros. summation ... 39061-190; Def. summation ... 42515-616

  The Netherlands:
    Military aggression against:
      Pros. ... 11629-12345; Def. ... 24763-27116; 36964-78; Pros. summation ... 39328-735; Def. summation ... 43050-222

  US:
    Military aggression against:
      Pros. ... 9263-11628; Def. ... 24763-27116; 36964-78; Pros. summation ... 39519-735; Def. summation ... 43050-222

  USSR:
    Military aggression against:
      Pros. ... 7213-8182; 31824-32199; 38197-575; Def. ... 22400-24762; 28062-84; 37103-63; Pros. summation ... 39736-976; Def. summation ... 42697-850

Air Raid Defense General Headquarters ... 612

Alcohol Monopoly (*See:* Government Monopolies)

Amau Declaration ... 9395; 25928-29

  Harada-Saionji memoirs concerning ... 37662-63

  Hirota-Lindley conversation concerning ... 29579-85

  Hirota's instructions after ... 29585-88

Ambon Islands (*See also:* GEA Policy; the Netherlands):

  Atrocities at ... 13928-14065; 40168-69; 40202-03; 40232-35; 40265-67; 40293-94; 40314-16; 40338-39

Andaman and Nicobars (*See:* Free Indies; GEA Policy):

  Atrocities at ... 13185-200; 30195-213; 30239-46; 40235-36; 40267; 40316

Anti-Comintern Pact (*See also:* Collaboration among Germany, Italy and Japan):

  Conclusion of, report concerning ... 5931-32; 5958-67

  German mediation in China Incident ... 5983-85; 5987-90; 5993-6000; 6002-15; 38750-51

  German proposal for negotiation for, Japan's reaction to ... 33716-27; 33730-59; 33767-70; 33772-810

  Harada-Saionji memoirs concerning ... 37767-68; 37770-71; 37773; 37779; 37782-84; 37789-92; 37804-05

Hiranuma (Defendant) ... 30333-36; 34009-10

Hungary and Manchuria, participation of ... 6037-45

Itagaki (Defendant):
  Aff. and test. concerning ... 30010-11; 34141-45
  Harada-Saionji memoirs concerning ... 37767-68; 37782-841 (*See also:* 30491-94; 30497-98)

Anti-Comintern Pact *(Cont.)*

   Kido (Defendant):
     Aff. and test. concerning ... 30864-66; 31528-31; 31567-69
     Harada-Saionji memoirs concerning ... 37804-05

   Matsuoka (Defendant):
     Conferences with Goering concerning ... 6533-37
     Conferences with Hitler concerning ... 6477-80; 6537-45
     Conferences with Ribbentrop concerning ... 6498-532; 6546-52

   Military Collaboration between Germany and Japan ... 6157-58 (*See also:* Collaboration among Germany, Italy and Japan)

   Oshima (Defendant):
     Aff. and test. concerning ... 33700-13; 33716-27; 33730-59; 33767-70; 33772-810; 33976-79; 33984-88; 33997-34014; 34077-149; 34318-23; 34337-39; 34340-43; 35400-05; 35429-36
     Appointment of ambassador to Germany, telegram concerning ... 34340-43
     Conference with Himmler ... 6026-28
     Conference with Himmler, Oshima's denial concerning ... 33764-67; 33770-72; 33923-24; 33991-97; 34331
     Conference with Ribbentrop ... 6459-68
     Harada-Saionji memoirs concerning ... 37767-68; 37770-71; 37773; 37779; 37782-84; 37789-92; 377804-05
     Interrogations concerning ... 5910-25; 6021-29; 7891-92
     Military attache, as ... 33983-86; 34100-02; 34111-13; 37055-79
     Relations with Germany under, aff. and test. ... 33393-94; 33961-64; 33976-79; 34062-66; 34070-77; 37055-79; 37080-100
     Secret agreement with Germany ... 6095-102; 22539-50; 33987-88; 34002-07
     Telegrams received by, concerning ... 34116-19

   Privy Council meeting concerning ... 5968-69; 6037-45

   Shiratori (Defendant):
     Aff. and test. concerning ... 6083; 16914; 33131-32; 33736-39; 33747-51; 34084-86; 34121-28; 34824-25; 34907-17; 35085-87; 35097-109
     Appointment of ambassador to Italy, aff. and test. ... 6083; 6092; 16914; 34907-17; 35031-35; 35088-91
     Harada-Saionji memoirs concerning ... 37779; 37782-84; 37808-09 (*See also:* 30491-94; 35040)
     Relations with Germany ... 34849-903

   Relations with Italy ... 34824-27

   Togo (Defendant):
     Absence from Tokyo when Italy joined pact ... 35416
     Aff. and test. concerning ... 34092-100; 34122-25; 34912; 35342-43; 35391-94; 35403; 35408-15; 35453-57; 35464-66; 35486-87; 35522-26; 35642-50; 35657-58

Anti-Japanese Traitors—Slaying Band ... 4639-40

Applications and Motions (*See also:* Tribunal Ruling, Applications and Motions):

   Defense:
     Affidavits:
       Cross-ex., presentation of affidavits for ... 11311-12; 11338-39
       Grew's affidavit, addition to ... 10206-08
       Interrogations of defendants in lieu of ... 26267-74
       Okawa, Mrs., affidavit, leave to file, concerning med. ex. ... 16993-95
       Revised affidavit, be offered at a later date ... 29376
       USSR pros. affidavits, production of ... 8086
     Anti-Comintern Pact, be stricken from the record ... 6049
     Chamber:
       Offensive language, exception for, question concerning ... 17782
       Proceedings in, be made part of the record of transcript ... 3154; 36986
     Changkufeng:
       USSR pros. evidence concerning, be stricken from the record ... 7782-86
     Cross-examination:
       Affidavits, presentation of, for cross-ex. ... 11311-12; 11338-39
       Scope of ... 2664-67
       USSR pros. wit., cross-ex. of, for rebuttal, be reserved until further ex. of USSR pros. doc. ... 38425
     Defendants:
       Admission of defendants made after completion of conspiracy against other defendants ... 2782-84
       Ambassadorial immunity ... 5894-98
       Calling of Shimada concerning Togo testimony ... 36963-64
       Consultation with Counsel during recess ... 3879
       Conventional war crimes, defendants be linked with atrocities case ... 11237-80
       Documents, acceptance of, only if defendants are presenting their evidence ... 30115-16
       Evidence of death of Nagano ... 14306-07
       General motion to dismiss on behalf of all defendants ... 16663-712
       General motion to dismiss on behalf of all defendants, renewal of ... 38946-47

INDEX TO MILITARY TRIBUNAL PROCEEDINGS 3

Individual case, defendants, reconsideration of tribunal ruling concerning ... 19751-54
Individual motion to dismiss ... 16275; 16277-661
Interrogations of defendants in lieu of affidavits ... 26267-74
Interrogation of Muto, reading of excerpts from, be suspended ... 3441
Interrogation of Oshima, correction of errors in, tribunal ruling concerning ... 5919-20
Lack of jurisdiction by tribunal ... 120-36; 180-92; 195-215; 220a-32; 280-85
Medical ex. of ... 1535-36
Motion to dismiss on behalf of eleven defendants ... 16262
Motion to disregard testimony of Tominaga on ground testimony given on direct ex. to interrogatories ... 16260
Opening statement for Dohihara and Hiranuma be permitted ... 17007-08
Opening statement, individual defendants be permitted to object to ... 18660
Recalling of Shimada ... 35859; 37022-24
Redirect ex. of, on behalf of other defendants, exception to, tribunal ruling concerning ... 20099

Defense counsel:
Additional American def. counsel ... 1838-41
Blakeney to make objection as second counsel for Umezu ... 2152-53
Conference with defendants during recess for further cross-ex. ... 3879
Def. ind. motion to dismiss, def. counsel's right to make objection to pros. statement concerning ... 16770-72
Documents, def. counsel's right to object to ... 13206; 26323
Documents, def. counsel's right to receive copies of certificate of ... 6907-08
Japanese def. counsel to confer re counsel Smith's withdrawal from proceedings, recess for ... 17777-80
Pros. statement, def. counsel's right to object to ... 16770-72
Reading doc. into evidence ... 1809
Re-direct ex., suspension of, until def. be supplied with copies of doc. ... 22660
Warren, counsel, for Hiranuma ... 16331
Wit., direct-ex. of, def. counsel's right to conduct, before pros. presentation of case ... 1354-55; 1549

Dismissal of indictment:
Bill of particulars re Hiranuma, Matsuoka, Shigemitsu, Togo and Umezu not contained in ... 307-15
General motion to dismiss on behalf of all defendants ... 120-303; 16663-712; 38940-44
General motion to dismiss on behalf of all defendants, renewal of ... 38946-47
Individual motions to dismiss ... 16275; 16277-661
Lack of jurisdiction of tribunal ... 120-36; 180-92; 195-215; 220a-32; 280-85

Motion to dismiss on behalf of eleven defendants ... 16262
Motion to dismiss on some of changes ... 13577-79
Question of law, to file brief of authorities on ... 34376

Documents:
Acceptance of, only if defendants are presenting their evidence ... 30115-16
Authenticity of, information concerning ... 11891-92
Certificate, def. counsel's right to receive copies of ... 6907-08
Copies of, reconsideration of tribunal ruling concerning ... 22559-62; 22564-67
Doc. be stricken from the record (See also: Evidence be stricken from the record) ... 14904
Examination of ... 1041
Identification of ... 19460-62; 29880
Individual case, in, presentation of doc. ... 19171-73; 19175
Judicial notice for def. doc. ... 36970-72
Number be given prior to pros. presentation of ... 13508-09
Order, modification of, concerning def. doc. ... 6833-39
Photostatic copies, substitution of for the originals, tribunal ruling concerning ... 3071-72
Presentation of doc. in full ... 4113; 22871; 36922-23
Probative value of ... 20811-12
Reading of doc. into evidence ... 1809; 9353; 18115

Dohihara (Defendant):
Opening statement for Dohihara, reserve right to make ... 17007-08

Evidence:
Certification of, def. counsel's right to receive copies of ... 6907-08
Evidence be stricken from record ... 23732-33; 23785-87; 23857-58; 32914-15; 35364
Mitigation, in ... 37367
Pros. summation of, be stricken from the record ... 12069
Scope of, to be offered in def. ind. case, reply to pros. application concerning ... 28098

Extra-comment be stricken from record ... 16003; 16011
French Indo-China, atrocities in, be stricken from record ... 15471-72
Grew, affidavit by, addition to ... 10206-08
Harada-Saionji memoirs, three versions of, production of ... 37522; 37526-28

Hiranuma (Defendant):
Counsel Warren be permitted for ... 16331
Kido's diary, entirety, be offered on behalf of ... 1932
Opening statement for Hiranuma, reserve right to make ... 17007-08
Transfer from Sugamo Prison to Tokyo Imperial Hospital ... 2128-29

Applications and Motions *(Cont.)*
  Defense *(Cont.)*
    Itagaki (Defendant):
      Judicial hearing against prisoner of war ... 285-92
    Interrogations of defendants:
      Admissibility of ... 25667
      Admissibility of, on behalf of other defendants, tribunal ruling concerning ... 2898
      Affidavits, in lieu of ... 26267-74
      Correction of errors in interrogation of Oshima, tribunal ruling concerning ... 5919-20
      Reading of excerpts from interrogation of Muto be suspended ... 3441
      Re-direct ex. of defendants by counsel on behalf of other defendants ... 20099
    Interrogations of witnesses:
      Record of, be submitted to the tribunal ... 1566
    Judicial hearing:
      Prisoners of war (Itagaki, Kimura, Muto, Sato), against ... 285-92
    Judicial notice:
      Def. doc., for ... 36970-72; 36973-78; 37173-75
    Kido (Defendant):
      Diary by, inspection of ... 1931-32
      Diary by, presentation of the entire text of, on behalf of Hiranuma ... 1932
      Diary by, pros. reading of excerpts from, tribunal ruling concerning ... 1930
      Evidence in mitigation ... 37367
    Kimura (Defendant):
      Judicial hearing against prisoner of war ... 285-92
    Litvinov's diary:
      Entire text, production of ... 22871
    Matsuoka (Defendant):
      Confinement in sanitarium, and name stricken from indictment ... 327-28
    Muto (Defendant):
      Interrogation of Muto, reading of excerpts from, be suspended ... 3441
      Judicial hearing against prisoner of war ... 285-92
    Nagano (Defendant):
      Death, evidence of ... 14306-07
    Nomonhan (or Nomonghan):
      Maps of, def. counsel be supplied with copies of ... 23721
    Okawa (Defendant):
      Medical examination of ... 1535-36
      Mrs. Okawa's affidavit, leave to file, concerning med. ex. ... 16993-95
      Name stricken from indictment ... 329-32
    Opening statements *(See also:* Defense; Defendants):
      Copies of, in English and Japanese, def. counsel's right to receive ... 8180
      Def. opening statement of Pacific war case be postponed until after recess ... 24165
      Def. opening statement def. counsel's right to object to ... 17009
      Delivery of, to def. 24 hours in advance ... 8242
      Dohihara's and Hiranuma's, reservation of right to make ... 17007-08
    Oshima (Defendant):
      Ambassadorial immunity ... 5894-98
      Interrogation of Oshima, correction of errors in, tribunal ruling concerning ... 5919-20
    Prosecution:
      Question to prosecutor ... 1466-67
      Summation of doc. be stricken from record ... 12069
    Pu-Y'i (Pros. witness):
      Evidence of handwriting of, be stricken from record ... 15552-53
      Retention of, in Tokyo, for further ex. ... 4351-52
    Recesses ... 12332-36; 13878-92; 16997-98; 17777-80; 18956-58; 19091-99; 23874-77; 23880-83
    Re-direct examination:
      Defendants of, on behalf of other defendants, exception to tribunal ruling concerning ... 20099
      Suspension of, until def. counsel be supplied with copies of doc. ... 22660
      Tribunal ruling concerning ... 1386
    Ribbentrop:
      Evidence of, be stricken from record ... 23732-33; 23785-87
    Sato (Defendant):
      Judicial hearing against prisoner of war ... 285-92
    Shimada (Defendant):
      Calling of, concerning Togo testimony ... 36963-64
      Recalling of ... 35859; 37022-24
    Tamura (Def. witness):
      Qualification of, as an expert ... 17885-86
    Tojo (Defendant):
      Re-examination of ... 18060-64
    Tribunal:
      Def. wit., court jurisdiction over voluntary ... 9336-37
      Member, challenging the participation of ... 92-97; 2346-49
      USSR pros., what can be proved by ... 7397-98
    Tribunal rulings:
      Def. ind. case, reconsideration of tribunal ruling concerning ... 19751-54
      Def. motion to dismiss on behalf of eleven defendants, exception to tribunal ruling concerning ... 16263
      Def. wit., modification of order concerning ... 6833-39
      Judicial notice for def. doc. ... 36970-72; 36973-78; 37173-75
      Re-direct examination ... 1386
      Re-direct examination of defendants on behalf of other defendants, exception to tribunal ruling concerning ... 20099

Witness note, use of ... 3896
Umezu (Defendant):
    Counsel Blakeney to make objection as second counsel for ... 2152-53
USSR general case, be reopened for additional evidence ... 31841-42
USSR prosecution:
    Documents, entire presentation of ... 36922-23
    Evidence, Changkufeng, be stricken from the record ... 7782-86
    Reopening of case for additional evidence ... 31841-42
    Statement of what can be proved by ... 7297-98
    Witnesses, cross-examination of, for rebuttal be reserved until further ex. of USSR pros. doc. ... 38245
    Witnesses, presentation of status concerning ... 7578; 7581-82; 7710; 8091; 8135; 8162; 8173
    Witnesses, production of ... 6301-06; 7581; 7710; 8135; 8162; 9087-89; 10556; 10558-60; 10612; 10617-18; 10633; 10677; 11338-39; 11731-34; 12042-43; 12053; 13850; 13857; 13863; 13865; 14228; 31842-43; 32776-95; 38350; 38355-56
Witnesses:
    Address of, be presented to def. ... 4814
    Answers of ... 4013; 4085; 4117; 4243; 14312
    Answers of, be stricken from the record ... 861; 875; 4036; 4448; 8571; 14286; 14314; 14327
    Cross-examination, scope of ... 2664-67
    Def. wit., qualification of, as an expert ... 17885-86
    Def. wit., production of ... 33595; 35597
    Direct-examination of, def. counsel be permitted to conduct, before presentation of pros. case ... 1354-55; 1549
    Interrogation of wit. be submitted to the tribunal ... 1566
    Issuance of warrant for Col. Sugita (pros. wit.) ... 5687-88
    Notes, wit. not permitted use of ... 3896; 3947; 3965
    Order, modification of, concerning def. wit. ... 6833-39
    Pros. wit., production of ... 6301-06; 7581; 7710; 8135; 8162; 9087-89; 10556; 10558-60; 10612; 10617-18; 10633; 10677; 11338-39; 11731-34; 12042-43; 12053; 13850; 13857; 13863; 13865; 14228
    Pros. wit., retention of, in Tokyo for further ex. ... 4351-52
    Qualification of def. wit., as an expert ... 17885-86
    Recalling of ... 3353-54; 8937; 15542; 17753; 17864; 18087; 18114; 18507; 18613; 19061; 19067; 19470; 19490-91; 19662; 23455; 35859; 37022-24
    Re-examination of ... 18060-64; 23721
    Re-examination of defendant ... 18060-64; 23721
    Statement of, be stricken from record ... 15444
    Subpoena on, service of ... 8154-55; 8158; 8177
    Suspension of, until further revision of affidavits ... 21639; 22090; 22555; 24250

Prosecution:
    Affidavits:
        Burrett, Col., by, substituting for cross-ex. ... 3351-52
        Direct evidence, in form of ... 915-28
        Doc. annexed by ... 20766-70
        Excerpt from, use of, if affiant not in Japan ... 1842-57; 1869-71
    Budarin, pros. wit., be permitted to take stand ... 32551-52
    Cross-examination:
        Affidavit by, substitution of ... 1842-57; 1869-71; 3351-52
        Counsel, change of ... 30485-87
        Rules of, alteration (or modification) of ... 3819-20
    Defense individual case, limitation of scope of evidence in ... 28090-97
    Documents:
        Affidavit, annexation by ... 20766-70
        Paraphrasing of, without reading ... 1010-13; 1736
        Presentation of part of doc. def. has not produced ... 31663
        Reading of excerpt ... 3696-97
    Evidence:
        Affidavit, in form of ... 915-28
        Scope of, limitation of, in def. individual cases ... 28090-97
    Opening statement:
        Objection, pros. right to make, to any part of ... 17010
    Powell, John B.:
        Permission to testify in different phases of case ... 3202-07
    Procedures, rules of:
        Affidavit, use of, if affiant not in Japan, modification concerning ... 1842-57; 1869-71
        Doc., service of, modification concerning ... 1289-303
        Wit., appearance of, in courtroom, modification concerning ... 805-06
    Redirect-examination:
        Rules for ... 20090-93
    Shidehara's speech at Washington Conference, strike from record ... 38213-16
    Translation:
        Ko-a-in ... 4775
        Question of ... 1995
    USSR, prosecution:
        Cross-ex. of wit. concerning events prior to the indictment period ... 7323-24
        Judicial notice for Imperial Rescript on first Russo-Japanese war ... 38200
        Russian language, use of ... 7083

Applications and Motions (Cont.)
  Prosecution (Cont.)
    Witnesses:
      Admissibility of testimony, tribunal ruling concerning ... 3986
      Answer of, strike from the record ... 892
      Appearance of wit. in courtroom, rules of procedure, modification of ... 805-06
      Budarin, pros. wit. ... 32551-52
      Evidence, taking, by commission ... 1726-28
      Examination, extension of ... 2009
      Note, permission to use ... 883
      Out of order ... 4371-72
      Production of wit. without presenting more than aff. ... 2518
      Question, retranslation of ... 1995
      Releasing of, from further testimony ... 3721
      Retention of def. wit. in USSR custody until def. production of wit. ... 8155-56
      Subpoena, suppression of, for def. wit. until pros. testimony ... 8001-02; 8004; 8006-08
      Testimony of, on different phases of case ... 3202-07

Araki, Sadao (See: Defendants)

Armaments Bureau, Ministry of Navy ... 598

Army Aviation Headquarters ... 590-91

"Army Explains War Bill," Article Entitled ... 8791-801

Army Land Survey Department ... 589

Army Press Section ... 585

Asia (See: Greater East Asia, Greater East Asia Co-Prosperity Sphere)

"Asia, Europe, Japan," book by Okawa ... 15605-08

Atrocities: Violations of Laws and Customs of Warfare and Laws of Humanity: Pros. ... 12345-15496; Def. ... 27117-27963; 28085-88; Pros. summation ... 39992-40537; Def. summation ... 42618-42691; (See also: Individual Responsibility; Defendants; Prisoners of War)

  Ambon Islands (NEI) ... 13928-14065; 40168-69; 40202-03; 40232-35; 40265-87; 40293-94; 40314-16; 40338-39

  Andaman and Nicobars (Free Indies) ... 13185-13200; 30195-213; 30239-46; 40235-36; 40267; 40316

  Borneo (NEI) ... 12043-44; 12047-53; 13312-16; 13344; 13420-49; 13492-95; 13499-504; 13505-28; 27536-95; 27599-619; 30195-213; 30247-50; 40168-72; 40203-06; 40236-39; 40267-69; 40294-98; 40316-18; 40340-46

  British North Borneo and Sarawak ... 13311-453 (See also: Borneo)

  Burma-Thailand ... 5358-5610; 11403-426; 12963-13111; 15500-02; 30195-213; 31722-48; 34466; 36421-22; 40206-08; 40239-44; 40269-73; 40298-300; 40318-19; 40346-49; 42658-61; 43664-66

  Celebes (NEI) ... 13845-927; 40173-75; 40208-10; 40244-45; 40273-75; 40300-01; 40319-22; 40349-52

  China:
    Civilian and others (included: murder, massacre, torture, rape, wanton destruction of properties); Pros. ... 3886-4998; 14156-96; Def. ... 20558-67; 20827-59; 21133-22090; Pros. summation ... 40115-167; Def. summation ... 42666-67; 42854-938
    Changsha ... 21794-804; 27493-98; 40160-61
    Chungking ... 21476-85
    Hangchow ... 21764-67
    Hangkow ... 3376-414; 21582-627; 21640-47; 21695-726; 21743-63; 21768-85; 30300-03
    Hong Kong ... 4648-49; 13112-84; 13304-11; 27513-33; 40177-83; 40214-17; 40250-51; 40278-79; 40304-05; 40325-26
    Hopei Province ... 4614; 40161-63
    Hsuchow ... 21695-726
    Hunan Province ... 4611-13; 40160-61
    Hungyang ... 21798-804
    Jehol Province ... 4656; 40164-65
    Kiangsu Province ... 4608-09; 40158-59
    Kwangsi Province ... 4651-54; 40164
    Kwantung Province ... 4648-50; 27476-79
    Kweilin ... 21630-34; 21799-804; 21807-11
    Liuchow ... 4648; 4651-52; 4655; 21804; 21807-11; 27479½-92; 27499-502; 40164
    Nanking ... 2624-75; 3893-943; 4456-79; 4483-4548; 4552-89; 4593-604; 16130-36; 21443-74; 21559-81; 21885-948; 22826; 28243; 29969-30000; 32583-658; 32673-89; 32738-63; 33087-91; 33819-25; 33842-47; 33850-83; 36988-89; 40116-58
    Peiping ... 4645; 4647
    Suiyuan ... 27486-92; 27503-07; 40165
    Taishan ... 27486-92; 27503-07
    Tungchow ... 20827-59
    Wuchow ... 27479½-92
    Wuyuan ... 27508-12
    Yunan ... 2619-23; 40166

  Formosa (Japan) ... 13207-27; 14489-90; 14518-20; 14708-27; 40211-13; 40248-49; 40276-77; 40302-03; 40324; 40355-56

  FIC (France) ... 7176; 7181-82; 7193-94; 15291-472; 40303-04; 40324-25; 40356-61

Hainan ... 13201-07; 40213-14; 40249-50; 40277-78; 40304; 40325; 40361

Hong Kong (British Commonwealth) ... 4648-49; 13112-84; 27513-33; 40177-83; 40214-17; 40250-51; 40278-79; 40304-05; 40325-26

Japan ... 14197-261; 14270-80; 16258; 28750-55; 40217-20; 40251-55; 40279-83; 40305-07; 40326-29; 40362-72; 42669-72

Java (NEI) ... 13291-97; 13476-91; 13629; 13644-47; 13537; 13629; 13644-47; 13700; 30215-38; 30183-88; 40220-22; 40255-57; 40283-84; 40307; 40329-32; 40372-75

New Britain (NEI) ... 14104-30; 40188; 40257-58; 40284-86; 40308; 40332-33; 40375

New Guinea (NEI) ... 14066-103; 40188; 40222-24; 40258-59; 40286-87; 40308-09; 40333-34; 40375-76

Pacific Islands ... 14911-15047; 33515-22; 40201-02; 40231; 40293; 40314; 40382-83

Philippines ... 15196-281; 27324-34; 27625-54; 27723-42; 27761-85; 27820-21; 32936-38; 33075; 33141-50; 40384-481; 42662-64

Singapore and Malaya (British Commonwealth) ... 5624-53; 5671-76; 12883-962; 13454-76; 27397-411; 30215-46; 40188-95; 40224-28; 40259-60; 40287-90; 40309-11; 40334; 40376-79; 43657-58

Solomon, Gilberts, Naru and Ocean Islands ... 14130-53; 33422; 40195; 40260-61; 40290; 40334-35; 40279

Southern Regions ... 1319; 5418-19; 13193-200; 12312-16; 13344; 13504; 13537; 13573; 13629; 13644-47; 13700; 13750; 13784; 13820; 13913-34; 27565; 28722-33; 30195-213; 30215-50

Sumatra and Banka Islands (NEI) ... 13297-303; 13554-604; 13733-820; 27532; 27655-79; 30195-246; 32935-36; 33061-65; 33121-33; 40229-30; 40261-63; 40290-92; 40311-13; 40335-37; 40379-82

Timor and Lesser Sunda Islands (NEI) ... 13821-44; 40198-201; 40230-31; 40264-65; 40292-93; 40313-14; 40337-38; 40382

USSR ... 15483-96

Offenses against survivors of torpedoed merchant ships ... 15088-196

"Ascot" (British) ... 15155; 15163-67
"Behar" (British) ... 15182-83
"British Chivalry" (British) ... 15154; 15159-61
"Daisy Moller" (British) ... 15154; 15158-59
"Jean Nicolet" (US) ... 15095-148
"John A. Johnson" (US) ... 15148-51
"Nancy Moller" (British) ... 15155; 15167-68
"Richard Hovey" (US) ... 15088-94
"Sutley" (British) ... 15154-55; 15161-62
"Tjisalak" (Netherlands) ... 15155; 15169-75

Opium and narcotics, use of; Pros. ... 3886-4998; Def. ... 18630-20485; Pros. summation ... 39177-90; 39309-25; Def. summation ... 42666-67; 42546-57; 42854-938

China:
  Central China ... 4845-80
    Conditions in, report ... 4853-54; 4865-66
    Purchase of Iranian opium ... 4860-63
  North China ... 4751-4819
    Chahar ... 4779-81; 4788-90
    Chahar, North ... 4785-88
    Conditions in ... 4751-58; 4813-19; 4903
    Control system ... 4776-78
    Jehol ... 4780-81
    Peiping ... 4800-01; 4810-13
    Suiyuan ... 4779; 4788-90
    Tsinan ... 4793-95
    Tunghsian ... 4800-01
  Occupied China ... 2648-75; 4663-72; 4926-28
    Nanking ... 2539-48
    Tientsin ... 2624-92
  South China ... 4820-51
    Amoy ... 4827; 4830; 4834-36
    Canton ... 4837-44
    Shanghai ... 4845-50
Far East ... 20251-53; 20273-87
Formosa ... 4831; 4901; 20271-72
Korea ... 4706-11; 4906; 4911
Manchuria ... 2786-2816; 4039-43; 4257-58; 4408; 4667-94; 4699-700; 4701-08; 4712-40; 4745-46; 4750-51; 4779; 4788-90; 4832-33; 4866; 4876-77; 4902-03; 4905; 4924-25; 4955-58; 5034; 15921; 20236-71; 20273-87; 20289-307; 29115-25; 32623-26

Sea atrocities ... 13228-311; 15088-196; 33294-96; 33311-12; 33371-74; 33416; 33418-22; 33420-26; 33540-22; 34670-89; 40482-97; 42673-75

Submarine warfare in Indian Ocean ... 15184-96

Violation of treaty provisions concerning hospital ships ... 15047-87
"Comfort" (US) ... 15055-64
"Hope" (US) ... 15049-54
"Op ten Noort" (Netherlands) ... 15065-87

Australia:

   POW, Australian, in the Far East ... 14901-02

   POW treatment, protest by ... 5521-26

Autonomous Movements, Five Northern Provinces, in China ... 2024-44; 2129-51

B

Banking Bureau ... 606

Banks:

   Central Bank for Commercial and Industrial Association ... 8393

   China:
      Bank of ... 3586-87
      Communication Bank of ... 3586-87

   Korea:
      Bank of ... 8416; 8444; 20468-69
      Industrial Bank of ... 8515

   Manchuria:
      Central Bank of ... 8416
      Industrial Bank of ... 8435-36

   Taiwan, Bank of ... 8443

Bataan Death March (*See also:* Atrocities; Philippines; POW and Civilian Internees):

   Summary ... 12668

   Testimony concerning ... 12610-39; 12673-724; 12738-75

   US protests ... 12821-27

Blockade:

   China coast:
      Shimada (Defendant), test. ... 34739-43; 34798-99; 34808-09

   Economic, ABD ... 25547-50; 25565-68
      Togo (Defendant), aff. ... 35690-92

   Regulations ... 21530-36

Boards:

   Audit ... 573-74; 33203-05

   Cabinet Information:
      Oka (Defendant), aff. ... 33383-84

   China Affairs (Koain):
      Muto (Defendant), test. ... 33203-05
      Opium in North China ... 4761-75; 4805-07

      Shimada (Defendant), aff. ... 34675
      Suzuki (Defendant), test. ... 35265-91
      Togo (Defendant), aff. ... 35747-48

   Field Marshals and Fleet Admirals (Gensuifu) ... 672

   Information ... 541-42; 6047-48; 6668-70; 8055-56
      Imperial Ordinance ... 17482-83

   Manchurian Affairs ... 540; 5113-14
      Hoshino (Defendant), aff. ... 29105-11
      Togo (Defendant), aff. ... 35748-49

   Opium Suppression ... 4876-77

   Peerage:
      Kido's (Defendant), resignation ... 30826-27

   Planning ... 540; 623-24
      Appointment:
         Kido's diary ... 9850-51
      Control associations and ... 35165-68
      Function of president:
         Suzuki (Defendant), aff. and test. ... 35237-42; 35292-93; 35296-99 (*See also:* 8290; 8403; 8476; 10204-05; 10213-14; 10228; 15963; 16930-31; 18358)
      GEA Ministry and:
         Togo (Defendant), aff. ... 35756-57
      Imperial Ordinance ... 17480-81
      New Planning Board ... 623-24
      POW Administration and:
         Suzuki (Defendant), aff. ... 35162-64
      Suzuki (Defendant) as president, aff. and test. ... 35175-76; 35196-97; 35213-20; 35225-27; 35234-47; 35291-93; 35296-301; 35319-23 (*See also:* 8290; 8403; 8476; 10024-25; 10213; 10228; 15963; 16930-31; 18358)

Borneo (*See also:* The Netherlands; Southern Advance; Southern Regions):

   Atrocities ... 12043-44; 12047-53; 13312-16; 13344; 13420-49; 13492-95; 13499-504; 13505-28; 40168-72; 40203-06; 40236-39; 40267-69; 40294-95; 40316-18; 40340-46)

   GEACPS ... 17912-18019

   POW treatment ... 27599-619
      Itagaki (Defendant), aff. and test. ... 30195-213; 30247-50

Brussels Conference ... 503

   Grew diary ... 29955-60

   Japanese statement ... 20984-89; 21000-06

Budget ... 605

Budget Committee (House of Representatives), Record of Meeting:

    Difference between public and political association ... 18164-67

    "Imperial Way," meaning of ... 18168-71

"Budget System of Japan," book entitled ... 568-69

Bureaus:

    Army Press (Imperial Headquarters) ... 34441-42

    Banking ... 606

    Convention ... 603

    Decorations ... 540

    Deposit Funds Management ... 607; 8550-52

    East Asia ... 602; 18160-63

    Education (Navy Ministry) ... 598

    Emergency Industrial Rationalization ... 8391

    Europe and Asia ... 602

    Executive ... 620-21

    Foreign Exchange Control ... 606

    Fuel ... 8296

    Functional ... 603

    Fund Employment (or Finance) ... 606

    General Affairs ... 589; 5116; 5187

    General Opium Amelioration ... 4879-80

    Geographic ... 602

    Historical ... 589

    Industrial ... 622

    Information (Foreign Affairs Ministry), Shiratori, chief of ... 35058-84; 35137

    Information (War Ministry) ... 15853-921; 34441-42

    Intendence ... 585

    Legal ... 585; Legal (Navy Ministry) ... 598

    Legislative ... 540; 15960; 16963; 35240-41

    Local Affairs ... 607

    Manchurian Affairs ... 621; 5187

    Medical (Navy Ministry) ... 598; (War Ministry) ... 585

    Military Affairs ... 582-83; 14285-422; 15951; 32332-41; 32452-54; 32944-65
        Muto (Defendant), aff. and test. ... 15863-921; 33084; 33092-93; 33108-09; 33115-23; 33126-29; 33199-205
        POW treatment, handling of protests ... 12872-73; 16085-90; 16097-101; 34311-37
        Privy Council and, ... 32958-59; 32963-65
        Sato (Defendant), chief of, aff. and test. ... 16087-88; 34381-96 (See also: POW Treatment and Military Affairs Bureau)
        Suzuki (Defendant), aff. ... 35192
        Tojo (Defendant), test. ... 15853-951
        Tripartite Pact and, ... 32994-96; 33110-11

    Military Preparations ... 585

    Military Service ... 584-85; 32948

    Mines ... 614

    Mobilization Plans ... 20674-744

    Monopoly ... 606

    Munitions ... 598

    National Prosperity ... 606

    National Savings Encouragement ... 606; 8546

    Navy Affairs:
        Oka (Defendant), director of ... 33289-94; 33385-87 (See also: 33303-18; 33336-55; 33403-04; 33411-14; 33422-24; 33459-64; 33470-83; 33506-29)
        POW administration and, ... 33294-96; 33311-12; 33371-74; 33416; 33418-20; 33424-26; 33504-22
        Submarine warfare and, ... 33422

    Operations ... 589

    Ordinance ... 585

    Planning:
        Hirota (Defendant), aff. and test. ... 29657-63

    Police ... 607; 18509-35

    POW Control ... 14839-89; 27198-99

    POW Information ... 594-95
        Camps ... 27803-78
        Function ... 14839-89; 34414-37
        Imperial Ordinance ... 14440-43; 17526-30; 35584
        Togo (Defendant), aff. ... 35768-69

Bureaus *(Cont.)*

    POW Information *(Cont.)*

        Treatment ... 5493-96; 5506-07; 5510-12; 14431-37; 14440-76

        Treatment and regulations ... 27182-90

    POW Intelligence ... 33126-29

    Public Hygiene ... 614

    Russian Emigrants ... 7240

    Shrine ... 607

    Social Welfare ... 614

    South Sea ... 602

        Business reports concerning FIC ... 6801-15; 6844-74

    Taxation ... 606

    Textbooks ... 613

    Treaties ... 603

Burma *(See also:* Burma-Thailand; The Netherlands; Southern Regions):

    Atrocities ... 12963-95; 12996-13049; 13051-55; 13057-111; 14629-55; 14658-61

    GEA Conference ... 18093-96; 36472

    GEACPS and, ... 17912-18019; 18032-61; 18064-88

    GEA Ministry ... 35765

    GEA policy:

        Tojo (Defendant), test. ... 36448-54

    Maw, Dr. Ba, speeches at GEA conferences ... 36453-54; 36472

    Policies toward, Japanese (*See:* Japan, Foreign policies)

    POW treatment ... 27536-95; 27599-619; 30195-213; 31722-48; 34466; 35772-73; 36421-22

        Itagaki (Defendant) ... 30195-213

        Kimura (Defendant), test. ... 31722-48

        Sato (Defendant), test. ... 34466

        Togo (Defendant), test. ... 35572-73

        Tojo (Defendant), test. ... 36421-22

    Preparation for operation ... 8191-93; 8457-63; 9010-54

    Treaties with Japan:

        Alliance Pact ... 36449-50

Burma-Thailand:

    Administrative responsibility for railway construction:

        Tojo (Defendant), aff. ... 36421-22

    Atrocities ... 5492-96; 5506-07; 5510-12; 5515-608; 11403-526; 12963-13111; 15500-02

    POW treatment ... 27438-42; 27536-56; 27743-50; 30195-213; 31722-48; 34466; 35772-73; 36421-22

    Report, Japanese government ... 5515-5608

        Itagaki (Defendant), aff. ... 30195-213

        Kimura (Defendant), aff. ... 31722-48

    Sato (Defendant), test. ... 34466

    Togo (Defendant), test. ... 35572-73

    Tojo (Defendant), test. ... 36421-22

C

Cabinet (*See:* Japan)

Cabinet Advisory Council ... 543-44

    Appointment of ... 623

    Creation of ... 622-24

Cabinet Committee, Plans for Economic Exploitations of Southern Regions ... 11944-59

Cabinet Conference (*See:* Japan, Conferences)

Cabinet Councillor:

    Matsui (Defendant), aff. and test. ... 33828-29; 33890-92

    Minami (Defendant), test. ... 32926-29

Cabinet Planning Board ... 5131-32; 5148-50; 5167-70 (*See also:* Board; Preparation for War)

Cabinet Secretariat, Chief:

    Duties of, Hoshino (Defendant), aff. ... 29191-95

    Hoshino (Defendant) as, aff. ... 29191-203

Canton (*See:* China)

Caroline Islands (*See:* Japan, Mandated Islands)

Central China Expeditionary Forces (*See:* China, Aggression against)

Central China Development Co. (*See:* China, Economic Aggression)

Central China Iron Mine Co. Ltd. (*See:* China, Economic Aggression)

Central China Promotion Co. Ltd. (*See:* China, Economic Aggression)

Central China Water and Electric Co. (*See:* China, Economic Aggression)

Central Cooperation Conference (*See:* IRAA)

Central Economic Council ... 544-45

Central Statistics Committee ... 544

Certificates:

    Illness of witness (Def.) ... 32881-82; 35589

    Non-availability of def. documents ... 20793-94; 23351; 26563-67; 27303-04; 29402; 29403; 29883; 29913-14; 29931; 29998; 32492; 32510; 32814-18; 32825; 32829; 32999; 33282; 33284-85; 33687-99; 34053; 34490; 34499-500; 34559; 34931-32; 35374; 36325; 36345-46; 36357; 36387; 36398; 36459-60; 37162-63

    Non-availability of Gen. Sakai (Def. wit.) by execution ... 36885

    Non-availability of Kwantung Army documents ... 23184-85

    Non-availability of pros. document ... 8076

    Status of affiants for def. cross-ex. ... 23154-65

Changkufeng Incident (*See:* USSR, Border incidents)

Chang Tso-lin ... 1743-53

    Affair ... 1810-1916; 1945-61; 2173-77

    Relations with Japan ... 1771-72

Chahar (*See:* Atrocities, Opium and narcotics)

Charts:

    Aluminum production in Japanese empire ... 8338

    Expansion of industry in Japan proper during 1931-41 ... 8556

    Expansion of precision bearing industry in Japan proper during 1931-41 ... 8357

    Gold production in Japanese empire during 1925-41 ... 8518

    Machine tool production and net imports in Japan proper ... 8356

    Total strength of Japanese army ... 9074-76

Chiang Kai-shek (*See:* China)

China:

    Aggression against (Pros. .. 3239-3886; Def. ... 20485-22399; Pros. summation ... 39191-325; Def. summation ... 42854-938)
    Anti-Japanese movement ... 4639-40 (*See also:* 20494-97; 20888-21133)
    Araki (Defendant):
        Cabinet decisions, lack of record, aff. ... 28536-37
        Expansion in China under Konoye cabinet, interrogation ... 15840-42
        Iwakuro aff. ... 18571; 18531-32; argument ... 36986-89
        Nanking, atrocities ... 36988-89
        Shanghai:
            Incident, statement ... 28270; 28432-34
            Landing of troops, cabinet meeting, interrogation ... 15843-45
        US rights in China, cabinet meeting, interrogation ... 15840-42
    Blockading of coast ... 21486-93
        Shimada (Defendant), aff. and test. ... 34739-43; 34798-99; 34808-09
    Bombing ... 34693-95; 34734-37; 34740-46
        Indiscriminate, Hirota (Defendant), test. ... 29948-53
        Nanking ... 21390-92
        Targets, aff. ... 21373-77
    Central China:
        Changsha:
            Atrocities (*See:* Atrocities, China)
            Bombing ... 34595; 34693-95
            Campaign, aff. ... 21794-804
            POW, aff. ... 27493-98
        Chungking:
            Air raid casualties and damages, statistics ... 3425
            Atrocities (*See:* Atrocities, China)
            Campaign, aff. and test. ... 21476-85
            Government, peace with, aff. and test. ... 32253-64; 32268-72
        Expeditionary forces ... 21695-739
        Nanking and, aff. and test. ... 21885-948
        Government, proposed organization of ... 22358-63
        Hangchow:
            Atrocities (*See:* Atrocities, China)
            Campaign, aff. ... 21764-67
        Hankow:
            Campaign, aff. and test. ... 21582-627; 21640-47; 21695-726; 21726-39; 21743-63; 21768-85; 30300-03
            Capture of, test. ... 3376-89; 3390-3414
        Hsuchow:
            Campaign, aff. and test. ... 21695-726
        Kwanganmen:
            Campaign, aff. ... 20558-67
        Nanking:
            Atrocities (*See:* Atrocities, China)
            Campaign ... 21443-74

China *(Cont.)*
  Aggression against *(Cont.)*
    Central China *(Cont.)*
      Nanking *(Cont.)*
        Matsui (Defendant), aff. ... 33819-25; 33835-83
      Capture of ... 3376-89
        Matsui (Defendant), aff. ... 33819-25; 33835-83
      Control of soldiers at, interrogation ... 3453-65
      Government ... 634; 22314-28
        Establishment, reason for ... 22341-50; 22367-72
        Japan's attitude toward ... 22375-76
        Platform ... 22364-66
        Policies ... 22336-38
        Purge movement ... 22383-85
      Incident, aff. and test. ... 2527-39; 2551-97; 2599-2615; 2624-75; 3505-09; 19596-612; 29969-30000; 36988-89
      Court martial, aff. ... 32674-77
      Instruction not to violate law ... 32688-89
      Itagaki (Defendant), aff. ... 30295-96
        (*See also:* 30078-84)
      Kaya (Defendant), test. ... 30640-41
      Kido (Defendant), aff. and test. ... 30841-42; 31477-526
      Matsui (Defendant), aff. and test. ... 33821-26; 33849-83; 33919-20
        (*See also:* 32583-658; 32673-88; 32738-63; 33087-91)
      Muto (Defendant), aff. ... 3087-91
      US official communication ... 4552-89
    Negotiations ... 20803; 20805-06
    Press release ... 3510-13; 32766-71
    Rape (*See:* Atrocities)
    Restoration government ... 5308-17
    Safety zone:
      Disorder by Japanese troops ... 4512-15; 4526-27; 4529-30
      Document ... 4508
      International committee for ... 4556-58; 4586-89
      Letter to Japanese embassy ... 4509-12; 4516-25; 4528-36
      Nanking campaign and ... 21468-74
    War crimes ... 4540-48
    Shanghai:
      Campaign, interrogation ... 3443-54; aff. ... 33814-19
      Campaign, plan for, test. ... 3376-89
      City Tatao government ... 5304-05
      Concession, International Settlement ... 10068-83; 10090-108; 10539; 10608-12
      Expeditionary Forces, aff. and test. ... 33812-19; 33838-42
      Incident, aff. ... 19576-91; 19731-49; 19773-20107; 20497-99
        Agreement for cessation ... 19571-73
        Araki (Defendant), aff. and test. ... 28122; 28270; 28432-34; 28455-71
        First ... 3239-40; 3252; 3261-62; aff. ... 34482-89; 34492-95; 34495-96
        Government, Japanese, statement ... 19559-69
        Kido diary ... 30757-59; 30762-64
        Koiso (Defendant), aff. ... 32221
        Matsui (Defendant), aff. ... 33814-19
        Origin of ... 3286-93
        Second ... 3241-45; aff. ... 21144-45
          Agreement for cessation ... 19571-73; 21133-34
          Joint commission of Shanghai, minutes ... 21178-200
          Testimony ... 3740-46; 3250-68
        Third ... 3245-47; 10608-12; 10644
          (*See also:* 3254; 10544; 10608; 10613; 27098-111)
      Landing of troops at, cabinet meeting, interrogation ... 15843-45
      War Zone Relief and Rehabilitation Association ... 5305-06

Atrocities (*See:* Atrocities, China; Atrocities, Opium and narcotics)

Chiang Kai-shek:
  Failure to overthrow, tel. ... 5983-6020
  Hostility of ... 30095-97
  Konoye speech ... 5255
  Negotiations with Itagaki (Defendant) ... 15735-38
  Peace with Japan ... 3591; 5983-6020; 15739; 22254-399

Chinese government regulations, international amity ... 20965-66

Collaboration with Germany against (*See:* Collaboration among Germany, Italy and Japan)

Communist:
  Activities against Japanese ... 20888-21133
  Party, history of ... 28035-62

Dohihara (Defendant):
  China Affairs Board, special committee on, test. ... 30107-38
  Chinese groups, collaborations with, tel. ... 4402-05
  Ching Teh-chen, supposed conversation with, aff. and test. ... 28627-46
  Puppet government, tel. ... 30114-15
  Relations with China, aff. ... 28687-95; article ... 28698
  Tientsin, action at, tel. ... 4401
  Tientsin consulate's telegrams, meaning of, aff. and test. ... 28648-66

Economic aggression (Pros. ... 4999-5906; Def. ... 20888-2113; Pros. summation ... 39295-39308; Def. summation ... 42854-938) (*See also:* Preparation for War)

Central China Development Co. ... 5341-44; 5500-02; 8277; 8475; aff. ... 21949-58
Central China, economic development by occupation ... 5268-77; 21949-58
Central China Iron Mine Co. Ltd. ... 5276-77
Central China Promotion Co. ... 543; 5008-09; 5227-28; 5252; 5261-66; 5281-82
Central China Water and Electric Co. ... 4426-35
China Affairs Board, regulation ... 5183-85
(See also: 4835)
China Affairs Bureau ... 5009; 5187
Construction, heavy, material, importation of ... 5339-40
Economic construction program ... 5003-05; 5010; 5038-41; 5104-05
Economic development by occupation ... 5258-66; 5268-77 (See also: 21949-58)
Economic exploitation ... 5105-10
Economic integration ... 8443-46
Financial plan, five year ... 5089-99
Hoshino (Defendant), interrogation ... 5119-82
Industrial development plan, five year ... 5005-06; 5099-5101; 5125-28; 5140-41; 5158-59
Industrial reconstruction ... 5278-82
Investment ... 5347
Mining and manufacturing industry plan, five year ... 5082-88
North China Development Co. ... 543; 5008-09; 5227-28; 5251-52; 5261-66; 5269-70; 5280-82; 5341-44; 8277; 8474; test. ... 3867-78
  Economic development and, aff. ... 21949-58
  Kaya (Defendant), aff. and test. ... 30642-46; 30701-04
North China economic development ... 5268-77
North China industrial control, method of ... 5270-76
North China Iron and Steel Corp. ... 5196-5207
North China Telegram and Telephone Co. Ltd. ... 5269
Treaties and agreements:
  Alliance Pact ... 5333-36; 36447-49
  Joint declaration of Japan-Manchukuo-China ... 5322-26 (See also: 21411-16)
  Sino-Japanese Basic Treaty ... 5327-30
  Sino-Japanese Secret Treaty ... 5320-21

Great Britain:
  Conference with Japan, concerning ... 21788-89
  Measures to protect foreign shipping, in ... 21540-42

Hashimoto (Defendant), articles by:
  "Build a State Union of China and Manchukuo with Japan as its Leader ... 15661-62
  "Solution of the Incident Depends on Expulsion of England" ... 15660-61; 15685-87

Hata (Defendant), aff. ... 28863-67 (See also: 1605-35)
  Foochow, Nanking, Shanghai triangle campaign, interrogation ... 3443-54

Hiranuma (Defendant), Tientsin crisis, aff. ... 29233-34

Hirota (Defendant):
  Cabinet, cause of resignation, aff. ... 29645-53
  Foreign policy of:
    Aff. and test. ... 29677-882; 29898-932
    (See also: 36997-99)
    Answer before Diet, aff. ... 29602-03; 29608; 29612
    Bombing, indiscriminate, attitude toward, test. ... 29948-53
    Speeches by, aff. ... 20868-70; 21346-48; 29452-61; 29591-99; 29640-42
    Telegrams by, aff. ... 29621-28; 29630-34
    Three principles, aff. ... 29625-28; 29630-34; 29635-37
    Wang, peace with, tel. ... 29569-77

Itagaki (Defendant):
  Chiang, hostility of, ... 30095-97
  No third power interference ... 15748-50
  Peace with, ... 15733-34; 15739; 30147-54
  Speech by ... 15741-43

Japan:
  Anti-Japanese movement ... 20494-97; 20888-21133 (See also: 4639-40)
  Army's position in Japan during 1932-37, aff. ... 20745-71
  Chinese Affairs Board, test. ... 30170-38; 34675; 35266-91; 35747-51
  Educational policy ... 3542-47
  Emergency measure in personnel administration ... 3487-88
  Foreign policy ... 20967-82; 21550-58; 29621-31; 29635-37; 29463; 29837-51; 31470-75
    Amau declaration ... 29579-88
    Anglo-Japanese conference re situation in China ... 21788-89
    Attitude toward third power property ... 21407-09
    China Incident ... 29855-57; 29898-913
    Great Britain's attitude toward ... 36054-58
    GEA policy, aff. and test. ... 21543-44; 36447-49; 36538-42
    GEA principles ... 32578-81; 32689-98; 32704-37; 33897-905; 33920-21
    Intention in China, statement ... 21423-26
    Konoye speech ... 5253-56
    Peace proposal to China, aff. and test. ... 1605-35; 15733-34; 15739; 20500-03; 21431-22090; 28863-67; 29916-17; 30147-50; 31114-16; 31245-48; 31412-66; 32220-27; 32253-54; 32268-72; 33189-95; 33486-90; 33826-28; 33844-45; 35747-48; 36187; 36206-12; 36538-42; 36634-36; 36691-94; 36863
    Relations with China, aff. and test. ... 29475-566; 36447-49; 36538-42

Kaya (Defendant), civilian ministers, purge of, after Incident, aff. ... 30534-49

Kido (Defendant):

China *(Cont.)*
  Kido (Defendant) *(Cont.)*
    Peace with China, aff. and test. ... 3114-16; 31418-66; 31638-39
    Withdrawal from China, Suzuki (Defendant) conversation with, aff. and test. ... 35205-13; 35251-54; 35325-32; 35304-06; 35311-12

  Koiso (Defendant):
    Peace with China, aff. ... 31245-48; 32253-54; 32268-72
    Speech by ... 2703-17

  Marco Polo Bridge Incident ... 2311-17; 3177-526; 3703-17; 5253-56; 20485-93; 20506-879; 29539-40; 29542; 29934; 30097-98; 32766-71; aff. and test. ... 20517-48; 20550-68; 20609-711; 29677-882; 29914-32
    Cabinet decisions ... 29817-30
      Negotiations ... 29916-17; 29921-22; 29926-29; 29934-47; 30095-97
      Settlement ... 29772-85; 33912-17
      Supreme, Central, command analysis of situation, aff. and test. ... 21970-22076
      Timetable ... 20506-07
    Defendants:
      Araki, interrogation ... 15840-42
      Dohihara, aff. and test. ... 28671-87; 28700-09
      Hirota, aff. and test. ... 29677-882; 29914-32; 36997-99
      Hoshino, article ... 15660-62; 15685-87
      Itagaki, aff. and test. ... 30293-311; 30317-20; 30410-43; 31284-86 (*See also:* 30085-92; 30098-138)
      Kaya, aff. ... 30639-40
      Kido, aff. and test. ... 30823-71; 30912-13; 31061-62; 31114-16; 31382-96; 31418-88; 31470-75 (*See also:* 30330-32)
      Koiso, aff. ... 32231-32; 32539-43 (*See also:* 3703-17)
      Matsui, test. ... 33912-17
      Minami ... 15764-68
      Muto, aff. ... 32931-32; 33085-91; 33095; 33672-76; 33680-81
      Oka, aff. and test. ... 33287-88; 33382; 33462-68
      Shimada, test. ... 34734-49; 34797-99; 34808-09
      Shiratori, test. ... 34825; 35087-89; 35109-15
      Suzuki, aff. and test. ... 35193-95; 35205-13; 35251-70; 35287-88; 35304-06; 35311-12; 35323-32
      Togo, aff. ... 35398-99; 35442-43; 35487-90; 35650-52; 35656-57; 35685-89; 35699-700; 35746-51; 35999-6001; 36013-24; 36054-58
      Tojo, test. ... 31252-66 (*See also:* 16226-31)

  Matsui:
    Attitude toward China ... 32738-62

    Central China Area Army, commander of, ... 33819-21; 33847-83
  Nanking:
    Campaign, aff. and test. ... 33819-21; 33842-47 (*See also:* 21885-948)
    Capture of, aff. and test. ... 33821-25; 33850-83
    Instruction not to violate law ... 32688-89
    Rape of (*See:* Atrocities)

Muto (Defendant), Nanking Incident ... 16130-36; 21885-945

New Regime ... 22254-399

North China:
  Affair, speech ... 20868-70; 20874-79
  Aggression in ... 2311-17
  Autonomous movements of five provinces, test. ... 2024-44; 2129-51
  Campaigns, aff. ... 21873-81
  Expeditionary Forces, aff. ... 21873-81
  Incident in 1935 ... 15771-73
  Japanese administrative policy toward ... 2740-43; 2746-48
  Japanese plans for dealing with ... 2721-26; 2748-50
  North China Political Council, test. ... 4955-57
  Peking, Provisional Government ... 5297-307
  Provisional government agrees with Wang's policy ... 22338-39
  Railways, military disposal of ... 3475-86
  Settlement of issue ... 36884
  Tientsin:
    Action at, tel. ... 4401
    Consulate's telegrams, meaning of, aff. and test. ... 28648-66
    Crisis, aff. ... 29233-34; 32941-43
    Movement of 1937, report ... 26863-64
    Provisional government, dissolution ... 20599-602
  Troops, Japanese and Chinese, disposition of, aff. and test. ... 20609-67

Oka (Defendant), peace proposal to China, test. ... 33189-95; 33486-90

Opium and narcotics (*See:* Atrocities, China)

Puppet Government ... 22306-12; 30114-15
  Sino-Japanese conversation ... 22254-94
  Wang Ching-wei, speech by ... 22330-32

Revolutionary Government ... 3589-90

Round-table of Sino-Japanese notables ... 30063-71

Shigemitsu (Defendant):
  Peace with China ... 15733-34; 29528-53
  Shanghai Incident ... 3252; 3261-62; 34482-89; 34492-96

Shimada (Defendant):
  Blockade, test. ... 34729-43; 34798-99; 34808-09

Bombing, test. ... 34734-37; 34740-46
China Affairs Board, aff. ... 34675
Chungking, bombing of, statement ... 34595; 34693-95

Shiratori (Defendant):
  Policy toward China ... 34840-44
  Wang Ching-wei regime, recognition of, aff. and test. ... 34960-61; 34979

Shrine for Japanese and Chinese soldiers, aff. ... 32765-66; 33835-37

South China:
  Foochow campaign ... 3443-54
  Hengyang campaign ... 21798-804
  Kweilin campaign, aff. ... 21630-34; 21799-804; 21807-11
  Luichow campaign ... 21800-04; 21807-11

Suzuki (Defendant):
  China Affairs Board, test. ... 35265-91
  Policy toward China ... 35177-88; 35234; 35256-65; 35338-41
  Wang Ching-wei regime, recognition of ... 3780; 35234; 35281-83; 35387-88

Togo (Defendant):
  China Affairs Board, aff. ... 35474-51
  Peace proposal to China, aff. ... 35747-48

Tojo (Defendant):
  Peace proposal to China, aff. and test. ... 36187; 36206-12; 32220-27; 36538-42; 36634-36; 36691-94
  Policy toward China under GEA policy, aff. and test. ... 31749-823; 36206-12; 36220-27; 36447-49; 36538-42; 36634-36; 36691-94

Treaties and agreements:
  Brussels Conference, Japanese statement ... 20984-89; 21000-06
  Chinese President's Declaration of 1913 ... 20605-06
  Dairen Conference of 1932, aff. and test. ... 20941-60
  Ho-Umezu Agreement ... 20781-90
  Hunchun Border Protocol ... 34499-507
  International Agreement of 1902 ... 20594-98
  International Agreement of 1912 ... 20602-04
  Joint Declaration, China-Japan-Manchukuo ... 5322-26
  Sino-Japanese Alliance of 1943, aff. ... 36447-49
  Sino-Japanese Basic Treaty of 1940 ... 5320-21; 5327-40; 36206-12; 36220-27; 36540
  Sino-Japanese Treaty, renouncing extraterritoriality ... 22387-89
  Tangku Truce, aff. and test. ... 20772-81

Umezu (Defendant):
  Chinese property ... 36889-90
  North China issue, settlement ... 36884
  Peace with China, interrogation ... 36863

USA (See: US, US-Japanese negotiations, Foreign policies)

China Incident (See: China, Marco Polo Bridge Incident)

Chinese Eastern Railway (CER) ... 3561; 3563; 35961; 35963

  Sale of:
    Admissibility of, tribunal ruling (rejected) ... 29441-45
    Aff. and test. ... 29319-33; 29387-90; 35417-23; 35485-86; 35490; 35630-33; 35949-69; 35973-75; 36129-30; 36139-40
    Agreement, signing of ... 29616-19
    Hirota-Litvinov message ... 29614-15
    Negotiation ... 29474; 29614
    Togo-Molotov negotiations, settlement of payment, aff. ... 35378-80

Civil Police ... 607-10

"Clear the Clouds from the East Asia Sky," article by Hashimoto (Defendant) ... 15657-59

Collaboration among Germany, Italy and Japan (Pros. ... 5848-6699; Def. ... 24165-666; 27964-28034; Pros. summation ... 39446-517; Def. summation ... 42940-43050) (See also: Germany; Italy; Japan)

  Anti-Comintern Pact:
    Conclusion of, report on ... 5958-67
    Economic cooperation in China ... 6017-19; 6604-20
    Germany's mediation to China ... 5983-85; 5987-90; 5993-6000; 6002-15
    Himmler-Oshima conference ... 6026-28
    Japan's aggressive policy in China, German attempts to avert ... 5991-92
    Negotiation ... 5939-40; 5957; 5968-72; 6037-45; 6047-48
    Pact and secret agreement attached thereto ... 5934-38; 5850-57
    Seventh Congress of Comintern ... 23741

  China, against:
    Collaboration ... 5983-6015
    Economic cooperation in ... 6017-19; 6588-602
    German preferential trade in ... 6623-24
    Japanese aggressive policy in, German attempts to avert ... 5991-92
    Ribbentrop-Oshima conference concerning econ. cooperation in ... 6588-91

  Cultural and Trade Agreement under Tripartite Pact:
    Cultural cooperation ... 6570
    Economic commission draft plan ... 6630-34
    Economic cooperation in China ... 6017-19; 6604-20
    Togo-Ribbentrop conversation ... 6588-91
    Togo-Weihl conversation ... 6591-6602

Collaboration among Germany, Italy and Japan *(Cont.)*

Decorations to Japanese officials ... 11352-58

East Asia:
    Arita speech ... 6148-49; 6238-40
    Japanese intention to establish new order in ... 6284-85
    Oshima-Weizsacker conversation ... 6456-58

FIC, against ... 6162-65; 6175; 6447; 7008-17; 7030; 7034-36; 7052-53; 7157-59
    Japanese attitude toward ... 6162-65
    Japanese demands for passage of troops ... 6295-98; 6955-57; 7067-68
    Japanese military aggression, German attitude ... 6175
    Japanese negotiation with, to establish bases ... 7046-48
    Japanese preparation ... 6162-68; 6175; 6560-61; 7008-16; 7030; 7034-36; 7052-53

Hata (Defendant):
    Tripartite Pact, aff. and test. ... 28944-93; 29406-18 *(See also:* 768; 1679; 6191; 6212; 33114-15; 33241-51; 33328-32*)*

Hiranuma (Defendant):
    Anti-Comintern Pact and, ... 34009-10
    Hiranuma cabinet, policies ... 30333-36
    Hiranuma cabinet, resignation ... 24202-04
    Tripartite Pact and, ... 16235; 30498-519; 31563-69

Hirota (Defendant):
    Tripartite Pact and, ... 30003-16; 30019-20

Itagaki (Defendant):
    Anti-Comintern Pact, test. ... 34010-11; 34141-45
    Congratulatory telegrams to Hitler ... 15745-46
    Tripartite Pact and, ... 15744-45; 16237-39; 31291-92

Kido (Defendant):
    Relations with Germany ... 34903-04
    Tripartite Pact and, ... 24450-67; 24489-560

Kimura (Defendant), German decorations to ... 16180-82; test. ... 31654-57

Muto (Defendant), Tripartite Pact and, aff. and test. ... 33110-18; 33218-29 *(See also:* 33676-78*)*

The Netherlands, German attitude toward ... 6159-62

Non-collaboration with Germany ... 6122-23; 6189-90; 6285-92; 7912; 9694-703; 24165-666; 27964-28034

Non-Separate Treaty:
    Ciano diary ... 6660-62; 6666-67
    Military agreement ... 6681-86
    Oshima-Hitler conversation ... 6671-80

Oshima (Defendant):
    Anti-Comintern Pact and, aff. and test. ... 33700-13; 33716-27; 33730-59; 33767-70; 33772-810; 33984-88; 33997-34014; 34077-149; 34318-23; 34337-39; 35400-05; 35429-36; 35447-51 *(See also:* 5910; 5912-25; 6021-26; 2028-29; 7891-92; 34116-19*)*
    Appointment as ambassador to Germany, tel. ... 34330-43
    Conferences:
        Ribbentrop, with ... 6459-68; 6992; 7903; 8033-34; 8176-77
        Weizsacker, with ... 6456-58
    Cultural agreement with Germany, aff. ... 33983
    Denial by, meeting Himmler concerning intelligence against USSR, aff. and test. ... 33764-67; 33770-72; 33923-24; 33991-97; 34331
    Economic agreement with Germany, aff. and test. ... 34044-45; 34222-31; 34267-69; 37080-100
    "German (Hitler's) Diplomacy," article by ... 34152-61
    German-Russian Non-Aggression Pact, aff. ... 34014-16; 34150-68; 34325
    Japan's refusal to attack USSR in 1941, interrogation ... 23558-60
    Letters:
        Ott, from, concerning minister in German embassy in Tokyo ... 6636
        Ribbentrop, to, concerning protest to Germany's signing Non-Aggression Pact with USSR ... 7911-12
    Military attache, as, aff. and test. ... 33983-86; 34100-02; 34111-13 *(See also:* 37055-79*)*
    Mixed special commission, aff. and test. ... 34042-45; 34204-09 *(See also:* 6417-20*)*
    Non-Separate Treaty, aff. ... 34036-41 *(See also:* 6638-42*)*
    Relations with Germany, aff. ... 33961-64; 33976-79; 34062-66; 34070-77 *(See also:* 35393-94; 37080-100*)*
    Secret Agreement, aff. ... 33987-88; 34002-07 *(See also:* 6095-102; 22539-50*)*
    Submarine transfer by Germany, aff. ... 34036-41 *(See also:* 6638-42*)*
    Submarine warfare, aff. and test. ... 34057; 34259-63 *(See also:* 15187-95*)*
    Telegram from Ribbentrop concerning war against USSR, Germany and Japan, preparation for ... 7870
    Tripartite Pact, aff. and test. ... 33978-79; 34018-21; 34168-204; 34209-16 *(See also:* 7916-19; 30336-38; 30487-519; 37055-79*)*
    "Tripartite Pact and USA," article by ... 34180-89

USSR-Japan, aff. and test. ... 33764-67;
33770-72; 33991-97; 34026-27; 34216-22;
34269-84; 34331 (See also: 6026-28;
6562-65; 7994-98; 10031-36)
USSR, war against, proposed entry of Japan
into ... 8014-20

Sato (Defendant), German decoration to ... 16180-
82; test. ... 34465 (See also: 34894-95)

Shigemitsu (Defendant):
Collaboration with Germany ... 24483-560
German decoration, not given to ... 24757
Tripartite Pact, speech about ... 8062; 8068
Tripartite Pact, tel. to Mussolini and Ribben-
trop ... 8066-67

Shimada (Defendant):
German decoration to ... 34629-33; 34674-75
Submarine warfare, order for, aff. and test.
... 34635-45; 34671-72; 34771-89;
34817 (See also: 15184)

Shiratori (Defendant):
Anti-Comintern Pact and, aff. and test. ...
33132; 33736-39; 33747-51; 34084-86;
34121-28; 34824-25; 34907-17; 35085-
87; 35097-109 (See also: 6083; 16914)
Appointment as ambassador to Italy, aff. and
test. ... 34907-17; 35031-35; 35088-91
(See also: 6083; 6092; 16914)
Collaboration with Germany ... 24479-82;
24489-560
German decoration to, aff. and test. ... 34891-
94; 34964 (See also: 11351-58)
German-Russian Non-Aggression Pact, aff.
and test. ... 34854-58; 34874-75; 35044-
47; 35092-93 (See also: 675-77)
Mussolini and Tripartite Pact ... 34918-30
(See also: 6476-80)
Relations with Germany ... 34849-903
Relations with Italy ... 34824-27
Tripartite Pact, aff. and test. ... 34826-27;
34849-58; 34875-78; 35047-50; 35125
(See also: 6082-83; 6097-102; 6103-11;
6130; 6141-43; 6265; 6296-98; 15744-45;
30491-519; 31239-40; 34168-70)

Singapore, German inducement to attack
... 6429-34

Southern regions, against:
Exploitations of resources by Germany
... 6988-90
Japanese military preparations ... 6293-94;
6560-61

Special air route to Germany from Japan,
tel. ... 7871-72

Submarine transfer by Germany to Japan
... 15186-95; 34671; aff. and test.
... 33967-73; 34045-48; 34259-60

Submarine warfare in Indian Ocean ... 15187-95

Suzuki (Defendant):
Attitude toward Germany, aff. ... 35190-91
Attitude toward Tripartite Pact, aff. and
test. ... 35190-91; 35255-56
German decoration to, aff. ... 35248-49 (See
also: 11353; 16180)

Thailand, against ... 6447

Togo (Defendant):
Anti-Comintern Pact, aff. and test. ... 35642-
50; 35657-58 (See also: 34092-100;
34122-25; 34912; 35342-43; 35391-94;
35403; 35408-15; 35453-57; 35464-66;
35486-87; 35522-26)
Collaboration with Germany ... 24468-79;
24489-560
Economic cooperation with Germany, aff.
... 35654-57
German decoration to, aff. ... 35625-26
(See also: 16944)
Non-Separate Treaty, aff. ... 35664; 35734-36
Relations with Germany, aff. and test. ...
35625-26; 35642-65; 35745-46; 35988-
99; 36038-42 (See also: 35342-43;
35391-94; 35403; 35408-15; 35429-31;
35437-45; 35453-59; 35464-67; 35486-
87; 35522-23)
Tripartite Pact, negotiation of, aff. and test.
... 35658-65; 35988-99; 36038-42;
37164-68 (See also: 35342-43; 35429-
31; 35437-45; 35453-59; 35466-67)

Tojo (Defendant):
German-Russian war, policy concerning, aff.
and test. ... 36254-65; 36807-08
Tripartite Pact, negotiation of, aff. and test.
... 36213-18; 36222-23; 36542-50;
36583-89; 36591-98; 36625-29; 36642-
45; 36769-72; 36791; 36807-08 (See
also: 6273; 11795; 31583-96; 31749-823;
33118-21; 33123-24; 33162-72; 33221-
22; 33226; 33345-50; 33524-31; 33542-
44; 33677-78; 33681-83; 34575-87;
35670-72; 35693-94; 35696-97; 35707;
35711-12; 35978-88)

Tripartite Pact (See also: Tripartite Pact)
Abe cabinet ... 24206
Background and purpose of ... 24351-66;
24371; 24374-78;
Cabinet decision ... 6271-72
Ciano diary ... 6092-93; 6095-97
Collaboration under ... 5975-81; 5983-85;
5990; 6264-65; 6449-56; 6468-69
Conclusion of ... 6148-49; 24277-576
East Asia, new order of, Japan's effort to
establish ... 6148-49; 6233-40; 6284-85
Four Minister Conference ... 6191
German efforts to negotiate with Japan ...
6098-102; 6127-33; 6141-42

Collaboration among Germany, Italy and
  Japan *(Cont.)*
  Tripartite Pact *(Cont.)*
    German-Italian agreement concerning Japan's
      participation ... 6115-19
    German navy report to Hitler ... 6459-68
    Goering-Mussolini conference ... 6112-14
    Hitler directive ... 6469-73
    Imperial conference ... 3629-43; 36190-92;
      36799
    Imperial rescript ... 6394-95
    Ito's commemoration speech ... 6412-17
    Japan cabinet change, German interest in
      ... 6150-58; 6257-67
    Japanese military preparations ... 6460-61;
      6456
    Japanese participation, German doc. ...
      6115-19
    Kurusu-Knoll conference ... 6170-73
    Kurusu-Weizsacker conference ... 6427-28
    Matsuoka-Ribbentrop conference ... 6498-
      532; 6546-52
    Matsuoka, trip to Europe ... 24578-87;
      24613-14
    Matsuoka-Weizsacker conference ... 6476-77
    Memorandum (Ott, Indelli, Matsuoka)
      ... 6417-20
    Military commission ... 24615-66
    Negotiations, renewal for ... 6278-82
    Oshima-Ribbentrop conference ... 6459
    Oshima-Stahmer conference ... 6323-27
    Oshima-Weizsacker conference ... 6456-58
    Sato (Defendant) trip to Berlin ... 24227-29
    Yonai cabinet, reason for fall of ... 6240-56

  US, against *(See also:* US, US-Japanese
    negotiation):
    German declaration of war on ... 24752-53
    Grew speech concerning Japan's policy in
      China ... 24313-25
    Japan's reaction to Grew speech ... 24326-31
    Matsuoka, explanation of Tripartite Pact
      ... 24335-39
    Relations with Japan under Tripartite Pact
      ... 24310-51
    Submarine transfer by Germany to Japan
      ... 15186-95; 34671
    Submarine warfare ... 15187-95
    Yangtze navigation, US opens ... 24216-19

  USSR, against *(See also:* USSR):
    German appreciation for Japan's efforts
      ... 7875-76; 7990
    German bad faith in negotiating with
      ... 24180-84
    German inducement to Japan to enter war
      against ... 6162-65; 6562-65; 6635-65;
      7984-86
    German-Russian Non-Aggression Pact
      ... 24185-89
      Japan's reaction to ... 6124-26
    Hiranuma cabinet, resignation of ... 24202-04
    Japan's inability to attack in 1941 ... 7971-72
    Japan's policy toward ... 7870; 7955-56;
      7961-69; 7975; 7978-84; 7993; 8071-74
    Treaties with Japan, German attitude to,
      ... 5939-40
    War with Germany, Japan's position in
      ... 7957-58

Combined Fleet Top Secret Operation Order,
  Japanese ... 11193-98; 11202; 11228-29;
  11232-33 *(See also:* US, Pearl Harbor
  Attack, US-Japanese Negotiations)

"Commentaries," Ito ... 554; 557; 559; 563; 575; 586

"Committee for the Maintenance of Peace and
  Order" ... 2755-56
Concordia Society, Manchukuo *(See:* Kyowa-Kai
  Society)

Conference Before the Throne (Gozen Kaigi) *(See:*
  Japan, Imperial Conference, Liaison
  Conference)

Conference for the Supreme Direction of the War
  (Supreme War Council) *(See:* Japan,
  Supreme War Council)

Conspiracy *(See also:* Tribunal, Law; Collaboration among Germany, Italy and Japan;
  Japan, Imperial Conference, Liaison Conference, Senior Statesmen Conference,
  Supreme War Council)

  Dohihara (Defendant), Itagaki arrangement of
    meeting with Pu Y'i ... 15726-29

  Hashimoto (Defendant), Tojo relationship with,
    ... 28765-66 *(See also:* 2056)

  Hata (Defendant):
    Resignation, cause of, aff. ... 29030-38
    Tojo, recommends, to War Minister ...
      36598-617
    War Minister, circumstances of, aff. and
      test. ... 28916-43; 29406-18 *(See also:*
      6191; 6212; 29076-79)

  Hirota (Defendant):
    Appointment of War and Navy ministers,
      change of rules for, aff. ... 29645-51
    Matsuoka policy and, aff. ... 30032-34
    Movement of rightist bodies concerning
      change of government ... 15790-97

  Hoshino (Defendant):
    Career, after resignation from Planning
      Board ... 29188-92
    Tojo cabinet, in ... 29203-07

  Itagaki (Defendant):
    Dohihara-Pu Y'i meeting, arrangement for
      ... 15726-29
    Koiso, meeting with, concerning Tripartite
      Pact ... 15815-18

Kaya (Defendant):
    Administration between civil and military ... 30627-32
    Civilian ministers, destruction of, after outbreak of China Incident ... 30534-39
    Tojo promise to, no war with US, aff. ... 30603; 30609-10

Kido (Defendant):
    Koiso and, ... 32433-36; 32473-75
    Shigemitsu, conversation with, concerning Japan's involvement in European war, test. ... 31216-32
    Shimada, appointment as Navy Minister, test. ... 34686-87
    Suzuki, conversation with, concerning withdrawal from China, aff. and test. ... 35205-13; 35251-54; 35304; 35306; 35311; 35325-32
    Tojo and, test. ... 35531-37

Kimura (Defendant), association with inner group ... 16179

Koiso (Defendant):
    Itagaki, meeting with, concerning Tripartite Pact ... 15815-18
    Kido and, test. ... 32433-36; 32473-75
    March and October Incidents and, ... 15676-77
    May 15 Incident and Okawa faction ... 15555-602
    Shigemitsu and, test. ... 32439-42
    Suzuki and, test. ... 32438-39

Matsui (Defendant), Supreme War Council, member of ... 33828-29; 33890-92

Minami (Defendant):
    Cabinet councillor and, aff. ... 32921-25
    Greater Japan Political Association, membership in ... 15786
    Japan Political Society and, aff. ... 32921-25
    Kokuhonsha and, test. ... 32274
    March Incident and, test. ... 31235-36
    October Incident and, test. ... 31235-36
    South Manchurian Railway president, party for, aff. ... 32809 (*See also*: 15753; 31705; 32215-16)

Muto (Defendant):
    Liaison between War and Navy ministers ... 16123
    Liaison Conference (*See*: Japan, Liaison Conference)
    Tojo policies ... 16127

Oka (Defendant):
    Liaison Conference (*See*: Japan, Liaison Conference)
    Political activities, aff. and test. ... 33356-63; 33410-11; 33422-24; 33457-68; 33476-85

Oshima (Defendant), aff. and test. ... 34048-52; 34068-69; 34364-66

    Matsuoka and, aff. and test. ... 34023-25; 34170-73; 34216-22; 34231-47; 34284
    Political activities, aff. ... 34018-19; 34372-75

Sato (Defendant), Tojo, relation with ... 16084-85

Shigemitsu (Defendant):
    Kido, conversation with, concerning Japan's involvement in European war, test. ... 31216-32
    Koiso and, test. ... 32439-42

Shimada (Defendant), aff. ... 34676-77
    IRAPS, aff. ... 34668 (*See also*: 11376)
    Liaison Conference (*See also*: Japan, Liaison Conference)
    Tojo cabinet, choice of Shimada in, aff. and test. ... 34635-45; 34671-72; 34771-89; 34817 (*See also*: 15184)

Shiratori (Defendant) ... 34827 (*See also*: 16765)
    IRAA and, aff. and test. ... 34828; 34963-64; 35019-26
    IRAPS and, aff. and test. ... 34828; 35006-07; 35053-54

Suzuki (Defendant):
    Imperial Conference (*See*: Japan, Imperial Conference)
    Imperial Rescript, declaration of war, aff. and test. ... 35246; 35312-18 (*See also*: 10685)
    Kido, conversation with, concerning withdrawal from China, aff. and test. ... 35205-13; 35251-54; 35304-06; 35311-14; 35325-32
    Koiso, test. ... 32438-39
    Konoye cabinet and, aff. and test. ... 35233-34; 35301-09; 35242-43 (*See also*: 16232; 16253)
    Konoye cabinet, resignation of, aff. and test. ... 35243-44; 35305-07 (*See also*: 10246; 10250; 16199)
    Liaison Conference (*See*: Japan, Liaison Conference)
    March Incident, aff. ... 35158-61; 35228-30 (*See also*: 1927; 1941)
    May 15 Incident and, aff. ... 35230-31 (*See also*: 16215)
    Political activities in 1930's, aff. ... 35158-61 (*See also*: 16927)
    Senior Statesmen Conference (*See*: Japan, Senior Statesmen Conference)
    Tojo cabinet, aff. and test. ... 35213-20; 35307-12

Togo (Defendant), aff. ... 35672-73
    Elder Statesmen Conference (*See*: Japan, Elder Statesmen Conference)
    Foreign minister, choice of, 1941, aff. and test. ... 35670-72; 35978-88; 37164-68
    Foreign minister, choice of, 1945, aff. and test. ... 35590-96; 35603-10; 35776-90; 35801-16; 39110-12

Conspiracy *(Cont.)*
  Togo *(Cont.)*
    Foreign Ministry, purge of, aff. and test. ... 35517-20; 35640-42; 35799-800 *(See also:* 6270; 6364; 16943)
    GEA Ambassador Conference *(See:* Japan, GEA Ambassador Conference)
    GEA Ministry, objection to establishment of, aff. ... 35525; 35574-79; 35755-65 *(See also:* 35556-57)
    Imperial Conference *(See:* Japan, Imperial Conference)
    IRAA, Central Cooperation Conference, aff. ... 35559-60
    IRAA, objection to, aff. ... 35741-42
    Liaison Conference *(See:* Japan, Liaison Conference)
    Matsuoka policy and, aff. ... 35517-19; 35521-24; 35738-39
    Senior Statesmen Conference *(See:* Japan, Senior Statesmen Conference)
    Supreme Council for Direction of War *(See:* Japan, Supreme War Council)
    Tojo, disagreement with, aff. ... 35740-42; 35752-64
    USSR, war against, refusal to participate in, aff. ... 35740-42; 35745-46
    War, termination of, in favor of, aff. and test. ... 35545-46; 35591-97; 35603-10; 35776-90; 35801-16; 36110-12

  Tojo (Defendant), test. ... 36574-77; 36598-617
    Army and politics, aff. ... 36473-80
    Cabinet meetings, army's view in ... 17869
    GEACP and, aff. ... 35752-54
    GEA Ministry, establishment of, aff. ... 35755-64
    Imperial Conference *(See:* Japan, Imperial Conference)
    Imperial Rescript, declaration of war, aff. ... 36404-07 *(See also:* 240-41)
    Kaya, promise to, no war against US, aff. ... 30603; 30609-10
    Kido and, test. ... 35531-37
    Konoye cabinet (second), participation in as War Minister, aff. and test. ... 36176-81; 36572-76; 36598-617 *(See also:* 31749-823)
    Konoye cabinet (third), downfall of, aff. ... 36293-307 *(See also:* 10289-90)
    Liaison Conference *(See:* Japan, Liaison Conference)
    Ogikubo Conference, aff. ... 36178-81
    Oka and, test. ... 33457-61
    Prime Minister, naming of ... 16199-211
    Senior Statesmen Conference *(See:* Japan, Senior Statesmen Conference)
    Togo, disagreement with, aff. ... 35740-42; 35752-64
    Tojo cabinet *(See:* Japan, Cabinet)
    War Minister, choice of, aff. and test. ... 36176-81; 36572-76; 36598-617 *(See also:* 31749-823)
    War, termination of, objection to, aff. ... 35807-16

  Umezu (Defendant):
    Cabinet formation by Gen. Ugaki ... 15798-800
    Military cliques, attitude toward, aff. ... 36843-45; 36851-83; 36958-61

Constitution, Japan ... 1238; 17470-76

  Emperor and, test. ... 31322-50; 31376-81; 31398-404

Constitutional Organization, Japan *(See:* Japan, Constitutional organization)

Control Association ... 625-26; 8403; 35241

  Planning Board and, ... 35165-68

Conventional War Crimes *(See:* Tribunal, Law; Preparation for War)

Crime Prevention Section ... 610

Crimes against Humanity *(See:* Atrocities; Tribunal, Law; POW)

Crimes against Peace *(See:* Aggressions; Tribunal, Law; Preparation for War)

"Crossing the Border Incident" ... 1682

Cultural Undertakings Department ... 604

Customs Bureau ... 606

D

"Dai-Asia-Shugi" (or "Greater Asia Principles"), Article Entitled ... 32715-19; 32730-33 *(See also:* Greater Asia Association; Greater Asia Development League; Greater Asia Doctrine)

Dai-Nihon Seinento (or Dai Nippon Seinen To, Great Japan Youth Association):

  Affidavit concerning ... 28781-86; 28797-98; 28818-19 *(See also:* 15680-81)

  Interrogation concerning ... 15677-78

Dai Nippon Asia Association *(See:* Dai Nippon Asia Development League; Greater Asia Association)

Dai Nippon Asia Development League *(See:* Greater Asia Association)

  Activities and duties of, affidavit and testimony concerning ... 33832-33; 33896-906

Dai Nippon Sekisei Kai

  Interrogation concerning ... 15676; 15680-81

INDEX TO MILITARY TRIBUNAL PROCEEDINGS

"Declaration of Hashimoto Kingoro," Article by
  Hashimoto (Defendant) Entitled ...
  15693-95

Declaration of War ... 10686-88; 35246; 38312-18

Defendants:

  Araki, Sadao:
    Indictment (Counts 1-19; 23-36; 44-47; 52-55)
      ... 33-45; 48-53; 59-61; 66-67
    Judgment ... 49774-76
    Plea ... 101
    Responsibility, governmental ... 686-89; 5900
    Responsibility, individual, by prosecution ...
      11302-401; 14262-910; 15560-16260; by
      defense ... 28106-592; 36978-89
    Sentence ... 49854
    Summation, individual, by prosecution ...
      40568-616; by defense ... 45471-709;
      45899-46051

  Dohihara, Kenji:
    Indictment (Counts 1-44; 51-55) ... 33-60;
      66-71
    Judgment ... 49777-79
    Plea ... 101
    Prosecution final statement ... 48215-36
    Responsibility, governmental ... 690-99; 6268
    Responsibility, individual, by prosecution ...
      11302-401; 14262-910; 15560-16260;
      by defense ... 28592-764
    Sentence ... 49854
    Summation, individual, by prosecution ...
      40617-60; by defense ... 43738-857

  Hashimoto, Kingoro:
    Indictment (Counts 1-19; 27-32; 34-36; 44-55)
      ... 33-45; 49-53; 59-71
    Judgment ... 49780-82
    Plea ... 101
    Responsibility, governmental ... 699-701
    Responsibility, individual, by prosecution ...
      11302-401; 14262-910; 15560-16260;
      by defense ... 28764-852
    Sentence ... 49854
    Summation, individual, by prosecution ...
      40662-68; by defense ... 44359-561

  Hata, Shunroku:
    Indictment (Counts 1-17; 19; 25-32; 34-36;
      44-55) ... 33-45; 49-53; 59-71
    Judgment ... 49783-85
    Plea ... 101
    Responsibility, governmental ... 701-04;
      5900-01; 6268
    Responsibility, individual, by prosecution ...
      11302-401; 14262-910; 15560-16260;
      by defense ... 28853-29064; 29077-79;
      29394-418
    Sentence ... 49854
    Summation, individual, by prosecution ...
      40688-779; by defense ... 43264-492

  Hiranuma, Kiichiro:
    Indictment (Counts 1-47; 51-55) ... 33-61;
      66-71
    Judgment ... 49786-87
    Plea ... 101
    Responsibility, governmental ... 704-06;
      5901; 6268
    Responsibility, individual, by prosecution ...
      11302-401; 14262-910; 15560-16260;
      by defense ... 29208-340
    Sentence ... 49854
    Summation, individual, by prosecution ...
      40780-846; by defense ... 43857-928

  Hirota, Koki:
    Indictment (Counts 1-17; 19-25; 27-33; 35-47;
      52-55) ... 33-61; 67-71
    Judgment ... 49788-92
    Plea ... 101
    Responsibility, governmental ... 706; 5901
    Responsibility, individual, by prosecution ...
      11302-401; 14262-910; 15560-16260;
      by defense ... 29340-30038; 36990-37019
    Sentence ... 49855
    Summation, individual, by prosecution ...
      40847-924; by defense ... 44154-71

  Hoshino, Naoki:
    Indictment (Counts 1-17; 19-25; 27-35; 37-44;
      52-55) ... 33-60; 67-71
    Judgment ... 49793-95
    Plea ... 102
    Responsibility, governmental ... 710-14;
      6048; 6268
    Responsibility, individual, by prosecution ...
      11302-401; 14262-910; 15560-16260;
      by defense ... 29064-207; 37047-51
    Sentence ... 49855
    Summation, individual, by prosecution ...
      40925-84; by defense ... 44823-900

  Itagaki, Seishiro:
    Indictment (Counts 1-19; 23-36; 45-47; 51-55)
      ... 33-45; 48-53; 60-61; 66-71
    Judgment ... 49796-800
    Plea ... 102
    Prosecution final statement ... 48237-48
    Responsibility, governmental ... 715-17;
      5902-03
    Responsibility, individual, by prosecution ...
      11302-401; 14262-910; 15560-16260;
      by defense ... 30040-526
    Sentence ... 49855
    Summation, individual, by prosecution ...
      40984-41023; by defense ... 45109-350

  Kaya, Okinori:
    Indictment (Counts 1-17; 19-22; 27-32; 34;
      37-47; 53-55) ... 33-46; 50-61; 68-71
    Judgment ... 49801-02
    Plea ... 102
    Responsibility, governmental ... 722-25;
      5902-03; 6048

Defendants *(Cont.)*
   Kaya, Okinori *(Cont.)*
      Responsibility, individual, by prosecution ... 11302-401; 14262-910; 15560-16260; by defense ... 30527-710
      Sentence ... 49855
      Summation, individual, by prosecution ... 41024-46; by defense ... 45717-899

   Kido, Koichi:
      Indictment (Counts 1-17; 19-55) ... 33-71
      Judgment ... 49803-06
      Plea ... 102
      Responsibility, governmental ... 725-26; 5902-03; 6268-69
      Responsibility, individual, by prosecution ... 11302-401; 14262-910; 15560-16260; by defense ... 30710-31648
      Sentence ... 49855
      Summation, individual, by prosecution ... 41047-129; by defense ... 46424-774

   Kimura, Heitaro:
      Indictment (Counts 1-17; 20-22; 27-32; 34; 37-44; 53-55) ... 33-46; 50-59; 68-71
      Judgment ... 49807-10
      Plea ... 102
      Responsibility, governmental ... 727-32; 6048
      Responsibility, individual, by prosecution ... 11302-401; 14262-910; 15560-16260; by defense ... 31649-823
      Sentence ... 49855
      Summation, individual, by prosecution ... 41129-64; by defense ... 44562-645

   Koiso, Kuniaki:
      Indictment (Counts 1-18; 26-32; 34; 36; 44; 48-51; 53-55) ... 33-44; 50-53; 59-60; 65-71
      Judgment ... 49811-13
      Plea ... 102
      Responsibility, governmental ... 733-35; 5902-03
      Responsibility, individual, by prosecution ... 11302-401; 14262-910; 15560-16260; by defense ... 32199-551
      Sentence ... 49855
      Summation, individual, by prosecution ... 41165-206; by defense ... 44648-820

   Matsui, Iwane:
      Indictment (Counts 1-17; 19; 25-32; 34-36; 44-47; 51-55) ... 33-45; 49-53; 59-61; 66-71
      Judgment ... 49814-16
      Plea ... 102
      Responsibility, governmental ... 735-37; 5902-03
      Responsibility, individual, by prosecution ... 11302-401; 14262-910; 15560-16260; by defense ... 30527-710
      Sentence ... 49856
      Summation, individual, by prosecution ... 41207-275; by defense ... 47127-274

   Matsuoka, Yosuke:
      Indictment (Counts 1-17; 23-36; 38-44; 51-55) ... 33-44; 48-53; 55-60; 66-71
      Plea ... 102

   Minami, Jiro:
      Indictment (Counts 1-18; 27-32; 34; 44; 53-55) ... 33-44; 50-53; 59-60; 68-71
      Judgment ... 49817-18
      Plea ... 103
      Responsibility, governmental ... 740-42
      Responsibility, individual, by prosecution ... 11302-401; 14262-910; 15560-16260; by defense ... 32799-929; 33530-666
      Sentence ... 49856
      Summation, individual, by prosecution ... 41276-310; by defense ... 43928-44153

   Muto, Akira:
      Indictment (Counts 1-17; 19-24; 26-34; 36-47; 51; 53-55) ... 33-61; 66-71
      Judgment ... 49819-21
      Plea ... 103
      Responsibility, governmental ... 742-47; 5902-03; 6269
      Responsibility, individual, by prosecution ... 11302-401; 14262-910; 15560-16260; by defense ... 32930-33285; 33666-84
      Sentence ... 49856
      Summation, individual, by prosecution ... 41311-90; by defense ... 44901-45006

   Nagano, Osami:
      Indictment (Counts 1-17; 20-24; 27-34; 37-44; 53-55) ... 33-60; 68-71
      Plea ... 103

   Oka, Takasumi:
      Indictment (Counts 1-18; 27-32; 34) ... 33-44; 50-53
      Judgment ... 49822
      Plea ... 103
      Responsibility, governmental ... 751-61
      Responsibility, individual, by prosecution ... 11302-401; 14262-910; 15560-16260; by defense ... 33285-530
      Sentence ... 49856
      Summation, individual, by prosecution ... 41391-471; by defense ... (unable to include in index)

   Okawa, Shumei:
      Indictment (Counts 1-18; 27-32; 34) ... 33-44; 50-53

   Oshima, Hiroshi:
      Indictment (Counts 1-17; 20-22; 27-32; 34; 37-44; 53-55) ... 33-46; 50-60; 68-71
      Judgment ... 49823-24
      Plea ... 103
      Responsibility, governmental ... 765-68 5905; 6048
      Responsibility, individual, by prosecution ... 11302-401; 14262-910; 15560-16260;

by defense ... 33687-810; 33922-34376;
35440-50; 37053-100
Sentence ... 49856
Summation, individual, by prosecution ...
41471-595; by defense ... 46409-23;
46780-47126

Sato, Kenryo:
Indictment (Counts 1-17; 20-22; 27-32; 34;
37-44; 48-50; 53-55) ... 33-46; 50-60;
65-66; 68-71
Judgment ... 49825-27
Plea ... 103
Responsibility, governmental ... 768-75; 5905
Responsibility, individual, by prosecution ...
11302-401; 14262-910; 15560-16260;
by defense ... 34376-467
Sentence ... 49856
Summation, individual, by prosecution ...
41596-620; by defense ... 45006-34

Shigemitsu, Mamoru:
Indictment (Counts 1-18; 23-25; 27-32; 34-35;
48-50; 52-55) ... 33-44; 48-53; 65-71
Judgment ... 49828-32
Plea ... 103
Responsibility, governmental ... 775-78
Responsibility, individual, by prosecution ...
11302-401; 14262-910; 15560-16260;
by defense ... 34468-565
Sentence ... 49857
Summation, individual, by prosecution ...
41621-58; by defense ... 46296-407

Shimada, Shigetaro:
Indictment (Counts 1-17; 20-22; 27-32; 34;
37-44; 53-55) ... 33-46; 50-60; 68-71
Judgment ... 49833-34
Plea ... 103
Responsibility, governmental ... 778-81; 6049
Responsibility, individual, by prosecution ...
11302-401; 14262-910; 15560-16260;
by defense ... 34565-821
Sentence ... 49857
Summation, individual, by prosecution ...
41659-709; by defense ... 45351-470

Shiratori, Toshio:
Indictment (Counts 1-17; 27-32; 34) ... 33-44;
50-53
Judgment ... 49835-37
Plea ... 104
Responsibility, governmental ... 781-83;
5905; 6048
Responsibility, individual, by prosecution ...
11302-401; 14262-910; 15560-16260;
by defense ... 34822-35154
Sentence ... 49857
Summation, individual, by prosecution ...
41712-812; by defense ... 46052-296

Suzuki, Teiichi:
Indictment (Counts 1-17; 19-22; 25-32;
34-47; 51-55) ... 33-46; 49-61; 66-71

Judgment ... 49838-39
Plea ... 104
Responsibility, governmental ... 783-87
Responsibility, individual, by prosecution ...
11302-401; 14262-910; 15560-16260;
by defense ... 35155-342
Sentence ... 49857
Summation, individual, by prosecution ...
41813-67; by defense ... 45037-109

Togo, Shigenori:
Indictment (Counts 1-17; 20-22; 26-32; 34;
36-44; 51; 53-55) ... 33-46; 50-60; 66-71
Judgment ... 49840-42
Plea ... 104
Responsibility, governmental ... 787-91;
5905; 6049
Responsibility, individual, by prosecution ...
11302-401; 14262-910; 15560-16260;
by defense ... 35342-36145; 37025-46;
37164-68
Sentence ... 49857
Summation, individual, by prosecution ...
41868-(unable to include in index);
by defense ... 47722-986

Tojo, Hideki:
Indictment (Counts 1-24; 26-34; 36-44;
48-55) ... 33-60; 65-71
Judgment ... 49843-48
Plea ... 104
Responsibility, governmental ... 791-97;
5905; 6049
Responsibility, individual, by prosecution ...
11302-11401; 14262-910; 15560-16260;
by defense ... 36146-839
Sentence ... 49857
Summation, individual, by prosecution ...
(unable to include in index); by defense
... 47274-720

Umezu, Yoshijiro:
Indictment (Counts 1-19; 26-32; 34; 36; 45-51;
53-55) ... 33-45; 50-53; 60-71
Judgment ... 49849-51
Plea ... 104
Responsibility, governmental ... 798-803; 5905
Responsibility, individual, by prosecution ...
11302-401; 14262-910; 15560-16260;
by defense ... 36840-962
Sentence 49858
Summation, individual, by prosecution ...
(unable to include in index); by defense
... 47987-48109

Defense:

Applications and motions (*See:* Applications and
Motions, Defense; Tribunal Ruling, Applications and motions, def., denied;
def., granted)

Arguments to president of tribunal:
Comment:

Defense *(Cont.)*
  Arguments to president of tribunal *(Cont.)*
    Comment *(Cont.)*
      Def. case, length of ... 18979
    Inquiry:
      Evidence, def. presentation of, during cross-ex. of wit. ... 3048-49; 3052-53; 3055-56
    Objections:
      Interrogation of def. wit., method of ... 17858-59; 17881; 17926; 18516-18; 18531; 18584; 18622-23; 18801-04; 18811-13; 20053; 20097-98; 21331-33; 24464-66; 24470-71; 26123-24; 26919; 27052; 27328-29; 27331; 31263; 33166; 33238; 33240-41; 33275-76; 33279-81; 33456-57; 35336-37; 36514; 36812-14
      Interrogation of pros. wit., method of ... 3055-56; 3058; 3064; 3086-87; 3089; 3091-92; 3108-09; 3134-35; 3198-99; 3382-83; 3403; 3409; 3812-13; 4065; 4072-73; 4146; 4206-07; 4211; 4219; 4442; 4628; 7470; 10870-72; 10875-77; 10883; 11064-65; 11069-70; 11076-78; 11081-86; 11089-90; 11093; 11095; 11104; 11108-09; 11114; 11121; 11125; 11129; 11133; 11147-48; 11273; 11486; 11488; 11498; 11567; 11612-13; 12254-56; 12290; 12313; 12336-37; 12340-41; 12664; 14321-22; 14392; 14441-42; 14953-54; 15131-32; 15456; 15877; 15892-93; 15927-28; 15937-38; 16156; 16172-73
    Opening statements:
      Def. gen. opening statement (Part II), presentation of ... 17109
      Def. opening statement (Japanese constitution), presentation of ... 17544-47
    Re-direct examination of def. wit., method of ... 22072-73; 23261; 23847; 26701; 34818; 35150
    Rejection of def. doc. ... 17515-16; 18023-24; 18791-92
    Warnings:
      Def. counsel, that observations are out of order ... 2155
      USSR, not to insult, in def. opening statement ... 21871-73

  Arguments vs. pros. applications and motions:
    Affidavits, admission of, reconsideration of tribunal ruling concerning ... 32565-66; 32776
    Affidavit, def. doc. must be annexed to ... 20766-69; 20771
    Doc., presentation of part omitted by defense ... 31664-65
    Witnesses, while on stand, be enabled to testify in different phases of case ... 3203-07

  Arguments vs. pros. objections:
    Affidavits in entirety, presentation of ... 21745-47; 22084-90; 22436-38; 22552-55; 22882-86; 22889-91; 22991-92; 23091-92; 23291-97; 23569-74; 23617-26; 23628; 23633-35; 23653-55; 23861-63; 23866-68; 23933-35; 23949-50; 24245-50; 24253-54; 24266-68; 25049; 25246-49; 25415-20; 26234-43; 26461-62; 26464½-65; 26546-50; 26983-84; 27042-45; 27893-94; 27950; 28050-52; 28068-72; 28074-75; 28477; 28481; 28518-20; 28534-35; 28541-43; 28560-61; 28563-64; 29237-40; 29320-21; 29373; 29378; 29405; 29419-21; 29423-25; 29672-77; 30052-54; 30140; 30142-43; 30148-49; 30536; 30542-43; 30546; 32478-82; 32521-24; 32800-01; 32882-84; 32945-46; 32974; 32975-76; 33058; 33068-69; 34535; 34549; 36933-34; 36999-37000; 37002-05; 37008; 37011
    Affidavits in part, presentation of ... 20749-50; 20773-74; 21148-50; 21158-59; 21165; 21245; 21440-42; 21501-02; 21560; 21636-39; 21650-52; 21697; 21765; 21973; 22100-01; 22104; 22256; 22258-59; 22715; 23013-14; 23028-29; 23495-99; 23501-03; 23974-75; 24283-85; 24387-92; 25266-68; 25904-06; 25910-11; 26509-10; 26552-53; 26560; 26614; 26655-56; 26743-44; 26778-80; 26870; 26879; 27246-47; 27250-51; 27487; 27654; 27804; 27819; 27828; 27832; 28018-19; 28522; 28555-56; 28674-75; 28865-66; 28868; 29007-08; 29032-40; 29138; 29230-32; 29257-58; 29681-82; 29900; 29915; 30004; 30022-24; 30029-31; 30076; 30079-80; 30099-100; 30567-68; 30575; 31618-21; 31626-30; 31636; 31691-92; 31746; 31750; 32487-88; 32497-501; 32545-46; 32801-02; 32872-73; 32891; 32941; 32977; 34398-99; 34401-02; 34833; 34952-55; 34992-94; 35180-81; 35375-76; 35590; 35594; 36841-42; 36848-49; 36850; 36892; 36991-93; 37014-16
    Affidavits in entirety, presentation of, for sur-rebuttal ... 38616; 38709; 38712-13; 38721-22; 38807-08; 38834-35; 38843-46; 38866; 38868; 38894
    Affidavits, service of ... 22979-82; 22984-85; 23023; 23280-81; 23425-26; 23651; 24233-34; 24380-81
    Ambassadorial immunity, facts of, introduction of ... 34355; 34557-58
    Defendants, re-direct ex. of, in behalf of other defendants ... 20092; 20094-105
    Documents:
      Authenticity of ... 17288-89; 19786; 21805-06; 20220; 21388; 24566-70; 24800-07; 24811-13; 24815-16; 24819-31; 24833-37; 26843-44; 26962-63; 28591
      Presentation of ... 15457; 15925; 15931; 17274-75; 17277-80; 17282-83; 17288-89; 17301-03; 17307; 17337-39; 17342; 17356-57; 17359; 17395; 17411; 17421-23; 17463; 17601-02; 17605-22; 17629-34; 17644-45; 17657-61; 17668-73; 17675; 17689-91; 17867; 17901-02; 18030-31; 18099-100; 18172; 18174; 18383-84; 18386-87; 18402; 18406-11; 18414; 18417; 18422; 18424;

18426; 18428; 18433; 18586-92; 18594;
18597; 18696-97; 18765-70; 18773-75;
18777; 18790; 18793-95; 19137-38; 19141-
42; 19144; 19159-60; 19178-82; 19188-89;
19191-94; 19199; 19204; 19215-17; 19318;
19404-05; 19478; 19489; 19520-21; 19539;
19597; 19614-15; 19620; 19664-65; 19687-
88; 19692-94; 19699-700; 19720; 19722-
23; 19726-27; 20215-17; 20219; 20238-39;
20241; 20263-67; 20456-58; 20509-10;
20512-16; 20549-50; 20589-92; 20606-08;
20795-98; 20801-02; 20804; 20807-09;
20816; 20826; 20860-61; 20866-67; 20871;
20882; 20884; 20886; 20940; 20961; 20964-
65; 20966-67; 20994-95; 21007; 21012;
21013; 21015-16; 21018; 21020-23; 21035;
21037-40; 21043; 21045-57; 21065-68;
21074-78; 21083-85; 21087-91; 21093;
21098-102; 21104; 21107; 21109; 21112-
13; 21116-18; 21120-22; 21124; 21126;
21128; 21132; 21137-38; 21140-43; 21342;
21345; 21348-49; 21357; 21359-62; 21369;
21377-78; 21389; 21393-95; 21404; 21406;
21410; 21417-21; 21427-29; 21431-33;
21494-96; 21545-49; 21727; 21733; 21745;
21805-06; 21813; 21816-21; 21824-26;
22300-01; 22373; 22377; 22379-82; 22450;
22452-56; 22461; 22463; 22467; 22474;
22476; 22497-99; 22504-08; 22511-13;
22532-33; 22535; 22537-39; 22556-57;
22568-69; 22571-72; 22693-94; 22703;
22705; 22707-12; 22801-02; 22820; 22822-
23; 22837-39; 22848-50; 22864-67; 22877;
22920-22; 22970-72; 23084-85; 23145-46;
23148; 23178; 23182-83; 23187-88; 23481-
82; 23548-49; 23584-87; 23645-47; 23649-
50; 23723; 23727-29; 23731-32; 23734;
23736-37; 23739-40; 23742-47; 23749;
23752; 23754-56; 23758-61; 23763-65;
23776-79; 23783-84; 23954; 24201; 24220-
23; 24225; 24260; 24271-72; 24274-76;
24283-85; 24311; 24340-51; 24374; 24575;
24590-99; 24601-06; 24608-09; 24611;
24652-57; 24669-70; 24672-75; 24677-80;
24683-84; 24686-87; 24690; 24731; 24800-
07; 24811-13; 24815-16; 24819-26; 24841;
24843-50; 24906-07; 24942-48; 24964-65;
24967; 25084; 25089; 25101-02; 25105-08;
25111-14; 25116-17; 25120-26; 25128;
25130-36; 25138-39; 25141-51; 25160-67;
25170; 25172; 25175-77; 25182-88; 25195-
97; 25216-19; 25221; 25223-26; 25231-40;
25298-301; 25303; 25313-15; 25319; 25329-
30; 25334-35; 25350; 25358; 25367; 25374-
75; 25389-90; 25393-94; 25399-402; 25405-
07; 25438; 25456-63; 25465-67; 25474-82;
25484-85; 25487-94; 25501-09; 25514-24;
25541-44; 25546; 25553-59; 25562; 25580-
83; 25588-92; 25594-98; 25600-04; 25607;
25611; 25613-16; 25623; 25627-30; 25632-
36; 25639-41; 25643-44; 25646; 25663-65;
25737-38; 26216-17; 26253; 26358-60;
26381-84; 26431; 26450-52; 26604-06;
26608-09; 26770-71; 26773; 26778-80;

26962-63; 27079-82; 27845; 27960-61;
28024-25; 28039-40; 28042-45; 28100-06;
28242-43; 28248-50; 28272-73; 28416;
28422; 28431; 28436; 28445; 28472; 28483;
28513-15; 28521; 28538-40; 28551-52;
28569-71; 28578; 28588; 28697-98; 29248-
49; 29251-52; 29380; 29386; 29434-35;
29445-47; 29450-51; 29462; 29464; 29467;
29471-72; 29473; 29567-69; 29578; 29589-
90; 29604-05; 29607-11; 29620; 29624-25;
29629; 29632; 29643; 29655-56; 29664-66;
29884; 29895-97; 29933; 29947-49; 29954;
29961-63; 30048-49; 30058; 30146; 30544;
32550; 32700-03; 32838; 32853-57; 32917-
18; 33059; 33955-57; 34032-33; 34335-36;
34346-48; 34355; 34357-58; 34491-93;
34493; 34503-05; 34527-28; 34539-40;
34681-82; 34847; 34856-57; 34858; 34860;
34868; 34870; 34871-72; 34881; 34883;
34885; 34889; 34897; 34995-96; 35137;
35352-57; 36886-87; 37018
Presentation of, for surrebuttal ... 38597-98;
38601-02; 38604-06; 38608; 38611-14;
38622-23; 38627; 38629; 38633-36; 38638;
38640-42; 38647; 38650; 38653; 38657-58;
38662-64; 38668-69; 38676; 38684-85;
38693-94; 38696-99; 38749-54
Service of ... 18919-22; 19486-88; 19540-41;
19553-54; 19620; 19801-05; 24333-34;
26608-09; 26774-75; 26962
Extra-comment ... 22691; 24194; 33673;
33715-16
International law, facts of, introduction
... 34355; 34557-58
Interrogation of def. wit., method of ... 17720-
22; 17764-66; 17799-800; 17857; 17860-
62; 17875-77; 17896; 17925; 18068;
18075-77; 18249; 18316; 18520-23; 18534;
18609; 18817; 18877-78; 18885; 18898-
900; 18914; 20079; 20094-95; 20097-98;
20736; 20739; 20741; 22151; 24459-61;
24469-70; 24475-77; 26584; 26681; 26683;
27051; 27330; 27332; 27462-65; 27716;
27719; 28246; 28255; 28278-82; 29024;
29430-33; 29743-44; 29994; 31219; 31221;
31227-28; 31233; 31761; 32858; 33167;
33348; 33350; 33442; 33750; 34387-88;
34390-92; 34836-37; 34856; 34858; 34860;
34868; 34870-72; 34881; 34883; 34885;
34889; 34897; 34971-72; 35010; 35828;
35837; 35842-44; 35867; 36493; 36511;
36513-14; 36530-31
Interrogation of pros. wit., method of, ...
873-74; 2486-93; 2497-99; 2502-06; 2509-
12; 3073-74; 3076-77; 3080-81; 3095;
3104; 3106-07; 3110; 3113; 3412-13; 3832-
34; 3838-39; 3845; 3851; 4198; 4307; 4967;
8579-80; 10873-75; 10899-901; 10978-79;
11521; 11623-24; 12247; 12309; 12327;
12663; 14339-40; 14390; 14411; 14857;
14938; 14947; 31894-95; 31914-15; 31935-
36; 31940-41; 31948-49; 31957; 31963-64;
31971; 31976; 31980-81; 31984; 31986;
31988-90; 32020; 32025-26; 32091; 32129;
32161-62; 32178; 32186

Defense *(Cont.)*
   Arguments vs. pros. objections *(Cont.)*
      Interrogation of pros. wit. for rebuttal, method of ... 37448; 37468; 37476; 37478
      Johnston book "Twilight in the Forbidden City," presentation of ... 4181
      Maps, introduction of, during def. testimony of def. wit. ... 23838-42; 23852-55
      Opening statements:
         Presentation of def. ... 17118-19
         Presentation of part of def. ... 20478-79; 22411-12
      Re-direct examination of def. wit., method of ... 21321-22; 21327; 21330-31; 21334; 22069; 24553; 24559-60; 24658-63; 26906; 27226; 29563-64; 29996; 30010; 32456; 32457; 33798-99; 33805-06; 33810; 35151-52; 36118-19; 36121; 36828; 36831-34; 37159
      Re-direct examination of def. on behalf of other defendants ... 20092; 20094-105
      Witnesses, answers of ... 22451-55; 36609

   Arguments vs. pros. statements:
      Pros. counsel, replacement of, for cross-ex. of Muto (Defendant) ... 33237-38
      Witnesses, arrival of, for cross-ex. in USSR pros. case, announcement concerning ... 31213-14; 32240-42; 32314-17; 32321-22

   Arguments vs. tribunal rulings:
      Affidavits, def. wit. must give his evidence in ... 19100-01
      Document, already in evidence, def. counsel not permitted to read ... 17169-75; 17178-84
      Evidence:
         Applicability of, in the general case to all defendants ... 25874½-90
         Chinese communism rejected as defense for Japanese action ... 22442-49
         Defendant, answer of, when interrogated be used against other defendants ... 16105-06
         Defendant gives once in his individual case ... 19733-45; 19747-49; 19751-61
         Harada-Saionji Memoirs, admission of, not accepted during pros. rebuttal ... 38633-36
         Hearsay evidence, admissibility of ... 29711-13; 29717-18
         Interrogation of defendants, admission of, against other defendants ... 16105-06
         Opening statement, def. gen., defense right to present ... 17005-06
      Witnesses:
         Answer of ... 23685
         Def. wit. must give his evidence in affidavits ... 19100-01

   Argument vs. USSR objection to presentation of affidavit in surrebuttal ... 38848

   Arguments vs. USSR pros. applications and motions:
      Documents:
         Presentation of, at a later date ... 16114-15
         Presentation of, from Japanese government offices without authentication ... 361-62
      Exhibits, all, presented in evidence be numbered consecutively ... 362-63
      Judicial notice for document set out in schedule A and B of charter (Art. 13a) ... 363-69

   Objections to defense by defense:
      Affidavits:
         Presentation of ... 35568
         Presentation of, against other defendants ... 37027-28
         Presentation of part of ... 31117
      Document, presentation of ... 17280-81
      Opening statement, general division ... 17115-17
      Re-direct examination of def. wit., method of ... 31247
      Witnesses, interrogation of, method of ... 35598-99

   Objections to French prosecution:
      Document, presentation of, for rebuttal ... 38182-83; 38190; 38580
      Evidence, presentation of, after close of French case ... 15291
      French case, presentation of, in French language ... 6700-07; 6736-91

   Objection to Netherlands prosecution:
      Netherlands case, presentation of, by counsel for the Netherlands ... 11629-31

   Objections to president of tribunal:
      Absence ... 32661-66; 32668-72
      Participation as member ... 92-97

   Objections to prosecution:
      Affidavits:
         Affiants later executed, by ... 7308-09; 7601-02
         Affidavits taken by commission ... 33530-32; 33536-39; 33544; 33553-60; 33567-89
         Ballantine, by ... 10714-16
         Def. wit. evidence must be in form of ... 21058-62; 21064
         Form of ... 930-39; 1031; 1034-35; 1079; 3333
         Murakami Keisuke, by ... 7572-73
         Presentation of ... 1157-58; 1316; 1319-33
         Presentation of, for rebuttal ... 37445; 38132
         Presentation of, after close of pros. case ... 31999-32004; 32386-87; 32419-21
         Presentation of, without correction of errors ... 31827
         Presentation of, without cross-ex. ... 916-18; 3352; 4451-55; 4851; 7448; 7500; 7525-26; 10083-88; 10138; 23788-803

Prisoner of war case, in ... 2289-90
Reading of ... 2324
Semynov, by ... 7311-14
Substitution of, for testimony ... 915-28;
    1400-01; 2527-30; 2556; 3352; 4451-55;
    4459-60
USSR affidavit, presentation of, without
    cross-ex. ... 23788-803
Applications and motions:
    Counsel, change of, during cross-ex.
        ... 30485-87
    Doc., paraphrasing of, without reading
        ... 1014-17; 1735-36
    Doc., service of, amendment of rules
        concerning ... 1296-98
    French language, use of ... 6700
    Rule 6 b (1), exemption from compliance
        with ... 1846-57; 1860-61
    Witnesses:
        Powell be allowed to testify in cases
            other than specified ... 3202-07
        Presentation of, without presenting
            more than affidavit ... 2519-26
        Subpoena by def. of witness in USSR
            custody ... 8177.
        Subpoena, suppression of, until pros.
            testimony ... 8002-05; 8010
Cross-examination:
    Affidavits:
        Cross-ex. by ... 3007-09; 10065-66
        USSR affidavit without cross-ex. ...
            23788-803; 32556-57
    Date prior to 1928, concerning ... 887-88
    Evidence, presentation of, in lieu of
        ... 28287
    Evidence, type of ... 4548-51
    Japanese, use of, in ... 3007-09
    Pros. application to change counsel during
        cross-ex. ... 30485-87
    Scope of ... 3895; 3913-14; 4006
Defendants (*See also:* Individual defendants):
    Evidence, applicability of, in def. gen. case
        to all defendants, tribunal ruling denying
        ... 25891-92; 25897-99
Def. general objection to presentation of pros.
    doc. of order list into evidence for
    rebuttal ... 37893-95
Def. individual case, scope of evidence to be
    offered, pros. application concerning
    ... 28265-67
Documents:
    Authentication of ... 2823-24; 3415-21; 3603-
        04; 3699-700; 4858-60; 6731-32; 6820;
        6827; 6831; 7000; 7639-41; 7645; 7977;
        9219-20; 9222-24; 9333-35; 9671; 9674;
        9723-24; 11213; 11227; 15642-44; 30416;
        37230; 37518-25; 37531
    Certificate, form of ... 11816
    Excerpts of ... 1060; 2197-98; 2213-15; 2728-
        40; 7699-700; 7941-43; 7946; 7948-50;
        9521-22; 10153-55; 14437-38
    Extra-comment on ... 1754-55; 6984-87;
        7400-01; 7648-50; 7677; 7730-31; 7764;
        7817; 7824; 7834-37; 8135; 9509; 10157;
        10222-23; 10259-62; 10299; 10346-47;
        10353; 10477; 11761-62; 13483; 13811;
        15980
    Presentation of ... 687-88; 762-65; 790;
        1316; 1319-22; 1924; 2199-208; 2264-67;
        6440-43; 7340; 7343; 7346; 7351; 7455-56;
        7507; 7522; 7665-66; 7725-27; 7738; 7865-
        66; 7879-81; 7920-21; 7925; 8023-24; 8034-
        36; 8939-40; 9481; 9485; 9496-97; 9508;
        9775-77; 10053-54; 10083-87; 10109-10;
        10138-39; 10620-21; 11345-46; 11405-07;
        11730; 11775-76; 11783-86; 11819-20;
        11967-69; 12067; 12126-28; 12380-81;
        12642; 12645; 12649; 12681; 12688-89;
        12751-52; 12770; 12893; 12946; 13605;
        13661; 14906; 15185-86; 15427; 15602;
        15604; 15608; 15642; 15754-55; 15804-05;
        15807-11; 15814-15; 16069-71; 16073-74;
        16077; 16079-80; 16082-83; 17809; 29157;
        30398-400; 30402; 30671; 31496-99; 31502-
        05; 31689; 33202; 33469; 33473; 33504;
        33599-600; 33795-96; 34116; 34118; 34241-
        42; 34246; 34290; 34291; 34308-09; 34315-
        16; 34371; 34425-26; 34706-07; 34785-86;
        35260-61; 36879; 36901-02; 36916
    Presentation of, after close of case
        ... 29814-17
    Presentation of, during testimony ... 26295;
        26329-31; 32351-54
    Presentation of, for rebuttal ... 37233-34;
        37241-43; 37247; 37254-55; 37258-59;
        37264; 37268-72; 37275-77; 37280-84;
        37298-304; 37307-14; 37318; 37320-21;
        37324; 37327-28; 37336-37; 37339; 37342-
        43; 37346-50; 37366; 37371; 37375; 37377-
        78; 37380-83; 37385; 37392-93; 37396;
        37401; 37404-06; 37408; 37411; 37413-16;
        37421; 37425-32; 37436-37; 37439-40;
        37547; 37553-56; 37558-60; 37562-71;
        37573-74; 37576-77; 37579; 37582-86;
        37588-93; 37595-97; 37601-03; 37605;
        37608; 37618; 37622-25; 37636; 37638;
        37644-46; 37648-49; 37651-52; 37655-57;
        37659-60; 37664; 37667-79; 37683-86;
        37688; 37690-91; 37695; 37700-01; 37703-
        08; 37713-17; 37734-36; 37740-42; 37745-
        46; 37750-51; 37753; 37759-63; 37765-66;
        37769; 37771-72; 37774-75; 37778; 37780;
        37785-87; 37793-98; 37801-03; 37806;
        37810; 37813-14; 37817-22; 37827-28;
        37830-31; 37835-38; 37840-41; 37843-45;
        37849; 37851-52; 37854; 37856-60; 37863-
        64; 37868-70; 37873-74; 37876-79; 37893-
        99; 37903-05; 37908-10; 37914-15; 37918-
        19; 37922; 37928-30; 37936; 37938; 37940-
        41; 37947-48; 37954; 37956-57; 37959-60;
        37966; 37969-70; 37973-80; 37982-83;
        37985-86; 37988; 37991-93; 37999; 38004-
        05; 38008-11; 38013-15; 38028-29; 38061-
        64; 38070; 38072; 38076; 38084-85; 38090;
        38092; 38096-98; 38103-06; 38110; 38113-
        15; 38126; 38157-59; 38163-65; 38170-73;
        38177-80; 38182-83; 38187; 38190
    Reading of, without being presented for iden-
        tification ... 24067-68; 24076; 24095

Defense *(Cont.)*
  Objections to prosecution *(Cont.)*
    Documents *(Cont.)*
      Service of ... 691; 719-22; 1043-46; 1060; 1066-67; 1119-24; 1131-32; 1180-86; 1283-85; 1453; 1723-25; 1731-32; 1594-96; 1598-603; 1756-67; 2197-208; 2254-55; 2264-67; 2279-82; 2291-93; 2694-701; 2714-15; 2745-46; 2960-61; 3415-16; 3426-27; 5613-18; 6045; 6047; 6083-89; 6090; 6093; 6282-83; 6322-23; 6404; 6688-91; 7304-05; 7322-23; 7334; 7337-38; 15634; 22619-20
      Summary doc. of interrogation of Japanese officers ... 8999-9010
      Translation of: *(See:* Translation)
      Typographical errors in ... 1174; 1433-34; 1467-38; 2028; 2744; 2912-15
    Evidence:
      Admissibility of, for rebuttal, pros. state. concerning ... 37178-87; 37197-202; 37205-07
      Allison case, presentation of ... 9508
      Atrocities, admissibility of, unless conspiracy has been established ... 2628-29
      Chao Seng letter, presentation of ... 4910-11
      Conventional war crimes, commission of ... 11405-07
      Crimes against peace and humanity ... 11405-07
      Cross-ex., in lieu ... 28287
      Cumulative evidence, presentation of ... 2651-52; 9531-32
      Defendants, major positions held by ... 5901
      Film reels, presentation of part of ... 13712-13
      German decorations to defendants, presentation of ... 11345-46; 11348-49
      Harada-Saionji Memoirs:
        Authentication of ... 37518-25; 37531; 38737-42
        Presentation of ... 37506-07; 37508-09; 37535-44; 37547; 37553-56; 37558; 37559-60; 37562-67; 37568-69; 37570-71; 37573; 37574; 37576-77; 37579; 37582-83; 37584-85; 37585-86; 37588; 37589; 37590; 37591; 37592-93; 37595; 37596; 37597; 37601-03; 37605; 37608; 37618; 37622-23; 37624-25; 37636; 37638; 37644; 37645-46; 37648-49; 37651-52; 37655-57; 37659; 37660; 37664; 37667-68; 37669; 37670; 37671; 37672; 37673-74; 37675-76; 37677; 37678; 37679; 37683; 37684-86; 37688; 37690; 37691; 37695; 37700-01; 37703; 37704; 37705-08; 37713; 37714-17; 37734-35; 37736; 37740-41; 37742; 37745; 37746; 37750-51; 37753; 37759; 37760; 37761-62; 37763; 37765-66; 37769; 37771-72; 37774-75; 37778; 37780; 37785-87; 37793-94; 37795-96; 37797-98; 37801-03; 37806; 37810; 37813-14; 37817; 37818; 37819-22; 37827-28; 37830-31; 37835; 37837; 37838; 37840-41; 37843; 37844-45; 37849; 37851-52; 37854; 37856-57; 37858-60; 37863-64; 37868-70; 37873-74; 37876-78; 37879; 38633-36; 38638; 38640-42; 38647; 38650; 38657-58; 38662-64; 38668-69; 38676; 38693-94; 38696
        Presentation of, not accepted during pros. rebuttal ... 38633-36
      Identical evidence in different doc. ... 3578-80
      Japanese-German Cultural Agreement, concerning ... 6572
      Japanese-Russian Non-Aggression Pact, Japan's refusal to sign ... 7713
      Kido (Defendant) diary, entirety, not served on def. for translation ... 1922-23
      Konoye speech, presentation of, on behalf of defendants ... 3575
      Maps:
        Nomonhan map ... 22617; 22636
        Soviet Far East ... 7302
        Testimony, during presentation of ... 23700-01; 23712-14; 23716
        World ... 7354-56
      Matsuoka (Defendant) book ... 2185
      Opium of, be stricken from record ... 4671-72
      Oshima (Defendant), concerning ... 5894-98; 11405-07
      Panay Incident, concerning ... 3514-17; 9481
      Picture exhibit, method of identification of ... 1193
      POW treatment in Burma and Siam, concerning ... 5612-13
      Prosecution evidence, type of ... 4548-51
      Pu-Y'i, original notes of ... 4228
      Sato (Defendant) speech, presentation of, in behalf of self ... 3603-04
      Scientific Research Institute for Total War, interrogation concerning formation and purposes of ... 7413
      Shimizu evidence, relevancy of ... 1405-06
      Shintoism, interrogation concerning truth of ... 4008-09
      Siberian intervention, presentation of, for rebuttal ... 38208-12; 38214-15; 38219; 38221
      Tokyo Gazette, excerpt from ... 6731-32
      Tripartite Pact in USSR case, presentation of ... 7906-07
    Extra-comment *(See:* Documents, extra-comment on)
    Interrogation of defendants:
      Admission of ... 2225-32
      Hashimoto, reading excerpt from ... 5152-53
      Oshima, concerning Japanese-German Alliance ... 5907-09
      Oshima, without presentation of entire interrogation ... 5916-17
      Reading of excerpts from ... 3433-35
      Shigemitsu, presentation of ... 2897

Tojo ... 10703-05
Translation mistakes ... 10465-66
Translation of, in prison ... 2210-17
Interrogation of witness (*See also:* Witnesses):
Japanese officers after war, summary doc. ... 8999-9010
Judicial notice:
Japanese aggression in Lake Khasan ... 7895-96
Tripartite Military Alliance ... 6120-22
Opening statement concerning theory of law ... 477-89
Re-direct examination:
Def. re-direct ex. of def. wit., interruption of ... 21691
Def. re-direct ex. of pros. wit. ... 14963; 26344-45; 26602; 31921-24; 31926; 32137; 32145; 32149-50; 32192; 32194; 32197
Def. re-direct ex. of pros. wit. for rebuttal ... 37501; 37510-11; 37516
Re-opening of case, Japanese-German collaboration ... 7862
Statements:
Affidavits in USSR case without cross-ex., concerning ... 32556-57
Def. motion to dismiss, concerning ... 16937-38
Evidence, admissibility of, for rebuttal ... 37178-87; 37197-202; 37205-07
Stimson, Henry, testimony of, by affidavit ... 10065-66
Summing-up:
Conclusion of case, before ... 1139-45; 1252
Testimony of def. wit., during ... 27268
Translation:
Chinese into Japanese and into English ... 2299-306; 2309-10
Doc., of ... 840-41; 850; 1095; 1174; 1216-17; 3572-74; 3652; 4389; 4405; 4660; 15762; 15769-70; 15783-84
Errors in pros. doc. ... 1180; 1216-17; 2217
Kido (Defendant) diary, whole not translated ... 1922-23
Mongolian doc., of ... 38529-31
Witnesses:
Answers of ... 2054; 2412; 2440-41; 2536-37; 13534; 13953
Answers not responsive to question ... 2004-05; 2032; 4004
Ballantine, reading of notes by ... 10727-29
Coates on behalf of Hirota (Defendant) ... 11402
Comment on past history ... 5047
Conclusions and opinions of ... 13534; 13953
Credibility of wit., attack on ... 4993
Def. wit. testimony in form of affidavit ... 21058-62; 21064
Errors, correction of, in affidavit during pros. testimony ... 31828; 31831; 31833
Interrogation of def. wit., method of ... 17587; 17806; 17810-11; 17828-31; 17934-35; 17939-41; 17943-44; 17946-47; 17949; 17952; 17957; 17961; 17966-67; 17971-75; 17977; 17981; 17984; 17987; 18018; 18038; 18055; 18058-59; 18159-60; 18332; 18476; 18478-80; 18492-93; 18496; 18500; 18563; 18570; 18853; 18863-65; 18870; 19071; 19088; 19361; 19364-65; 19444-46; 19454; 19457-58; 19460; 19607-08; 19610; 19641-42; 19650; 19807; 19817-18; 19820; 19851; 19853-54; 19872-73; 19889-92; 19904-05; 19910-11; 19926-27; 19941; 19946-47; 20128; 20152-53; 20539; 20541; 20638-40; 20645; 20648-50; 20664-65; 20712; 20947; 21206; 21208; 21217-18; 21223; 21240; 21274; 21284; 21291-92; 21316; 21576; 21578; 21665; 21670; 21716-17; 21945; 22019; 22025; 22029-30; 22033; 22050; 22190; 22192; 22224; 22626-27; 22644; 22744; 22748-49; 22776-77; 22785-86; 22788; 22959; 22964-65; 23043; 23073-74; 23212; 23214-15; 23242-43; 23408; 23411; 23529; 23681; 23895; 24009; 24011; 24023; 24027; 24061-62; 24081-82; 24087-88; 24090; 24101-02; 24104; 24107; 24111; 24493; 25288-89; 26136; 26141; 26638; 26644; 26685-87; 26697; 27195-96; 27220-21; 27266; 27441; 27549; 27711-12; 27769; 27780; 27871; 28317; 28323-24; 28327-28; 28330; 28335; 28342-43; 28347; 28351; 28353-54; 28367; 28379; 28382; 28388; 28390-91; 28393; 28401-02; 28467; 28494-95; 28623; 28642; 28652-53; 28655; 28660; 28662; 28719-20; 28732; 28900; 28923; 28942; 28948; 28953; 28955; 28958; 28970; 28988; 28990; 29092; 29280-81; 29285; 29287; 29293; 29296; 29298-99; 29511; 29546; 29548-49; 29759; 29796; 29804; 29853; 29984; 29987; 30396; 30403; 30404-06; 30446; 30681; 30685; 30704; 31304; 31324-25; 31327; 31350-51; 31377; 31381; 31387; 31399; 31434; 31459; 31469; 31490; 31523-24; 31533-34; 31557; 31560; 31603; 32277; 32279; 32286; 32297; 32336-37; 32348-49; 32389; 32398; 32403-04; 32411; 32901; 32903; 32909; 33030; 33035; 33185-87; 33199; 33266; 33311; 33317; 33327-28; 33330-31; 33372-74; 33453-54; 33465; 33483; 33492; 33497; 33517; 33519-20; 33591; 33593; 33637; 33646-47; 33971; 34092-93; 34100; 34108; 34163; 34216; 34229; 34264; 34271; 34312-13; 34433; 34435; 34456-57; 34459; 34577-78; 34580-81; 34583; 34596; 34598-99; 34613-15; 34619; 34640; 34702; 34704-05; 34709-10; 34720; 34731; 34734-35; 34741-42; 34745; 34748; 34753; 34764-69; 34915-16; 34977-78; 34980-82; 34997; 35025; 35065-66; 35111; 35124; 35300; 35400-02; 35526; 35886-87; 35902; 35910; 35938; 36088-89; 36536; 36570-72; 36804; 36873-76; 36882; 36952-53; 36955; 37041; 37070-72

Defense *(Cont.)*

  Objections to prosecution *(Cont.)*

    Witnesses *(Cont.)*

      Interrogation of pros. wit., method of ... 834-37; 890-91; 895; 1150-51; 1384; 1387; 1391; 1438; 1673-74; 1954; 1959; 1965; 1997-98; 2002; 2011; 2018-19; 2023; 2043; 2531; 2533-35; 2540-44; 2546; 2561-63; 2570; 2646; 2681; 3223; 3226; 3231-32; 3256-57; 3284; 3506; 3738-39; 3752-53; 3856; 3864; 3866; 3960; 4029; 4034; 4414; 4421; 4428; 4432; 4439; 4773; 4979; 4993; 5356; 5367; 5370; 5602-03; 7517-19; 7585; 7768; 7770; 7772; 7775-76; 10733; 11172; 11444; 11446-48; 11529; 11537; 13007; 13558; 13560-61; 13595; 14285; 14294; 14840-41; 14923-24; 14935-37; 14965; 15225; 15288; 15440; 15443; 15860; 15862; 15869

      Notes, reading of ... 2657; 10727-29

      Notes, use of ... 883-85; 2039

      Out of order ... 11397-98; 11400

      Qualification of ... 806; 828; 830-32; 836-37; 898; 994-96

      Recalling of ... 14282-84; 15852

      Subpoena of ... 1774-75

      Testimony in Japanese ... 3007-09

  Objections to tribunal rulings:

    Affidavits, def. wit. must give evidence in ... 19091-95

    Cross-ex. of hostile wit. ... 20048

    Cross-ex., limitation of, by def. counsel ... 3066-69

    Evidence:

      Applicability of, in general case to all defendants ... 25891-92; 25897-99

      Cumulative ... 12089; 12092

      Mitigation, in ... 2155

  Objections to USSR prosecution:

    Affidavit, presentation of ... 8086

    Affidavit, presentation of, for rebuttal ... 38235-36; 38286-88; 38416-19

    Documents:

      Excerpts, reading of ... 7699-700

      Excerpts, use of, without presenting original ... 7748; 7750

      Part of, presentation of, into evidence ... 7621; 8126-27; 8135

      Presentation of, for rebuttal ... 38198-99; 38203-05; 38208-12; 38218-21; 38224-28; 38241-43; 38247-49; 38255-57; 38260-61; 38263-65; 38268-70; 38401-05; 38407-08; 38507-13; 38518; 38520-21; 38523-26; 38529-31; 38884; 38884-87

    Evidence:

      Japan's attack on USSR in 1945 ... 7539; 7665-66

    Koiso, inaccurate evidence concerning ... 7702-03

    Interrogation of def. wit., method of, for rebuttal ... 38430-34; 38544

    Map, Nomonhan, authenticity of ... 7844; 38342-43; 38350-52; 38354-56; 38358

  Statements (*See also:* Defense Counsel):

    American defense counsel, use of, reason for ... 38937-40

    Cross-examination by more than one counsel ... 36534

    Evidence, limitation of, in summation ... 43813-15

    Harada-Saionji memoirs, authenticity of ... 38737-42

    Indictment, mistranslation of ... 86-88; 92

    Language arbiter's apology for remarks, acceptance of ... 4302

    Mitigation, evidence in ... 38915-16; 38922-23

    Mongolian language, interpretation of ... 38396

    Offensive language to prosecuting countries in def. summation, tribunal warning concerning ... 42693-94 (China); 42695-96 (USSR); 43469-71

    Oshima evidence, references to ... 34335-36

    Summation:

      Evidence, limitation of ... 43813-15

      Procedure ... 38590-92

    Togo, limitation of charges against ... 35348-49; 35950-51; 35954

    USSR witness, permission to return to USSR ... 9835

Defense Counsel:

  American defense counsel:

    Improper conduct of, president's remarks concerning ... 19928-29

    Use of, reason for ... 38937-40

  Attempts at addressing tribunal at opening of def. case ... 17114

  Blakeney, appearance of, as additional American counsel for Togo ... 2296

  Brooks, withdrawal of, as counsel for Okawa ... 1433

  Cunningham apology for slur on USSR ... 34366-69

  Introduction of ... 76-77; 84-195; 325-26; 491-92

  McManus apology for conduct ... 28363

  Smith:

    Offensive language, use of, to tribunal ... 17774

    Refusal to apologize ... 27726-28

Diaries:

  Count Ciano:

    No separate peace treaty among Germany, Italy, and Japan ... 6660-62; 6666-67

    Tripartite Military Alliance ... 34921-25; 34927-30; 34947-48

Tripartite Pact ... 6092; 6095-97; 7910; 7922-24

Great Secret Diary of Manchuria ... 30392; 30394-95
    Concerning Manchurian Incident ... 32834-45

Great Secret Diary of War Ministry:
    Minami's discipline concerning improper conduct of young officers in 1931 ... 32810-12
    Non-availability of certain volumes of, ... 32817
    Sworn deposition concerning ... 27112-16
    Testimony concerning ... 32443-45

Grew:
    Brussels Conference ... 29955-60
    Hirota's attitude toward Matsuoka's foreign policy ... 30036
    Japan's indiscriminate bombing in China ... 29948-53
    Panay Incident ... 29964-65

Kido:
    Anti-Comintern Pact ... 7890; 30866
    Cabinet change ... 16220-21; 16231-33; 16240-46
    Changkufeng Incident, cabinet meeting concerning ... 30854-55
    China affairs and Germany ... 16222-31
    China Incident ... 16217; 16252; 31392-93
    China, peace with ... 30834-37; 30853; 30858-59
    Chinese government, negotiation with ... 15733-34
    Dismissal of Professor Yanaibara ... 30833
    Dismissal of university professors ... 30842
    Doolittle air raid ... 14607
    Education Council ... 30832-33
    Emperor and foreign policy ... 30797; 30799-800
    Emperor and Japan's withdrawal from League of Nations ... 30794-97
    Emperor's attitude toward Japan's south advance ... 30917
    Emperor's instructions to Tojo and Oikawa ... 31021; 31025
    Emperor's instructions to Tojo concerning early termination of war ... 31056-57
    Emperor's message concerning termination of war ... 31181-83
    Emperor's talk with Tojo concerning Terauchi cabinet, formation of ... 31102-03
    Emperor's views of Lord Keeper of Privy Seal ... 30803
    Emperor's wishes to promote friendly relations with China ... 30754-55
    Emperor's worry over increased activities of younger militarists ... 30802
    February Incident ... 30806-18
    French Indo-China ... 6824-25; 16250
    French Indo-China, French reaction to Japanese advance into ... 6971
    French Indo-China, Japan's action in ... 7049-50
    French Indo-China, Japan's diplomatic relations with ... 10156
    French Indo-China, Japan's policy toward ... 11744-47
    French Indo-China, Japan's ultimatum to ... 6972-73
    General staff, military activities of, during July 1940 ... 6259-60
    German-Japanese collaboration ... 11363-64; 11367-71
    German-Soviet Non-Aggression Pact ... 24189
    German-Soviet war ... 10024-25
    German-Soviet war, announcement of outbreak of ... 10021-23
    German-Soviet war, Japan's position concerning ... 9979-81
    German-Vichy negotiations concerning FIC ... 9998
    Higashikuni cabinet, consideration of ... 10276-79; 10282-83
    Higashikuni cabinet, formation of ... 31201-02
    Higashikuni cabinet, peace talk ... 31203
    Home Ministry post ... 16233-34
    Imperial Conference, concerning preparation for war ... 10214-15
    Imperial Conference, July 2, 1941 ... 10144-45
    Imperial Conference, August 14, 1941 ... 31192-94
    Imperial Conference, September 6, 1941 ... 31019
    Imperial Conference, November 5, 1941 ... 10331-32
    Imperial General Headquarters, establishment and declaration of war ... 16220
    Imperial General Headquarters and Government, liaison between ... 16221-22
    IRAA (Imperial Rule Assistance Association) ... 16246; 16247-48
    Itagaki (Defendant), connection with Japanese activities in Manchuria ... 15731-32
    Itagaki and others attempt to negotiate with Chinese government ... 15733-34
    Japanese atrocities at Hong Kong, Eden's address in Parliament ... 14606
    Japanese-British conference of 1939 ... 30878
    Japanese-German collaboration ... 11363-64; 11367-71
    Japanese southern advance for oil supply ... 10199-202
    Japanese spirit ... 16216-17
    Kido, advice to Emperor concerning friendly relations with USSR ... 30842; 30914-15
    Kido, appointment as Education Minister ... 30826; 30828-29
    Kido, attitude toward Japanese-US relations ... 30943-44; 30949
    Kido, attitude toward Matsuoka's resignation and US relations ... 30936
    Kido, drafting procedure of Senior Statesmen's Conference ... 30790
    Kido, effort toward cabinet change (third Konoye) ... 10295

Diaries *(Cont.)*
  Kido *(Cont.)*
    Kido, favor of cooperation with US and Great Britain ... 30791
    Kido, opinion concerning appointment of Kan-In (Imperial Prince) to post of Chief of General Staff ... 30750-51
    Kido, opposition to fascism ... 30818
    Kido, position in constitutional government ... 30740-41
    Kido, recommending Konoye as Lord Keeper of Privy Seal ... 30890-91
    Kido, recommending Konoye as premier ... 30819
    Kido, reform plan of local administration system ... 30869-70
    Kido, resignation as chief secretary to Lord Keeper of Privy Seal ... 30821-23
    Kido, resignation as president of Board of Peerage ... 30826-27
    Kido, response to recommendation as Lord Keeper of Privy Seal ... 30895-96
    Kido, talk with Emperor, concerning Matsuoka's visit to Europe ... 30920
    Kido, talk with Emperor, concerning Navy's intention for war ... 31045-46
    Kido, talk with Emperor, concerning Pacific war ... 31055
    Kido, talk with Emperor, concerning Philippine's battle ... 31111-12
    Kido, talk with Emperor, concerning Tripartite Military Alliance ... 30909-10
    Kido, talk with Emperor, concerning US-Japanese relations ... 30940-42; 31034-35
    Kido, talk with Itagaki, concerning China Incident ... 30852-53
    Kido, talk with Konoye, concerning possibility of war with US ... 10230
    Kido, talk with Shigemitsu, concerning European situation ... 31107-09
    Kido, talk with Shigemitsu, concerning termination of war ... 31114
    Kido, talk with Tojo, concerning preparation for war with US ... 10222
    Kido, tentative peace plan ... 31147-52; 31155-58; 31160-65
    Kido, Tripartite Pact ... 30871-75; 30877-78
    Kido, view regarding war with US ... 10241-42
  Koiso cabinet, formation and fall of ... 11381-87
  Konoye cabinet ... 30857-58
  Konoye cabinet, crisis in ... 10274-79
  Konoye cabinet, reorganization of ... 30850-52
  Konoye cabinet, second, fall of ... 30936-37
  Konoye cabinet, second, fall of and formation of third Konoye cabinet ... 10166-68
  Konoye cabinet, third, fall of ... 10291-92
  Konoye cabinet, third, fall of and naming of Tojo as premier ... 16199-211
  Konoye, intention to resign as premier ... 30956-57
  Konoye, peace envoy to USSR ... 31166-67
  Konoye, resignation as premier ... 30829-30; 30846; 30848-49

League of Nations ... 16231
Liaison Conference ... 10314; 30617
Lord Keeper of Privy Seal, appointment of ... 16249
Lord Keeper of Privy Seal, responsibilities of ... 30761; 30787-88; 30791-97; 30887-90
Lord Keeper of Privy Seal, role of, in formation of cabinet ... 30734-35
Makino, resignation as Lord Keeper of Privy Seal ... 30801
Manchukuo government, establishment of ... 30751-52; 30761-62
Manchuria prior to Incident ... 30728-29
Manchurian Incident, army's policy toward ... 30742-43
Manchurian Incident, outbreak of ... 30730-31
March Incident ... 30770-72
Matsuoka, diplomacy of ... 30905
May Incident and forming new cabinet ... 30776-87
Midway, Japan's defeat at ... 31065
Minami, inspection of situation in Manchuria and Mongolia .. 16213-14
Minami, lecture on Manchuria before Emperor ... 19924-25
Need for strong national government to combat military, 1931 ... 30744-47
Netherlands East Indies (NEI) and Singapore ... 11718
Nine Power Treaty ... 16218
October Incident ... 30737-40; 30742; 30772-74
Pacific war ... 31068-69
Pearl Harbor attack, results of, report concerning ... 11309
Planning Board, appointment of president ... 9850-51
Political party cabinets ... 16215
Political situation in Japan, 1944 ... 31077; 31079
Potsdam Declaration, acceptance of ... 31174-80; 31186-88
Pro-Axis policy, abandonment of ... 24206
Rebellion, August 15, 1945 and broadcast of termination of war ... 31198-200
Saionji, intention to have Konoye as president of House of Peers, Kido as Vice Grand Chamberlain ... 30774-76
Saionji, recommendation of Inukai as premier ... 30748-50
Saionji, views of Senior Statesmen's Conference ... 30787-89; 30791-93
Sakurada Gate Incident ... 30753
Senior Statesmen, proposed audience of ... 31113-14
Senior Statesmen's Conference ... 16187-91; 31081-101
Senior Statesmen's Conference, April 1941 ... 31122-42
Senior Statesmen's Conference, October 1941 ... 30991-92; 31005-18
Senior Statesmen's Conference, November 1941 ... 31039-43
Shanghai Incident ... 30757-59; 30762-64

INDEX TO MILITARY TRIBUNAL PROCEEDINGS 33

Southward advance ... 11744-47
Soviet-German peace maneuvers, Tojo-Kido talk concerning ... 11309
Soviet-German Non-Aggression Pact ... 24189
Soviet-German war ... 10021-25
Soviet-German war, Japan's position in ... 9979-81
Suzuki cabinet, decision of, to accept Potsdam Declaration ... 11393
Suzuki cabinet, formation of ... 11390-93
Termination of war ... 31076
Thailand, Japan's policy toward ... 11744-47
Tojo cabinet, fall of ... 11378-80; 31080
Tojo cabinet, policy of ... 11372-76
Tojo, forming Higashikuni cabinet ... 30983-84
Tojo, promotion to full general ... 10293
Tripartite collaboration ... 9875
Tripartite Military Alliance ... 16235-39
Ugaki, resignation as Governor General of Korea ... 30759-60; 30767-69
US, early peace with ... 31066; 31071
US, Japan's policy toward, July 1941 ... 11184-86
US-Japanese negotiations ... 10233; 10246-48; 16197-98; 16253; 30950; 30952-53; 30956; 30960-61; 30963-64; 30966-71; 30998; 31034-35; 31039
US-Japanese relations ... 10026-28; 10429-30
US, President Roosevelt's personal message to Emperor ... 10683-84; 16192-93
US, preparation for war against ... 10231-32; 10389-90; 10452-54; 10468; 10523; 10541-42
US, proposal for treaty with Japan, concerning status quo in Pacific ... 11708-11
USSR, Japan's policy toward ... 7911
USSR-German Non-Aggression Pact ... 24189
USSR-German peace maneuvers, Tojo-Kido talk concerning ... 11309
USSR-German war ... 10024-25
USSR-German war, announcement of outbreak of ... 10021-23
USSR-German war, Japan's position in ... 9979-81
Yonai-Arita cabinet, fall of ... 6240-56
Wakatsuki cabinet, formation of ... 30725-28

Kido diary, translation question ... 9998-9999; 10000; 10023; 10025; 10028; 10037-39; 10295-96; 10455-60; 10685; 11309; 14951-53; 16193-95; 16217-18; 16254; 17812-13; 20097-99; 36610

Litvinov:
Changkufeng Incident ... 22804-19; 22826-36; 22852-62; 22903-09; 22913-17; 23906-11
Talk with Japanese Foreign Minister Yoshisawa ... 22678-82

Smetanin, Japan's neutrality after Soviet-German war ... 7956-57

Documents, Burning of:

Changkufeng and Nomonhan ... 22759-800

General staff ... 7677-78; 7683-88

Moscow embassy ... 22844-46

Testimony concerning ... 22067-76

Top secret ... 14701-06
Introduction, argument ... 21648-58

Document Section (*See:* Ministry of Foreign Affairs, Secretariat)

Doolittle Fliers:

Court martial of:
Hata (Defendant), aff. and test. ... 14613-29; 28867-915; 29038-58; 38059-60
Order for ... 27908
Record ... 27917

Execution of ... 27905-06; 27912-17
Kido diary ... 38616-17; 38621-22
Sato (Defendant), aff. and test. ... 29038-58; 32960-61; 34447-49; 34462-64
Tojo (Defendant), test. ... 14599-606

Investigation, report of:
Kimura (Defendant), interrogation ... 27903-04

Military regulations for punishment:
Hata (Defendant), interrogation ... 14662-65
Tojo (Defendant), aff. and test. ... 36419-20; 36490-91; 36820 (*See also:* 27908)

Verdict ... 27904-05; 38059-60

E

East Asia Research Institute ... 15561 (*See also:* Japan, Organizations)

Eastern Hopei Anti-Comintern Autonomous Council ... 1685; 20665; 20757-59; 20835-38

Economic Aggressions (*See:* Aggressions; Preparation for War)

Economic and Cultural Agreements under Tripartite Pact (*See also:* Collaboration among Germany, Italy and Japan):

Cultural agreement ... 6570

Cultural committee program ... 6579-83

Economic agreement ... 5850-51; 6621-27; 8055-56; 34267-69

Economic commission draft plan ... 6630-34

Economic cooperation between Germany and Japan in China ... 6017-19; 6585-602 (*See also:* 34044-45; 34222-31; 34267-69; 35654-57)

Economic and Cultural Agreements under Tripartite Pact *(Cont.)*

    Mixed special commission ... 6417-20
        Oshima (Defendant), test. ... 34042-45; 34204-09

    Oshima (Defendant), aff. and test. ... 33983; 34044-45; 34222-31; 34267-69; 37080-100 *(See also:* 6636)

    Privy Council meeting ... 6573-75

    Togo (Defendant), test. ... 35654-57 *(See also:* 34044-45; 34222-31; 34267-69)

Economic Preservation Section ... 611

Economic Programs and Policies *(See:* Japan, Internal policies; Preparation for War)

Education Investigation Committee ... 344

Education Ministry *(See:* Japan, Constitutional Organizations)

Educational Council ... 30832-33

Elder Statesmen (Genro) ... 677-78

Elder Statesmen (Jushin) ... 679; 30020-27

Elder Statesmen's Conference *(See:* Japan, Conferences)

Election Law *(See:* Japan, Legislation and Laws)

"Emergency Japan," film entitled *(See:* Propaganda, Censorship and control of press and publication)

Emperor:

    Cabinet, formation of:
        Tojo (Defendant), test. ... 36379-83

    Chief of Naval General Staff, appointment of:
        Shimada (Defendant), test. ... 34810-12

    China Incident, action in:
        Kido (Defendant), test. ... 30844-45

    Constitution:
        Kido (Defendant), test. ... 31322-50; 31376-81; 31398-404

    Diplomatic policy:
        Kido (Defendant), test. ... 30882-83

    February Incident:
        Kido (Defendant), test. ... 30806-09; 30811-16

    Hostility, notification of opening of ... 10480
        Tojo (Defendant), test. ... 36799-803

    Imperial Conference:
        Kido (Defendant), test. ... 31362-73

    Imperial rescript, declaration of war ... 240-41
        Tojo (Defendant), test. ... 36404-07

    Imperial rescript, termination of war:
        Kido (Defendant), test. ... 31198-200

    Japan's southern advance, attitude toward:
        Kido (Defendant), test. ... 30915-19

    Japan's withdrawal from League of Nations:
        Kido (Defendant), test. ... 30794-97

    Kido, evaluation of:
        Kido (Defendant), test. ... 30826-27

    Kido, tentative peace plan of:
        Kido (Defendant), test. ... 31152

    Lord Keeper of the Privy Seal:
        Kido (Defendant), aff. ... 30803

    Manchurian Incident ... 1539-48
        Kido (Defendant), test. ... 31296-322

    Militarists, younger, increased activities of:
        Kido (Defendant), aff. ... 30802

    Pearl Harbor attack:
        Shimada (Defendant), test. ... 34708-24

    Power and duty of ... 1539-48
        Kido (Defendant), test. ... 31322-50; 31376-81; 31398-404

    Pres. Roosevelt message to:
        Kido (Defendant), test. ... 31604-11
        Tojo (Defendant), test. ... 36410-11

    Supreme Command:
        Tojo (Defendant), aff. ... 36379-83

    Tojo, instruction to, concerning early termination of war:
        Kido (Defendant), test. ... 31055-57

    Tripartite Pact:
        Kido (Defendant), aff. ... 30909-11

    Ugaki's private report to ... 3580-90

    US:
        Negotiation with:
            Oshima (Defendant), ... 33344-45
        Relations with:
            Kido (Defendant), aff. ... 30936
        War with:
            Tojo (Defendant), test. ... 36780-81

    USSR, relations with:
        Kido (Defendant), test. ... 30914-15

War:
    Declaration of, decision concerning:
        Togo (Defendant), test. ... 36126-27
    Great Britain, with:
        Tojo (Defendant), test. ... 36780-81
    Termination of:
        Kido (Defendant), test. ... 31055-57; 31181-83; 31198-200
        Togo (Defendant), test. ... 35784-90; 35807-16; 36138-39

    War Minister, appointment of:
        Kido (Defendant), aff. ... 30882-83
        Tojo (Defendant), test. ... 36598-625

Espionage:

    Australia ... 9063

    British New Guinea and Solomons ... 9062

    Consular at Hawaii as aid to naval attack ... 11203-25; 11296-97

    The Netherlands ... 9059

    Philippines ... 9058

"Establishment of Order in Greater East Asia," book entitled ... 15619-31

Executive gaps and conflicts ... 663-71

"Expel the British Influence from the Far East," article by Hashimoto (Defendant) ... 15659-60; 15681-85

Extra-Constitutional Organs and Offices ... 671-83

Extraordinary Fund Adjustment Law (*See:* Japan, Legislation and Laws)

Extraordinary War Expenditures Accounts ... 8542

F

February 15 Incident ... 15588-89

February 26 Incident:

    Kido (Defendant), aff. ... 30804-18

    Military clique ... 36476-77

    Muto (Defendant), aff. ... 33084

    Tojo (Defendant), aff. ... 36476-77; 36481-82

    Umezu (Defendant), aff. ... 36843-45; 36860-61; 36865-83; 36958-61

Federal Mongolian Autonomous Government ... 635 (*See also:* Mongolia)

Federal Reserve Bank of China ... 5223-26; 8436; 8444-45

Films (*See also:* Propaganda, Censorship and control of press and publication):

    "Australia Calling" ... 13709-11

    "Nippon Presents" ... 13707-08; 13714-32

    Testimony ... 11562-209; 18598-613; 18614-28

Five Ministers Conference (*See:* Japan, Conferences)

Five Year Industrial Development Program in Manchukuo ... 5005-06; 5125-28; 5140-41; 5158-59 (*See also:* Japan, Internal policies, Manchuria)

    Outline of ... 5069-82

    Outline of the revised plan for financing ... 5089-99
    Outline of the revised plan for mining and manufacturing industry ... 5082-88

Five Year Plan for Important Industries ... 8264-70; 8436-37; 8443-44; 8483-87; 8513; 8518-29; 8545-46; 8552; 18272 (*See also:* Japan, Internal policies)

Five Year Plan for Production of War Materials ... 8184-94; 8261-63; 8317; 8348; 8351-52; 8360-79; 8382-90; 8437-44; 18272-341

Foochow (*See:* China)

Foreign Affairs Ministry (*See:* Japan, Constitutional organization)

Foreign Relations Board of Information ... 5190-93

Foreign Service ... 604-05

Formosa (*See also:* Taiwan):

    Aerial operations, preparations for ... 33214-17

    Atrocities ... 13207-27; 14489-90; 14518-20; 14708-27; 14211-13; 40248-49; 40276-77; 40302-03; 40304; 40355-56

    Formosa Pharmaceutical Co. ... 4901

    Japan's domination of economic structure of ... 8842-43

    Opium and narcotics ... 4831; 4901; 20271-72

    Opium regulations ... 20258-61

    POW, internment of ... 14489-90; 14518-20; 14708-27

Formosa *(Cont.)*

   Training in ... 8984-85

France and French Indo-China (FIC):

   Aggression against: Pros. ... 6708-7212; Def. ... 26829-947; Pros. summation ... 39519-755; Def. summation ... 43050-175 *(See also:* Preparation for War; US-Japanese Negotiations):

      Agreement with Japan, circumstances leading to conclusion of ... 6939-48 *(See also:* Treaties and agreements)

      Attack on ... 8977-78 *(See also:* Southern advance)

      Collaboration with Germany *(See also:* Collaboration among Germany, Italy and Japan):

         Demands, Japanese, on FIC, Ott-Ribbentrop telegram concerning ... 6295-98

         Interest, Japanese, in FIC, Ott-Ribbentrop telegram concerning ... 6162-65

         Japan desire for German influence in FIC ... 6981-82

         Military aggression, Japan attempts to obtain German view on, Ott-Ribbentrop telegram concerning ... 6175

         Resources, German exploitation of, in FIC ... 6988-90

         Southern advance, Japanese, into FIC, Oshima (Defendant)-Ribbentrop conversation ... 6295-98

         Troops, German refusal to remove, from FIC ... 6983

      Control of ... 7113-16

      Defense of, Franco-Japanese cooperation in Kato (Amb.)-Darlan (For. Min.), exchange of letters ... 7059-65

      Delivery of supply to troops in ... 8972-77

      Demands on ... 6295-98

      Hostilities, opening in FIC ... 10615-17; 10673-76

      Military bases, establishment of ... 7008-11; 7037-41; 7080-81; 7104-05

      Military employee, Japanese, injured by FIC soldiers, memorandum concerning ... 7001-07

      Negotiations with:

         Foreign office statement concerning ... 6829-31

         Notes of military and political agreement concerning ... 6886-918

      Occupation of ... 6711-17; 6722-24; 6733; 7030; 7043-44; 7053-54; 7107-09

      Pan-Asiatic League, activities of ... 7110-12

      Preparation for operation ... 9010-54 *(See also:* Preparation for War)

      Resistance movement ... 15459-68

      Siamese aggression ... 6718-21; 7157-59

         (See also: Thailand)

      Situation in ... 6725-30; 6824-25

      Southern advance into ... 6709-11; 6793; 6971; 6992; 7032-41; 7046-50; 7053-54; 7117-19; 7138-39 *(See also:* US-Japanese Negotiations)

      Thai-FIC border dispute, Japan's mediation plan concerning ... 6993-98; 34295-302

      Ultimatum on:

         Kido diary ... 7992-93

         US Secretary of State memorandum ... 6957-62

   Atrocities ... 7176; 7181-82; 7193-94; 15291-472; 40303-04; 40324-25; 40356-61 *(See also:* POW)

   Economic aggression against:

      Economic expansion into ... 6724-25; 7155-57

      Economic policy toward ... 6975-80; 10034-36; 10156; 10158-60; 10175-78; 10180-84; 10325-26; 10334-40; 10407-09; 11709-18; 11738-41; 11744-47; 11751-56; 11794-95; 11944-59; 11969-12007; 12038-39

      Economic problems in Ishizuka, explanation concerning ... 7133-36

      Military currency, use of ... 8652; 8993-98; 26971-80

      Terms of payment under Franco-Japanese agreement, Mitani-Laval letter concerning ... 7146-47

   Japan:

      Bombing in FIC ... 26879-87

      Collaboration with Germany in FIC, denial of ... 24685-715 *(See also:* Preparation for War)

      GEA conference and FIC ... 18032-61; 18064-88 *(See also:* GEA Policy; GEACPS)

      GEA ministry and FIC ... 35766-67 *(See also:* GEA Policy; GEACPS)

      Konoye message to Marshal Petain ... 36239-40

      Military agreement with FIC ... 35752 *(See also:* Treaties and Agreements)

      Navy and FIC ... 26908-33 *(See also:* 6191; 6212; 6262-63; 6350; 6476)

      Negotiations with FIC:

         Shiratori (Defendant), aff. ... 35050

      POW *(See:* Atrocities, Southern Regions; POW)

      Southern advance into FIC:

         Kido (Defendant), aff. ... 30905-07; 30911-13; 30915-20; 30923-24; 30933; 30939

         Koiso (Defendant), aff. and test. ... 32243-45; 32409-30; 32441-43; 32529-32

         Oshima (Defendant), aff. and test. ... 34022-23; 34191-200; 34284-317 *(See also:* 6459-73; 6552-53)

         Sato (Defendant), test. ... 16094-97

         Shiratori (Defendant), aff. 34960; 34964; 35050

         Suzuki (Defendant), ... 35198-99; 35216-20; 35244-46; 32294-96; 35300-01; 35309-12 *(See also:* 11943; 11947)

         Togo (Defendant), aff. and test. ... 10181-84; 26942-47; 35687-89; 35703-05; 36187-88; 36197-205; 36230-54; 36260-70; 36375-76; 36709-21; 36763-69; 36820-23

INDEX TO MILITARY TRIBUNAL PROCEEDINGS 37

    Tojo (Defendant), aff. and test. ... 35687-89; 35703-05; 36187-88; 36197; 36205; 36230-54; 36260; 36262-65; 36267-70; 36375-76; 36398-404; 36636-40; 36709-21; 36763-69; 36820-23
    Thai-FIC border disputes, mediation in ... 34295-302 (See also: 6993-98)
    Troops in FIC ... 26829-62; 26869-75; 26936-41 (See also: 6795; 6844; 7033; 7037; 7043; 7052; 7055; 7059)
        Franco-Japanese communique concerning ... 26908-33 (See also: 6191; 6262-63; 6350)
        Tojo (Defendant), aff. and test. ... 36187-88; 36197-205; 36763-69; 36820-23
    War with FIC ... 34550

    Treaties and agreements:
        Franco-Japanese Joint Defense concerning FIC ... 7104-05; 7121-32; 7140-54; 24688-89
        Franco-Japanese Military Agreement concerning FIC ... 6875-954; 6969-71; 7014-26; 7059-65; 7069-87; 7121-32; 35752
        Franco-Japanese Protocol, ratification of ... 7913
        Franco-Japanese Treaty of Residence and Navigation ... 7159-61

    US (See also: US-Japanese Negotiations, Foreign Policies; US):
        Negotiations with Japan concerning FIC ... 6957-62; 6964-68; 7058; 7079; 9719-22; 10047-50; 10235-40; 10402-09; 10418-19; 25753-55; 25808-10
        Neutralization of FIC ... 35703-08 (See also: Hull's Note of Nov. 26, 1941)
        Toyoda-Grew conversation ... 24691-99; 24703-16

Free Indies (Includes: Andaman and Nicobar Islands) (See also: GEA Conference; GEA Policy; Southern Advance; Southern Regions):

    Atrocities ... 13185-200; 30195-213; 30239-46; 40235-36; 40267; 40316

    Bose, speech by, at GEA conference ... 36471-72

    POW (See: Atrocities)

    Relations with Japan under GEA policy:
        Tojo (Defendant), aff. ... 36467-68

    Tojo (Defendant), speech at GEA conference ... 36468

G

General Affairs Board (Manchukuo) ... 5113-14; 5119-82

General Affairs Bureau (See: Bureaus)

General Opium Amelioration Bureau (See: Bureaus)

General Outline of the Economic Construction Program of Manchukuo ... 5003-05 (See also: Manchuria)

"General Outline of Sabotage Activities against Soviet Russia," report entitled ... 7624-30 (See also: USSR)

General Staff (See: Japan, Constitutional Organization)

Geneva Protocol (See: Treaties and Agreements)

Geographic Bureau (See: Bureau)

Germany (See also: Collaboration among Germany, Italy and Japan):

    Aggression, interpretation of ... 7875-76

    Boltz:
        FIC and Thailand, tel. ... 6447
        USSR-Japan Neutrality Pact, tel. ... 6554-56

    Ermandorf, USSR, Japan's military preparations ... 7982-83

    Goering:
        Conference with Matsuoka, collaboration with Japan ... 6533-37
        Conference with Mussolini, Tripartite Military Alliance ... 6112-14

    Hemmen:
        FIC rubber, tel. ... 7157-59

    Himmler, conference with Oshima, collaboration with Japan ... 6026-28

    Hitler:
        Conference with Matsuoka, collaboration with Japan ... 6477-80; 6485-98; 6537-45
        Conference with Oshima, No Separate Treaty ... 6671-80
        Directive, collaboration with Japan ... 6469-73
        "German Diplomacy," article by ... 34152-61
        Letter to Emperor, appointment of Ott as German amb. ... 6634-35

    Knoll, Conference with Oshima, relations with Japan ... 6170-73

    Kramarets, Memo by, USSR, Japan's military preparations ... 7965-66

    Mackensen:
        China Incident, collaboration with Japan ... 5990
        USSR, Japan's military preparations, tel. ... 7962-63

Germany *(Cont.)*

    Navy report, collaboration with Japan ... 6474-75

    Neurath:
        Economic cooperation with Japan, trade in China, memo. ... 6017-18
        Japan's aggressive policy in China, memo. ... 5991-92

    Ott:
        Conference with Matsuoka, Tripartite Military Alliance ... 6286-92
        Letters:
            China, German preferential trade in ... 6623-24
            Tokyo, Minister in German Embassy ... 6636
            Tripartite Military Alliance, negotiation ... 6396-401
        Telegrams:
            China Incident, collaboration with Japan ... 5987-88; 5993-6015
            Conference with Matsuoka ... 7008-09
            East Asia, new order of, Arita speech ... 6148-49; 6238-40
            FIC ... 6162-65; 6175; 7030; 7034-36; 7052-53; 7113-16
            FIC ... Japanese demands for passage of troops ... 6295-98; 6955-57; 7067-68
            Hiranuma declaration ... 6103-11
            Japanese cabinet change, Germany's interest in ... 6150-53; 6162-65; 6257-58; 6261-63; 6266-67
            Japanese government, unification of ... 6429-34
            NEI, German attitude ... 6159-62
            No Separate Treaty ... 6640-42
            Relations with Japan, strengthening of ... 6130; 6141-42; 6150-53; 6162-65; 6257-58; 6261-63; 6264-67
            Singapore, German inducement to attack ... 6429-34
            Tripartite Pact ... 6103-11; 7933
            US, stopping shipping of ... 8031
            USSR:
                German inducement to Japan to attack ... 6162-65; 6663-65
                Japan, inability to attack in 1941 ... 7971-72
                Japan, military preparations ... 7963-69; 7978-84; 8071-74
                Japan, policy toward ... 7961-62; 7971-72; 7975
                Japanese provision to Germany of information ... 7993
                USSR-German Non-Aggression Pact, Japan's reaction ... 6122-23
                USSR-German war, Japan's position ... 7957-58

    Ribbentrop:
        Conferences:
            Matsuoka, collaboration with Japan ... 6498-532; 6546-52
            Oshima, collaboration with Japan ... 6459-68
            Oshima, relations with Japan ... 6133-39
            Togo, economic cooperation in China ... 6588-91
        Letter, USSR-Japan treaties ... 5939-40
        Memo, relations with Japan ... 6133-39
        Report, Japan's military preparations ... 6477-80
        Telegrams:
            Aggression, interpretation of ... 7875-76
            Anti-Comintern Pact ... 5975-81
            Collaboration with Japan ... 5975-81; 6468-69
            FIC, Japan's negotiations with ... 7046-48
            Japanese cabinet change, German interest in ... 6157-58
            No Separate Treaty ... 6638-42
            Relations with Japan, strengthening ... 6127-30
            Tripartite Military Alliance, negotiations ... 6098-102; 6115-19
            Tripartite Pact ... 5157-58; 6098-102; 6638; 7902
            USSR, Japanese collaboration against ... 6562-65; 7870; 7955-56; 7990; 7993

    Stahmer, conference with Oshima, relations with Japan ... 6323-27

    Trautmann, China Incident, collaboration with Japan, tel. ... 5983-85

    Weihl:
        Conference with Togo, economic cooperation with Japan, trade in China ... 6591-6602
        Memos:
            FIC ... 6166-68; 6560-61
            Japan, military preparation against FIC and Malaya ... 6560-61

    Weizsacker:
        Conferences:
            Kurusu, collaboration with Japan ... 6427-28
            Matsuoka, collaboration with Japan ... 6456-58; 6476-77
            Oshima, collaboration with Japan ... 6427-28; 6981-82
            Oshima, USSR, China, British possessions in East Asia ... 6456-58
        Memos:
            Economic cooperation with Japan, trade in China ... 6018-19
            USSR-German Non-Aggression Pact, Japanese reaction ... 6124-26
        Telegrams:
            East Asia, new order of, Japan's intention to establish ... 6284-85
            Relations with Japan ... 6278-82

    Woemann:
        Southern regions, Japan's military preparations, memo. ... 6560-61
        Relations with Japan, tel. ... 6131-32

Government Monopolies ... 606

INDEX TO MILITARY TRIBUNAL PROCEEDINGS 39

Grand Chamberlain (Jijucho) ... 674-75

Great Britain and British Empire (Pros. 9263-11628; Def. ... 24763-27116; 36964-978; Pros. summation ... 39519-735; Def. summation ... 43050-175) (*See also:* Malaya; Preparation for War; Singapore; US, US-Japanese negotiation)

    ABD pressure against Japan ... 25448-50; 25532-34; 25547-50; 25565-68; 36244

    Anti-Japanese joint encirclement, formation of ... 34678-82

    Atrocities (*See:* Atrocities)

    China, attitude toward, test. ... 36054-58

    Conference with Japan, 1939, aff. ... 30878-82

    Economic blockade ABD against Japan, aff. and test. ... 34678-82; 35690-92; 36248-49; 36272-73; 36277-78; 36319-20

    FIC-Japanese relations, objection to, aff. ... 36249-50; 36375-76

    Hashimoto (Defendant), pro-British attitude ... 28765-66 (*See also:* 7647)

    Kaiso (Defendant), attitude toward, aff. ... 32544-47

    Ladybird Incident (*See:* Ladybird Incident)

    Malaya, protest vs. atrocities in ... 5653-55

    Military encirclement against Japan, formation of, aff. and test. ... 36246-48; 36262-63; 36273-77; 36338-44; 36723-28

    Military operational plan toward (*See:* US, Aggression against)

    Negotiation with Japan (*See also:* US, US-Japanese negotiation):
        Adjustment of pending problems with Japan ... 3585-86
        Application of Geneva Convention to POW and civilian internees ... 14754-90; 14836-38
        Togo (Defendant) and, test. ... 34791-92

    Notes exchanged with Japan, question of possible international renunciation of war ... 17361-72

    Offenses against survivors of torpedoed ships (*See:* Atrocities)

    Opening hostilities ... 10522-55; 10544-48; 10608-12; 10621-25; 10635-76; 10680-81; 10706-09

    Peace proposal, Japanese, via Sweden, Shigemitsu (Defendant), aff. ... 34559-64

    POW (*See:* POW and Civilian Internees)

    Relations with Japan (*See also:* US, US-Japanese negotiation) ... 9451-55; 9673-86; 9688-706; 9712-16; 9736-51; 9782-95; 9801-02; 9811-13; 9816-25; 9828-32; 9835-37; 9868-73; 10043-47; 10330-31; 10333-40; 10353-54; 10356-61; 10363-71; 10373-75; 10401-06; 10468-72; 10621-24; 10635-76; 10690-700; 15487-79
        Koiso (Defendant) and, aff. ... 32544-47
        Shigemitsu (Defendant), aff. ... 34511-34; 34545-47
        Togo (Defendant), aff. ... 35349-50; 35413-14; 35487-90; 35665-736

    Shigemitsu (Defendant):
        European war, attitude toward, aff. ... 34541
        Peace proposal to Great Britain via Sweden, aff. ... 34559-64
        Relations with Great Britain, aff. ... 34511-34; 34545-47

    Suzuki (Defendant), attitude toward ... 35190

    Togo (Defendant):
        Negotiation with Great Britain, test. ... 34791-92
        Relations with Japan, aff. ... 35349-50; 35413; 35487-90; 35665-736
        War, termination of, aff. and test. ... 35545-46; 35591-97; 35603-10; 35776-90; 35801-16; 36110-12

    War, termination of, aff. and test. ... 35545-46; 35591-97; 35603-10; 35776-90; 35801-16; 36110-12

"Government in Japan," book entitled ... 18117-30

"Great Manchurian Diary," Araki (Defendant) by ... 28380-81

"Great Manchurian Empire" ... 7605-15

Greater Asia Association (*See:* Japan, Organization)

Greater Asia Principle ("Dai-Asia-Shugi") ... 32578-81; 32689-98; 32704-37; 33897-905; 33920-21

Greater East Asia Ambassadors' Conference (*See:* Japan, Conferences)

Greater East Asia Co-Prosperity Sphere (SEACPS) (*See:* Japan)

Greater East Asia Ministry (*See:* Japan, Constitutional Organization)

Greater East Asia Policy (*See:* Japan, Foreign Policies)

"Greater East Asia Sphere under Imperial Influence," Hashimoto (Defendant), article by ... 7348-49; 12022-24; 15652-56

Greater East Asiatic Deliberative Council:

Document entitled ... 36441

Establishment of, aff. ... 36441-45

Okada, Tadahiko, interpellation at 79th Diet ... 36443

Greater East Asiatic Establishment Council, Togo (Defendant) objection to, aff. ... 35741-42

H

Hague Conventions (See: Treaties and Agreements; Tribunal, Law)

Hainan Island ... 6143

Atrocities (See: Atrocities)

Occupation of ... 6733; 26863-68

POW (See: POW)

'Hakko Ichiu' (See: Japan)

Hankow (See: Atrocities, China, Central; POW)

Harada-Saionji Memoirs (See: Defense; Prosecution; Tribunal Rulings):

Dictation of, aff. and test. ... 37461-534 (See also: 37461-97; 37517)

Harada's health ... 37448-52; 37457-58; 37464; 37490; 38686-90

Purpose of ... 37549-53

Translation question ... 31436-39; 37622-30; 37728-34; 37793-804; 38631-79; 38691-703; 38749-51

Harbin Special Service Agency:

Koiso (Defendant) and, test. ... 32990

White Russians, use of, test. ... 36757-60

Hashimoto, Kingoro (Defendant) (See: Defendants)

Hata, Shunroku (Defendant) (See: Defendants)

High Civil Service Committee ... 544

High Police ... 1264-65

Hiranuma, Kiichiro (Defendant) (See: Defendants)

Hirota, Koki (Defendant) (See: Defendants)

Historical Bureau (See: Bureaus)

"The Holy War," film entitled (See: Preparation for War; Propaganda, Censorship and control of press and publication)

Hong Kong:

Atrocities (See: Atrocities)

Military preparation for attack on ... 8980-83

POW (See: POW)

Honjo, Shigeru:

Testament ... 19243-47

"Truth of the Manchurian Incident," book by ... 19258-73

Hopei Chahar Political Council ... 1685

Formation of, Kwantung Army's position in ... 20759-61

Hoshino, Naoki (Defendant) (See: Defendants)

House, Law of (See: Japan, Legislation)

House of Peers (See: Japan, Constitutional organization)

House of Representatives (See: Japan, Constitutional organization)

Housing Section, Ministry of Welfare ... 614

"How to Rebuild the World," Hashimoto (Defendant), article by ... 15674-75; 15699-700

Hsuchow (See: China, Central)

Hunchun Border Protocol (See: Treaties and Agreements)

I

Imperial Conference (See: Japan, Conferences)

Imperial Diet (See: Japan, Constitutional organization)

Imperial Fuel Enterprise Co. ... 8291-92; 8532

Imperial General Headquarters (See: Japan, Constitutional organization)

Imperial Headquarters Conference (See: Liaison Bodies)

Imperial House Law (*See:* Japan, Legislation)

Imperial Household Office (*See:* Japan, Constitutional organization)

Imperial Petroleum Co. ... 8290-91; 8476-77; 8533-34; 16931; 35241-42

Imperial Precepts to Soldiers and Sailors ... 33284

Imperial Rescript on Declaration of War (*See:* Japan; War, Declaration of)

Imperial Rule Assistance Association IRAA (*See:* Japan, Organization)

Imperial Rule Assistance Political Society IRAPS (*See:* Japan, Organization)

Imperial Rule Youth Association (*See:* Japan, Organization)

Imperial Way "Kodo" (*See:* Japan)

Indictment ... 26-73 (*See also:* Tribunal, Law)

   Group I: Crimes against peace (Counts 1-36) ... 33-53
     Conspiracy (Counts 1-5) ... 33-38
     Planning and preparation of a war of aggression and a war in violation of international law treaties, agreements and assurances (Counts 6-17) ... 38-44
     Initiation of a war of aggression and a war in violation of international law, treaties, agreements and assurances (Counts 18-26) ... 44-50
     Waging a war of aggression and a war in violation of international law, treaties, agreements and assurances (Counts 27-36) ... 50-53

   Group II: Murder (Murder and conspiracy to murder) (Counts 37-52) ... 54-67

   Group III: Conventional war crimes and crimes against humanity (Counts 53-55) ... 67-71

Indonesia (*See:* The Netherlands)

Industrial Bank of Korea ... 8515

Industrial Bank of Manchuria ... 8435-36

Industrial Equipment Co. ... 8321; 8534

Industrial Preparation for War (*See:* Preparation for War, Industrial)

"Inevitability of the Renovation," Hashimoto (Defendant), book by ... 15687-93

International Law (*See also:* Tribunal, Law):

   Greater East Asia War and ... 35570-71

   Hostility, Togo's knowledge of commencement of, aff. and test. ... 35718-21; 35723-24; 35851-52; 35861-62; 36131-33

   Present state of ... 17594-697

   Togo (Defendant) view ... 20029

International Red Cross Committee, POW Treatment in Malaya and ... 5492-93

Itagaki, Seishiro (Defendant) (*See:* Defendants)

Italy:

   Anti-Comintern Pact (*See:* Collaboration among Germany, Italy and Japan)

   Ciano (*See:* Diaries, Ciano)

   Collaboration with Germany and Japan (*See:* Collaboration among Germany, Italy and Japan)

   Mussolini (*See:* Collaboration among Germany, Italy and Japan)

   No-Separate Treaty (*See:* Collaboration among Germany, Italy and Japan)

   Shigemitsu (Defendant), Tripartite Pact, telegram to Mussolini ... 8066-67

   Shiratori (Defendant):
     Anti-Comintern Pact and, aff. and test. ... 34824-25; 34907-17; 35085-87; 35097-109 (*See also:* 6083; 16914)
     German-Russian Non-Aggression Pact, aff. and test. ... 35044-47; 35092-93
     Italian ambassador, appointment to, aff. and test. ... 34907-17; 35031-35; 35088-91 (*See also:* 6083; 6092; 16914)
     Relations with Italy ... 34824-27
     Tripartite Pact, negotiation of, aff. and test. ... 34825-26; 34939-46; 34959-60; 34966-71; 34977-78; 34980-86; 35036-47; 35090-125 (*See also:* 6100; 16915-16)

   Togo (Defendant), relations with Italy ... 35416; 35664; 35734-36

   Tripartite Pact (*See:* Collaboration among Germany, Italy and Japan)

J

Japan:

   Conferences:
     Elder Statesmen Conference:

Japan *(Cont.)*
  Conferences *(Cont.)*
    Elder Statesmen Conference *(Cont.)*
      Hiranuma (Defendant), aff. and test. ... 29255-319
      Kido (Defendant) and ... 30795-96; 34687-90
      Togo (Defendant), aff. and test. ... 35711-12; 35801-07
    Five Minister Conference:
      China Incident ... 30413-40; 30444-49
      Tripartite Pact ... 30489-519
    Greater East Asia Ambassadors' Conference:
      Joint statement of ... 35579-82
      Togo (Defendant) and, aff. ... 35764-68
    Greater East Asia Conference:
      "Address Delivered before Assembly of Greater East Asiatic Nations," pamphlet entitled ... 36432
      Bose, Subha Chandra, speech at ... 36471-72
      Greater East Asia policy and, aff. ... 36468-72
      Laurel, Jose, speech at ... 36471
      Maw, Dr. Ba, speech at ... 36430-31; 36472
      November 6, 1943 conference, aff. ... 36430-31
      November 28, 1943 conference, aff. ... 36431-32
      Oka (Defendant) and ... 33322-23
      Testimony concerning ... 17912-18019; 18032-61; 18064-88
      Tojo (Defendant), speech at, aff. ... 36435-39; 36468
      Waitayakon, Prince Wan, speech at ... 36460-61
      Wang, Ching-wei, speech at ... 36448
    Imperial Conference:
      Army attitude toward, Tojo (Defendant), interrogation ... 17870-71
      China, Japan's policy toward ... 29837-51
      Conferences:
        January 11, 1938 ... 29837-51
        July, 1941 ... 10151-52
        September 6, 1941 ... 10220-21; 25810-11; 34577-83; 34600-02; 35203-04; 35207-08; 35224-25; 36271-82; 36295-309
        October 12, 1941 ... 10272-74
        November 6, 1941 ... 11936
        December 1-4, 1941 ... 10513-15; 10520-22; 26072-93; 36271-83; 36721-28; 36744-50
      Hostilities, notification of opening of ... 26271-83; 36721-28; 36744-50 *(See also:* 26702-04)
      Kaya (Defendant), aff. and test. ... 33098; 33180-88; 33255-58; 33269-71
      Kido (Defendant), test. ... 34600-02
      Muto (Defendant), aff. and test. ... 33098; 33180-88; 33255-58; 33269-71
      The Netherlands, Japan's policy toward ... 11936
      Oka (Defendant), aff. and test. ... 33289-90; 33339-40; 33411-14; 33471-75; 33491-94
      Oshima (Defendant), aff. ... 34027-28
      Shimada (Defendant), aff. and test. ... 34658-62; 34673-74; 34696-717
      Suzuki (Defendant), aff. and test. ... 35198-99; 35203-04; 35207-08; 35224-35
      Togo (Defendant), aff. and test. ... 35674-75; 35697-98; 35711-12; 35824-25; 35983-86; 36001-12; 36044-58; 36110-12 *(See also:* 10333)
      Tojo (Defendant), aff. and test. ... 36271-82; 36295-309; 36371-83; 36721-28; 36744-50 *(See also:* 10151-52; 10220-21; 10272-74; 10513-14; 10520-22; 26702-04)
      Tripartite Pact, conclusion of ... 6329-43; 36190-92; 36799
      US-Japanese negotiations ... 10151-52; 10220-21; 10272-74; 10513-14; 10520-22; 25810-11; 26072-93
      USSR, Japan's policy toward ... 7904; 7960-61
      War, termination of ... 35783
    Imperial Headquarters Conference *(See:* Liaison Bodies)
    Liaison Conference:
      Conferences:
        Jan. 30, 1941 ... 36231-35; 36764-69
        Feb. 3, 1941 ... 36213-16; 36769-72
        April 21, 1941 ... 36220-23; 36262-65
        June 22, 1941 ... 36257
        June 25, 1941 ... 36236-51
        July 27, 1941 ... 36184-88; 36542-688; 36798
        Aug. 4, 1941 ... 36268-70
        Nov. 1, 1941 ... 10173-74; 30610-15; 30617-19; 30651-55; 30657; 30661; 30705-06
        Nov. 20, 1941 ... 36398-400
        Nov. 22, 1941 ... 36356-57
        Nov. 27, 1941 ... 35706; 35710-11; 35830-34; 36077-97; 36357-59; 36389-91 *(See also:* 26097)
        Dec. 1-7, 1941 ... 10480-81; 35561-67; 35569-70; 35721-23; 36388-96
      FIC, Japan's policy toward, aff. and test. ... 36231-35; 36764-69
      German-Russian war, Japan's policy, aff. ... 36257
      Germany, negotiation with, aff. and test. ... 36213-16; 36769-72
      Hostilities, notification of opening of, aff. and test. ... 35714-17; 35834-62; 36116-19; 36389-91
      Hull, note of Nov. 26, 1941, aff. and test. ... 35830-34; 36077-97; 36357-59; 36389
      Italy, negotiation with, aff. and test. ... 36213-16; 36769-72
      Kaya (Defendant), aff. and test. ... 30610-15; 30617-19; 30651-55; 30657; 30661; 30705-06
      Kido (Defendant), aff. ... 30832; 30834-35; 30839-40; 30933
      Military operations, preparatory measures for, aff. ... 36398-400

Muto (Defendant), aff. and test. ... 33097-98; 33171-72; 33174; 33180
Oka (Defendant), aff. and test. ... 33336-55; 33389-90; 33411-14; 33440-47; 33491-94; 35677-79; 36058-96
Operational plans ... 35702-03
Oshima (Defendant), aff. ... 34027-28
Secretariat, duties of, aff. ... 33016-18
Shimada (Defendant), aff. and test. ... 34656-58; 34812-13; 35201-03; 35223; 35236; 35301-05; 35332; 36058-96 (See also: 10140; 10216; 10314; 10333; 10518)
Southern advance, policy ... 36231-51; 36398-400; 36764-69
Suzuki (Defendant), aff. and test. ... 35201-03; 35223; 35236; 35301-05; 35332 (See also: 10140; 10216; 10314; 10333; 10518)
Testimony ... 15282-90; 16140-74
Thailand, policy toward, aff. and test. ... 36231-35; 36764-69
Togo (Defendant), aff. and test. ... 34683-86; 34791-92; 35677-80; 35682-89; 35702-03; 35706; 35710-12; 35714-17; 35830-34; 35983-86; 36058; 36077-97; 36814-15
Tojo (Defendant), aff. and test. ... 36220-23; 36231-51; 36262-65; 36268-70; 36356-59; 36389-91; 36398-400; 36764-69 (See also: 10173-74; 10480-81)
US:
Final draft, Japan to, aff. and test. ... 35561-67; 35569-70; 35721-23 (See also: 3473)
Negotiation with ... 36220-23; 36262-65; 36268-70; 36356-57; 36388-96
War with, decision ... 16122
USSR, negotiation with, aff. and test. ... 36213-16; 36769-72
World situation, measures to meet change in ... 30184-88; 36542-688; 36798
Senior Statesmen Conference:
Hiranuma (Defendant), aff. ... 16187-91; 31079-105; 31120-43
Hirota (Defendant), aff. ... 30990-31018; 31079-105; 31120-43
Suzuki (Defendant), aff. ... 35223-24
Togo (Defendant), test. ... 29314-15
Tojo (Defendant), aff. and test. ... 29306-14; 31120-43; 36364-70; 36508-09
Supreme War Council (Supreme Council for the Direction of War) ... 629; 631-32; 672
Dohihara (Defendant), aff. ... 28735-37; 28744-45 (See also: 11352; 16179-80)
Imperial ordinance ... 35616
Matsui (Defendant), aff. and test. ... 33828-29; 33890-92
Military Affairs Bureau ... 32963-65
Togo (Defendant) ... 672; 681; 10297; aff. ... 35624

Constitution ... 17470-76

Constitutional organization:
Cabinet ... 545-48
Cause of resignation of 18 cabinets during indictment period ... 17127-29; 17755-865
Change of ... 16215; 16231-32; 16240-42
Composition of, and participation of defendants ... 17698-704
Conflict between Diet and ... 650-63
Decisions ... 2919-43; 8561-67; 8807-10; 17708-54; 18357-79; 28536-37; 36709
Formation of, role of Lord Keeper of Privy Seal ... 30724-25
Imperial ordinance ... 17477-80; 18176-88
Japanese constitutional system, in ... 650-57
Meetings, army views ... 17869
Procedure ... 545
Cabinet Advisory Council ... 543-44
Appointment of ... 623
Araki (Defendant) ... 15833-34
Creation ... 622-24
Cabinet Committee ... 11944-59
Cabinet councillor:
Matsui (Defendant), aff. and test. ... 33828-29; 33890-92
Minami (Defendant), aff. ... 32926-29
Cabinet Planning Board ... 5131-32; 5148-50; 5167-70
Cabinet Secretariat, Chief:
Duties ... 29193-95
Hoshino (Defendant) as, aff. ... 29191-203
Cabinets:
Abe, formation of ... 30884-85
Higashikuni (Prince), formation of ... 31198-203
Hiranuma (Defendant):
Army demands on ... 30120-22
Fall of ... 30882-83
Policies ... 29219-29; 30333-36
Tripartite Pact and ... 31563-69
Hirota (Defendant):
Fall of ... 29645-53
Formation of ... 30819-21
Koiso (Defendant):
Fall of ... 31081-105; 32244-45; 32250-56; 32416-27; 32463-67
Formation of ... 11384-87; 11390-93; 31114-19; 32532-44
Konoye (Prince) ... 30857-58
1st Cabinet, formation of ... 30894-95
2nd Cabinet, ... 31579-83; 36176-81; 36598-617
Fall of ... 6179; 6191; 6212; 6266; 28941; 30936-37; 33298; 36261-67; 36577-83; 36598; 36834-35
US-Japanese negotiations ... 36218-31; 36262-65
3rd Cabinet:
Fall of ... 30972-85; 33301-02; 33394-97; 35169-71; 36293-307
Formation of ... 30937-39; 33298
US-Japanese negotiations ... 36265-93; 36817-18
China Incident ... 31382-96; 31412-66; 31477
Interview with Roosevelt, arrangement of ... 33364-74
Personal message to Roosevelt ... 32979-90
Reorganization ... 30850-52

Japan *(Cont.)*
  Constitutional organization *(Cont.)*
    Cabinets *(Cont.)*
      Konoye (Prince) *(Cont.)*
        Resignation and Suzuki (Defendant) as messenger ... 35233-34; 35243-44; 35301-07 *(See also:* 10246; 10250; 16199)
        US-Japanese negotiations ... 31583-74
      Okada ... 30811
      Suzuki:
        Fall of ... 31197-99
        Formation of ... 31119
      Tojo (Defendant):
        Fall of ... 31077-82 *(See also:* 11377-80)
        Formation of ... 30990; 31018-19; 31024-27; 31597-604; 33170-72; 33320-21; 34378; 34404-11; 34444-46; 35169-71; 36307-16; 36504-08 *(See also:* 10291; 11142; 15873; 36683)
        Policy ... 11372-76
        US-Japanese negotiations ... 30955-90; 31021-32; 31037-44; 35215-20; 35224-25
      Wakatsuki ... 30725-28
      Yonai ... 30901-02; 31351-60
    Diet, Imperial ... 553-74
      Houses ... 555-59
        Peers ... 555-58
        Representatives ... 559-71; 17708-54
      Law ... 564-65
      Legislative power ... 555; 565
      Purpose and aims of ... 554
    General Headquarters, Imperial ... 673
      Directive concerning submarine warfare ... 27270; 27274-75; 27311-14; 27387-89
      Function of, aff. ... 33416
      Imperial ordinance ... 17513
      Interrogation concerning ... 14553-57
      Navy minister, function in, aff. ... 34626-28
      Organization of, aff. ... 33416; 36388
      Shimada and, aff. ... 34676
      Tojo and ... 14533-57
      Unification of, aff. ... 35234-35 *(See also:* 10024)
    General Staff:
      Administration in, test. ... 16140-74
      Chief of:
        Appointment of ... 34810-12; 30750-51; 36941-57
        Atrocities, receipt of report of, aff. and test. ... 36926-31
        Duties of Vice ... 33283
      College ... 588
      Estimate by:
        Japanese military strength in Manchukuo and Korea ... 23555-56
        Soviet Far East troop strength ... 23549-53
      Operational plans against USSR, aff. and test. ... 23302-89
      Regulation of ... 17509-10
      USSR, attitude toward, aff. ... 23298
    Lord Keeper of the Privy Seal:
      Chief Secretary to, resignation of, Kido diary ... 30821-23
      Imperial ordinance concerning ... 17536-37
      Kido (Defendant) as, aff. and test. ... 30723-28; 31292-96
      Makino, resignation as, Kido diary ... 30801
      Responsibility:
        Cabinet, formation of ... 30724-25
        Prime Minister, selection of ... 30761; 30786-97
    Ministries ... 574-618
      Agriculture and Commerce ... 629
      Agriculture and Forestry ... 617
      Commerce and Industry ... 616
      Education ... 612-13
      Finance ... 605-07
        Function ... 605
        Minister, responsibility of ... 605-06
      Foreign Affairs ... 600-07
        Administrative jurisdiction ... 6145-46
        Bureaus ... 602-03
        "Collection of Treaties," pamphlet ... 5034-35
        Department ... 600-02
        FIC, advance into ... 7138-39
        FIC, negotiations ... 6829-31
        Foreign policy ... 6975-80
        Foreign policy toward China ... 3590-99
        Imperial ordinance ... 17503-04; 34830-31
        Minister:
          Togo (Defendant) ... 35517-20; 35590-96; 35603-10; 35640-42; 35670-72; 35776-90; 35799-816; 35978-88; 37164-68
        National Policy ... 35699-700; 35817-18
        Secretariat ... 604
      Greater East Asia ... 580; 5009; 5186-89
        Establishment ... 11359-62; 12070; 17912-18019; 18032-61; 18064-88; 35247-48; 35318-19; 35525; 35556-57; 35574-79; 35755-64; 36441-42; 36445-46 *(See also:* 12071-95; 35557-58; 35757-59)
        Imperial ordinance ... 5186-89
        Jurisdiction ... 36446
        Planning Board, relation with ... 35756-57
        Wartime change in ... 618-22
      Home Affairs ... 607-12
        Bureaus ... 607
        Civil police ... 607-10
        Imperial ordinance ... 17520-21
        Institutions ... 612
        Sections ... 610-11
      Imperial Household ... 579-80
        Imperial ordinance ... 17535
      Justice ... 615-16
        Composition of ... 615-16
        Minister, qualification of ... 616
        Responsibility ... 615
      Navy ... 597-600; 26413-66
        Bureaus ... 598-99
        Establishment ... 597
        General Staff, Chief of ... 599-600
        General Staff Office ... 17510-12
        Imperial ordinance ... 17499-502

Minister:
  Appointment, change of rule for ... 29645-51
  Conference ... 34626-28; 36386-88
  POW responsibility (*See:* POW, Prisoners of War, Individual responsibility)
  Qualification ... 597
  Shimada (Defendant) ... 34569-602; 34649-52
  Special duties ... 597
Overseas ... 617-18; 580
  Abolition of ... 618
  Establishment, purpose for ... 617-18
  Imperial ordinance ... 17519-20
  Minister:
    Koiso (Defendant) ... 32528-32
    Togo (Defendant) ... 35674
Railways ... 617
  Minister ... 617
State ... 578-617
Transportation and Communication ... 614-15; 629
War ... 580-97; 31671-75
  Administrative power ... 585-86
  Bureaus ... 581-85
  General staff, organization ... 588-94; 16122; 16140-74
    Army Aviation Headquarters ... 590-91
    Bureaus ... 589
    Departments ... 589
    General Staff, Chief of ... 588
    General Staff College ... 588
    Military Aviation, Inspector General ... 590
    Military Training, Inspector General ... 589-90
    POW (*See:* POW)
  Imperial Headquarters, wartime ... 593-94; 14553-57
  Imperial Ordinance ... 17487-98
  Minister:
    Appointment ... 580-81
    Appointment, change of rule for ... 29645-51
    Appointment procedure ... 36598-625
    Hata (Defendant) ... 28916-43; 28994-29018; 29030-38; 29394-401 (*See also:* 6191; 6212; 19076-79)
    Imperial General Headquarters and Imperial General Headquarters Conference ... 36386-88
    Itagaki (Defendant) ... 30296-317; 30330-36; 30407-43
    Minami (Defendant) ... 23803-12 (19776-77)
    POW responsibility (*See:* POW, Prisoners of War, Individual responsibility)
    Tojo (Defendant) ... 36176-81; 36598-617; 36572-76 (*See also:* 31749-823)
  Organization of ... 31671-75
  POW administration (*See:* POW, Prisoners of War, Administration)

  Regulations ... 31658-62; 31665-67; 31769-84; 32484-85
  Vice Minister:
    Itagaki (Defendant) ... 30085-138
    Koiso (Defendant) ... 32223; 32277-80; 32443-52
    Power of ... 31715-21; 31749-823
  Welfare ... 613-14
    Housing section ... 614
    Responsibility ... 613-14
Privy Council ... 548-53; 640-41; 17708-54
  Aims of ... 548
  Composition of ... 548
  Function and powers ... 549-50
  Hoshino (Defendant) and ... 29132-35
  Imperial Ordinance ... 17516-17
  Investigation Committee meetings, aff. and test. ... 33289-90; 33340; 33411-14; 33501-04
  Legislative powers ... 851-53
  London Naval Limitation Treaty, Japanese naval opposition to ratification of ... 9161-68
  Meetings:
    Agreement concerning Joint Economic Committee, Manchuria-Japan ... 8418-31
    Anti-Comintern Pact ... 5968-72; 22480-94
    Anti-Comintern Pact, Hungary and Manchukuo participation in, ... 6037-45
    Arita report to ... 3590-99
    China Incident, report ... 15764-68
    Franco-Japanese Military Cooperation Protocol, conclusion of ... 7014-26; 7069-78; 7913
    FIC, Japan, economic expansion into ... 7155-57
    German-Italy-Japan Protocol, conclusion of ... 6034-36
    German-Japanese Cultural Treaty, conclusion of ... 6573-77
    Greater East Asia Ministry ... 7522-23; 12071-95; 35557-58
    Manchukuo-Japan Protocol ... 2972-94
    Suzuki (Defendant) and, aff. ... 35236-37 (*See also:* 7069; 7074; 10490; 11303)
    Termination of cooperative relations, Japan and various organs of the League of Nations ... 3641-51
    Thai-Japanese Protocol ... 7014-26
    Tripartite Pact, conclusion of ... 5968-72; 7927-28
    Tripartite Pact, negotiation ... 6191-6211; 6214-32; 36192-94
  Military Affairs Bureau and, aff. and test. ... 32958-59; 32963-65
  No Separate Treaty ... 11304-08
  Operation of ... 29132-35
  "A Record of the Privy Council Concerning the Ratification of the London Naval Treaty of 1930," book entitled ... 9170-74
  Thai-Japanese Treaty concerning Thai territories in Malaya, conclusion of ... 11364-67

Japan *(Cont.)*
  Constitutional organization *(Cont.)*
    Privy Council *(Cont.)*
      Togo (Defendant) and, aff. ... 35647-48
    Wartime changes in government administration ... 618-37
      Army and Navy General Staff, reorganized responsibilities of ... 630
      Cabinet Advisory Council, creation of ... 622-24
        New Planning Board:
          Creation of ... 623-24
          Functions of ... 623-24
        Wartime Economic Council:
          Appointment of ... 623
          Composition of ... 623
      Japanese occupied territory, administration of government of ... 633-36
      China, government of occupied ... 633-35
      China, government of republican, at Chungking ... 635
      China, national government of, at Nanking ... 634
      Kwantung leased territory ... 633
      Manchukuo ... 634
      Mandated Islands ... 633
      Mongolia, federal, autonomous government of ... 635
      South Pacific ... 633
    Liaison Committee, creation of ... 630-31
    Ministries:
      Agriculture and Commerce, creation of new ... 629
      Greater East Asia ... 618-22
        China Affairs Bureau ... 621
        Executive Bureau ... 620-21
        Industrial Bureau ... 622
        Manchurian Affairs Bureau ... 621
        Southern Regions Affairs Bureau ... 621-22
      Munitions: ... 625-36
        Control Association, creation of ... 625-26
        Purposes of ... 628-29
      Transportation and Communications, creation of new ... 629
    Supreme Council ... 632
    Supreme Council for the Direction of War, creation of ... 629; 631-32
    Wartime legislation ... 632-33
      National Mobilization Law ... 632-33
      New Peace Preservation Law ... 633
  Foreign policies:
    Burma (See also: Japan, Foreign policy, Southern regions) ... 10333-41; 10367-72; 10374-75
    China:
      Administrative policy toward North China ... 2728; 2740-43; 2746-48
      Economic policy ... 2828; 3543-47; 5010; 5258-66; 5268-82; 8561-67
      Narcotization policy in North China ... 4791-92
      Political policy ... 3590-99; 3612-39; 9506-08; 9510-13; 9516-20; 9522-30; 9542-47; 9549-53; 9565-67; 9635-42; 10026-28; 10034-37; 10090-108; 10111-28; 10370-71; 10336-38; 21550-58; 29261-63; 29621-31; 29635-37; 29837-51; 29855-57; 29898-913; 30001; 31470-75; 36187; 36206-12; 36220-27; 36538-42; 36634-36; 36691-94
    FIC ... 6877-80; 9691-703; 9718-22; 9771-72; 9778-80; 9782-87; 9791-92; 9797-98; 9811-13; 9833-34; 9843-48; 9998; 10034-36; 10041-42; 10047-50; 10111-37; 10145-48; 10152; 10156; 10158-60; 10175-78; 10180-84; 10235-40; 10251-52; 10323-28; 10367-72; 10383-86; 10402-09; 10411-14; 10418-19; 10430-37; 10469-72; 10526-27; 10532-33; 11719-28; 11738-41; 11744-47; 11751-56; 11794-95; 11944-59; 11961-66; 11969-12007; 12038-39; 36231; aff. and test. ... 36231-35; 36763-69
    Germany (See: Tripartite Pact)
    GEA & GEACPS, aff. and test. ... 36449-68; 36773-80; 36807
      Establishment ... 7411-12; 7425-29; 12010-21; 37047-51
      Management of territories ... 7406
      Scope and structure ... 7410
    Greater East Asia Co-Prosperity Sphere (GEACPS) ... 6976; 7431-34; 9389-92; 9395-402; 9427-28; 9446-50; 9516-20; 9542-47; 9549-53; 9572-89; 9608; 9643-46; 9652-57; 9662-63; 9683-86; 9688-89; 9691-703; 9712-16; 9782-87; 9803-06; 9821-25; 9828-32; 9843-47; 9871-73; 9879-83; 10043-47; 10090-108; 10111-37; 10141-42; 10145; 10204-05; 10301-07; 10363-65; 10391-98; 10414-17; 10452-54; 11628; 15675-76; 17026-34; 17912-18019; 18032-61; 18064-88; 35752-54; 37047-51
      Geographical limitations, Minami (Defendant), interrogation ... 15786-87
      Hashimoto (Defendant), interrogation ... 15675-76
      Meaning of ... 17026-34; test. ... 17912-18019; 18032-61; 18064-88
      Togo (Defendant), objection to idea of, aff. ... 35752-54
      Togo (Defendant), speech concerning, aff. ... 35754
      Tojo (Defendant), aff. ... 35752-54
      Tojo (Defendant), speech by ... 12034-41
    Greater East Asia policy:
      Burma, under, aff. ... 12034; 36448-54
      China, under, aff. ... 36447-49; 36538-42
      Foreign policy, under, aff. and test. ... 36449-68; 36773-80; 36807
      Free Indies, under, aff. ... 36434-39
      GEA Conference and, aff. ... 36430-32; 36468-72
      Main points of, aff. ... 36434-39
      Manchukuo, under, test. ... 36773-80 36807
      The Netherlands, under, aff. ... 36464-67
      Philippines, under, aff. ... 36454-56
      Thailand, under, aff. ... 36456-64
      Tojo (Defendant), aff. ... 36426-73; 36503-04; **36538-42; 36807**; 36820-23; 37773-80

Italy (*See:* Tripartite Pact)
Malaya (*See also:* Japan, Foreign policy,
    Southern regions) ... 9782-87; 9816;
    9833-34; 9848; 10158-60; 10333-41;
    10367-72; 11944-59; 11961-66; 11974-
    12007
Manchuria ... 2967-71; 5003-06; 5010; 5038-41;
    5052-69; 5099-101; 5125-28; 5140-41;
    5158-59; 7557-59; 8561-67; 9386-88;
    9406-11; 9413-15; 9418-20; 9481-83;
    10068-73; 10090-108; 10111-37
Mongolia, plan to control Outer Mongolia
    ... 7435-37
The Netherlands (*See also:* Japan, Foreign
    policy, Southern regions) ... 9652-57;
    9662-63; 9667-70; 9683-86; 9694-9703;
    9759; 9848; 10047-50; 10105-06; 10158-
    60; 10111-37; 10215-18; 10391-98; 10400-
    06; 10418-20; 12110-19; 12121-23;
    12221-25
1941 policies (includes: Policy toward Russo-
    German war, Tripartite Pact vis-a-vis
    US and Great Britain, USSR): ... 9756-66;
    9826-27; 9833-34; 9879-82; 9979-81;
    9987; 9999-10000; 10021-28; 10031-37;
    10051-52; 10156-60; 10165-68; 10170-74;
    10188-97; 10211-15; 10217-18; 10220-22;
    10224-33; 10241-42; 10246-48; 10251-79;
    10282-83; 10289-92; 10301-09; 10314;
    10316-28; 10330-40; 10347-50; 10363-71;
    10373-79; 10381-98; 10411-20; 10438-39;
    10452-54; 10461-65; 10480-91; 10493-
    522; 10530-31; 10538-41; 10690-700
Southern regions ... 6976-80; 9667-70; 9683-86;
    9691-94; 9798-800; 9851-61; 9891-903;
    9906-07; 9937-46; 9951-53; 9961-62;
    9974-78; 9982-83; 9988-95; 10005-19;
    10047-50; 10105-06; 10111-37; 10154;
    10235-40; 10323-28; 10333-34; 10374-75;
    10377-79; 10391-98; 10402-06; 10418-19;
    10461-64; 11944-59; 11961-66; 11969-73;
    36236-51; 36399-400; 36709-21; 36820-23
Thailand (*See also:* Japan, Foreign policy,
    Southern regions) ... 9782-87; 9801-02;
    9811-13; 9816; 9833-34; 9843-47; 10145-
    48; 10183-84; 10202-03; 10333-41; 10367-
    72; 10414-19; 10692; 11719-28; 11738-41;
    11744-47; 11751-56; 11944-59; 11961-66;
    36231-51; 36398-400; 36763-69
Tripartite Pact (*See also:* Japan, Foreign
    policy, 1941 policies) ... 6307-21; 9694-
    706; 9712-16; 9756-57; 9782-87; 9789-94;
    9801-02; 9811-13; 9821-27; 9843-48;
    9869-71; 9875; 9884-89; 9904-05; 9510-14;
    9918-32; 9940-42; 9987; 10021-25; 10031-
    36; 10043-47; 10111-37; 10153-60; 10170-
    71; 10185-86; 10260-61; 10301-10; 10324-
    28; 10333-41; 10366-75; 10383-86; 10391-
    98; 10469-72; 10692-93; 10701-02; 36213-
    16; 36769-72
US (*See:* US, Relations with Japan, US-
    Japanese negotiations)
USSR (*See:* Japan, Foreign policies, 1941
    policy; USSR)

Hakko Ichiu:
    Meaning of ... 17023-25; 17890-911; 18101-15;
        23931-47
    Use of ... 23956-62
Imperial way (Kodo):
    Meaning of ... 17028-29; 18101-15; 18168-71;
        23947-51
    Use of ... 23955
Internal policy:
    Economic:
        Economic conditions ... 18198-242
        Economic construction plan ... 5010;
            8561-67
        Economic planning ... 18357-79; 25197-215
        Educational and cultural ... 18438-507;
            18536-84; 18598-627
        Financial:
            Financial planning ... 8498-507; 8518-42;
                18446-62; 24934-41
            Financial plan and war expenditure ...
                25413-32
            Foreign trade ... 8193-95; 8477-522;
                24837-39; 24850-51; 25000-02; 25009-11;
                36965-68
            Gold embargo ... 24950-58
            Kaya (Defendant) and financial policy ...
                30551-81; 30619-23
            Monetary policy ... 8543-68
        Industrial:
            Companies:
                Imperial Fuel Enterprise Co. ... 8291-92
                Imperial Petroleum Co. ... 8290-91
                Industrial Equipment Co. ... 8332
                Manchurian Heavy Industrial Develop-
                    ment Co. ... 8293-94
                National Policy Co. ... 8187-92; 8299;
                    8322; 8416; 8470-77; 8530-35
                Nippon Substitute Fuel Producer Co.
                    ... 8293-94
                Taiwan Electric Power Generation Co.
                    ... 8277; 8473
            Electric power, state control of ...
                25056-58
            Legislation (*See:* Japan, Legislation)
            Oil situation in 1941, Nomura-Roosevelt
                conversation ... 25305-07
            Petroleum problem ... 25016-23
            Plans:
                Electric power, five year plan for,
                    ... 8274-75
                Important industries, five year plan for
                    ... 8264-70; 8436-37; 8443-44; 8483-
                    87; 8513; 8518-29; 8545-46; 8552;
                    18271-341; 24959-63
                Important industries, resume of policy
                    relating to execution of five year
                    program (1937) ... 8269-70; 8443-44;
                    8513; 8518-29; 8545-46; 8552;
                    18271-341
                Important industries, essentials of five
                    year program for (1937) ... 8264-68;
                    8436-37; 18271-341; 30547-49

Japan *(Cont.)*
  Internal policy *(Cont.)*
    Industrial *(Cont.)*
      Plans *(Cont.)*
        Materials, essential, regulatory plan for ... 8498-8507
        Productive power, outline of plan for expansion of (1935), Board of Planning, by ... 8270-77; 8288; 8297; 8320; 8322; 8326; 8336; 8352½; 8360; 8414; 18357-79
        War materials, five year plan for production of ... 8183-95; 8261-63; 8317; 8438; 8351-52; 8360-79; 8382-90; 8437-44; 18272-341; 30547-49
      Raw materials, need for ... 25394-95
      Rubber, lack of ... 25352-58
      Shipbuilding industry ... 24908-32
      Shipping industry ... 18342-55; 25042-44; 25047; 25303-05
      Steel problem ... 24979-94

  Legislation:
    Aircraft Manufacturing Law (3/1938) ... 8380
    Automobile Industry Control Law (5/29/1936) ... 8358-61; 25003-04
    Automobile Manufacturing Enterprise Law ... 8362
    Bank, Convertible, Note Law (4/11/1941) ... 8545
    Capital Flight Prevention Law (1932) ... 8480; 24969-71
    Chemicals, Synthetic, Manufacturing Law (1940) ... 8318; 25079-82
    Coal Distribution Control Law (1940) ... 8299
    Coal Sale Control Regulations ... 8298
    Coal Supply Control Law ... 25077-78
    Commercial Guild Law (9/1932) ... 8393
    Defense, National, Security Law ... 8208; 8805-06
    Elections, Law of ... 557-58
    Electric Distribution Control Law ... 8276-77
    Electric, National, Power Control Law ... 8187-88; 18243-70
    Export Control Law ... 25011-12
    Export and Import Bill ... 25039-41
    Export and Import, Temporary, Control Law ... 8488-90
    Foreign Exchange Act ... 25008-09
    Foreign Exchange Control Law (3/1933) ... 8480-82; 8490; 24972-74
    Foreign Trade Adjustment Law (8/1937) ... 8488; 25027-33
    Foreign Trade Controlling Law ... 25054
    Fuel, Imperial, Development Co. Law (8/1937) ... 8291-92
    Fund, Extraordinary, Adjustment Law ... 30569-70
    Fund, Temporary, Adjustment Law (9/10/1937) ... 855; 25045-46; 30559-60
    Gold Fund Special Account Law (8/10/1937) ... 8513-14
    Gold Production Law (8/10/1937) ... 8513-15; 8516; 25034-38
    Houses, Law of ... 17514
    Imperial House Law ... 17477
    Industrial Equipment Corporation Law (11/25/1941) ... 8407-10
    Industrial Guilds Law (1931) ... 8393
    Industries, Key, Control Ordinance (8/30/1941) ... 8404-07; 15963; 16930; 35240-41
    Industries, Major, Control Law (8/1931) ... 8391-93; 24968-69
    Iron, Cast, Manufacturing Facilities Restricting Regulations (9/23/1939) ... 8327-28
    Iron, Japan, Manufacturing Co. Law (4/6/1933) ... 8322; 8325; 24975-78
    Iron, Scrap, Distribution Controlling Regulations (11/21/1938) ... 8326; 18342-55
    Machine Tool Industry Law (1938) ... 8353-54; 25063-65
    Metals, Light, Manufacturing Law (4/28/1938) ... 8348-49; 25073-75
    Military Automobile Subsidy Law ... 8362
    Military Criminal Law ... 33283
    Military Secret Protection Law ... 8208
    Military, National, Service Law ... 37112-13
    Military Service Law (3/1939) ... 8207-08; 8802-05
    Minerals, Promotion Law (3/29/1938) ... 8297-98; 8325; 8346; 25058-61
    Mobilization, General, Law (4/1/1938) ... 8489-90
    Mobilization, National, Bill ... 25065-69
    Mobilization, National General, Law ... 632-33; 8197-98; 8207; 8395-406; 8558
    Mobilization, National, Law ... 25061-63
    Naval Service Law ... 31874-83; 31885-87
    Oil Resources Exploitation Law (3/28/1938) ... 8289-90
    Oil, Synthetic, Industry Law ... 8291-92; 25013-15
    Ordinances, Industrial:
      Corporate Accounts ... 8558
      Operation of Funds of Banks and Other Financial Institutions (10/19/1940) ... 8558
      Plan by Promoter of a Business for General Mobilization (7/26/1936) ... 8402
      Use and Expropriation Ordinance of Factories and Workshops (12/28/1939) ... 8403
    Parliamentary Member Election Law ... 33283
    Petroleum Control Law (1934) ... 8282-84; 24998-25000
    Rice, Emergency Trading in, Law ... 25044-45
    Shipbuilding Industry Law (4/15/1939) ... 8320-21
    Shipping Guide Law ... 24966
    Shipping, Temporary, Control Law ... 25053

Mandated Islands (includes: Jaluit, Kwajalein, Pagan, Palao, Palau, Ponape, Rota, Saipan, Taroa, Tinian, Truk, Wotje, Yap):
  Administration of ... 9158
  Atrocities in ... 14911-15047
  Exclusion of foreigners from, reports ... 9142-58

Fortification of ... 8208-13; 9076-159; 11189-202; 26466-542; 38115-25
   Privy Council meeting ... 9158B-E
   Shimada (Defendant), test. ... 34667-68
   Togo (Defendant), aff. ... 35738-39
Geographical features ... 9077-79
Terms of mandate ... 9081-84; 9269-70
Treaty with US concerning administration ... 9084-85
US photographing prior to war ... 25608-09

Operational plans:
   Combined Fleet top secret operational order ... 11193-98; 11202; 11228-29; 11232-33
   Kwantung Army special manuever "Kantokuen" ... 7581-86; 7598-600; 7730; 8082-84; 8087; 23134-84; 23189-263; 23270-79; 23282-86; 23302-88; 23390-424; 31824-931; 31959-62; 37128-34
   Kwantung Army headquarters directive ... 8081-82
   Military operational plans of 1941 ... 26982-27039; 27061-65; 36283-89; 36317; 36321-26; 36329-35; 36345; 36357-59; 36371-83; 36388-410; 36721-28; 36797-98; 36807-08; 36820-23
   Overall War Strength Experimental Station ... 8199
   Pearl Harbor operational plan (*See:* US, Pearl Harbor attack)
   Scientific Research Institute for Total War (*See:* Japan, Organization)
   Table top manuever ... 8202-04; 8891-925; 8930-36
   Theoretical manuevers for total war ... 8938-61
   Total Investigation Laboratory ... 8199
   Yamamoto plan ... 10188-90; 10194-95

Organizations ... 815-20; 17708-865; 18140-63
   Dai Nippon Asia Association (Greater Asia Association) aff. and test. ... 32578-81; 32689-98; 32704-19; 33829-31; 33892-906
   Annual reports of ... 32720-29
   Matsui (Defendant), lecture by ... 32733-37; publication by ... 32730-37
   Dai Nippon Asia Development League, activities and duties of, aff. and test. ... 33832-33; 33896-906
   Dai Nippon Sekisei Kai, Hashimoto (Defendant), interrogation ... 15676; 15680-81
   Dai Nippon Seineto, Hashimoto (Defendant), aff. and test. ... 15677-78; 28781-86 (*See also:* 15680-81); interrogation ... 15677-78
   East Asia Research Institute, purpose of ... 15651
   Greater Asia Association ... 32578-81; 32689-98; 32704-19; 33829-31; 33892-906
   Annual reports of ... 32720-29
   Matsui (Defendant), lecture by ... 32733-37
   Matsui (Defendant), publication by ... 32730-37
   Greater Japan Political Association, Membership of ... 15786

IRAA (Imperial Rule Assistance Association) ... 635-37; test. ... 1638-73; 17708-54; 18140-63
   Aims and purposes of ... 18132-39; 18164-67
   Central Cooperation Conference of, aff. ... 35559-60
   Hoshino (Defendant), and, interrogation ... 29166
   Japan Political Society and ... 32921-25
   Kaya (Defendant), and, aff. ... 30605-10
   Kido diary ... 16246-48
   Minami (Defendant), and, aff. ... 32921-25
   Muto (Defendant), and, test. ... 33476-81
   Nature of ... 18132-39; 18164-67
   Oka (Defendant), and, test. ... 33476-81
   Shiratori (Defendant), and, aff. and test. ... 34828; 34963-64; 35019-26
   Togo (Defendant), and, aff. ... 35559-60; 35741-42
IRAPS (Imperial Rule Assistance Political Society) ... 637; test. ... 1670-72; 17708-54; 18140-63
   Shimada (Defendant), and ... 11378; 34668 (*See also:* 11376)
   Shiratori (Defendant), and ... 34828; 35006-07; 35053-54
Imperial Rule Youth Association, aff. ... 15680-81; 28781-86; 28797-98; 28818-19
Japanese Federation of Young Men's Associations ... 30605
Japan Political Society, Minami (Defendant), aff. ... 32921-25
Jimmu Kai, principle of ... 15576-77
Kochisha, principle of, interrogation ... 15563-64
Kokuhonsha:
   Harada-Saionji memoirs ... 37561; 37567-68
   Hiranuma (Defendant) ... 32274-78
   Minami (Defendant), test. ... 32274
Kokusaku Kenkyu Kai (National Policy Investigation Association, Society for Study of National Policy):
   Administrative measures, committee for, aims of creation for, report concerning ... 7407-09
   Koiso (Defendant), and, test. ... 32273
   Members, active, list of ... 7399-403
   Relationship to GEA policy ... 36444-45; 36503-04
   Togo (Defendant), and, aff. ... 35613-16; 35626-27
   Zaibatsu and ... 7400-01
Kyowa Kai (The Concordia Society), test. ... 18798-881; 19968-71; 36756-57
   Active support to ... 7608-13
   Basic principle of ... 7606-08
   Functions of, aff. and test. ... 7596-600; 7603-04; 31838-39; 31890-97
   History of ... 7606
   Itagaki (Defendant), and, ... 30075-77
   Role played by, in construction of New Order ... 7614-15
National Policy Institute:
   Itagaki (Defendant), and ... 33095-96
   Muto (Defendant), and ... 33256-65

Japan *(Cont.)*
  Organizations *(Cont.)*
    Sakura Kai, aff. and test. ... 1961-63; 2057-59; 19664-85
      Hoshino (Defendant), interrogation ... 15675
      Police Affairs Bureau and ... 2188-92
      October Incident and ... 19664-85
    Scientific Research Institute for Total War (Research Institute for Total War) (September 30, 1940) ... 8198-207; aff. and test. ... 8820-87; 27066-77; 29181-87; 31996-32067
      East Asia, establishment of ... 7431-34; 7992; 11974-12007
      GEACPS:
        Establishment of, plan for ... 7423-29; 12010-12
        Forms of ... 7425-29
        Territories to be included in ... 7419-20
      GEA Policy and, aff. and test. ... 36441-45; 36503-04
      German-Russian war, Japan's attitude toward ... 7417
      Hoshino (Defendant), and ... 37047-51
      Research, basic, and study concerning total war ... 8816-19
      Siberia, including Outer Mongolia, plan to govern, secret publication of ... 7435-37
      Tojo (Defendant), and ... 31996-32013; 32041-58 *(See also:* 7575; 8816; 27066)
      USSR ... 7418-19
    Showa Kenkyu Kai (Showa Research Society) ... 30605-06

  Supreme Command ... 674
    Chain of command, Tojo (Defendant), aff. and test. ... 36412-13; 36837-39
    Independence of, Konoye memoirs ... 25670-72
    Tactics of, prior to and during China Incident ... 21970-76

  War, declaration of ... 10482-86; 10686-88

  "The Way of the Subject," translation of ... 1047-65

Japan Aeronautics Co. ... 8533

Japan Coal Co. ... 8299

Japan Electric Generation and Transmission Co. ... 8274-77; 8532

Japan Gold Production Enterprise Co. ... 8473-74

Japan Iron Manufacturing Co. ... 8322; 8531

Japan Political Society ... 32921-25

Japan Rice Co. ... 8532

"Japan's Decision to Fight" ... 7989; 9010-69$\frac{1}{2}$; 9255-61; 11920-21

"Japan's Mission in the Showa Era," Araki by ... 7828-29

Japanese Army and Navy Arsenals ... 8354-55

Japanese Army Ordinance and Aviation Arsenals ... 8354-55

Japanese Army Personnel Regulations ... 33059-60

Japanese-British Conference ... 30878-82

"The Japanese-English-Chinese War," article entitled ... 7345-46

Japanese Federation of Young Men's Associations ... 30605

Japanese Instruction in How to Interrogate ... 12779-80

Japanese Loans to Encourage Poppy Cultivation in Jehol, report ... 4699-700

Jehol Province *(See:* Atrocities, China)

Jehol (Manchuria):

  Opium ... 4779-81

  "Poppy Cultivation in, Japanese Loans to Encourage," report entitled ... 4699-700

Jimmu Kai, principle of ... 15576-77

Journal of Battle Actions of the Red Army General Staff Concerning Actions in the Lake Hassan Area ... 7813-16

Judgment ... 48414-49772

July 15th Incident of 1940, Kido and ... 30898-99

K

"Kantokuen" Kwantung Army Special Manuever *(See:* Japan, Operational plans)

Karafuto Development Co. ... 8476

Kawamura Incident ... 18882-19126

Kaya, Okinori (Defendant) *(See:* Defendants)

Khalkin Gol Incident *(See:* USSR, Border Incident, Nomonhan)

Kido, Koichi (Defendant) *(See:* Defendants)

Kimura, Heitaro (Defendant) *(See:* Defendants)

"Koain" *(See:* Boards, China Affairs; Japan, Constitutional organization)

"Kochisha" *(See:* Japan, Organization)

"Kodo" Imperial War *(See:* Japan)

Koiso, Kuniaki (Defendant) (*See:* Defendants)

"Kokuhonsha" (*See:* Japan, Organization)

"Kokusaku Kenkyu Kai" National Policy Investigation Association (*See:* Japan, Organization)

Korea:

    Airfields, increase of ... 7590

    Annexation of ... 17318-19

    Bank, Imperial, of ... 8515

    Barracks, increase of ... 7559

    Fortified district, construction of ... 7590-91

    Itagaki (Defendant):
        Korean Army, as commander of, aff. ... 30320-21
        POW and, aff. and test. ... 30159-73

    Koiso (Defendant):
        Korean Army, as commander of, aff. and test. ... 32232-33; 32390-400 (*See also:* 22742-43; 22751)
        Military bases, establishment of ... 7587-94
        Military dumps, construction of ... 7592
        Military strength, Japanese, in ... 23555-56; 23651-59
        Minami (Defendant), POW and, aff. ... 32919-21
        Opium and Narcotics in (*See:* Atrocities, Opium and narcotics)
        Order of battle, test. ... 23425-55
        Poppy cultivation, expansion of, report (*See:* Atrocities, Opium and narcotics)
        Ports, increase of ... 7559
        POW (*See:* POW, Administration, Camps)
        Resources, Japanese utilization of ... 8442
        Security measures in ... 9063-66
        Transportation (highways and railways), increase of ... 7588-89
        Troops, Japanese, increase of ... 7587-88
        USSR, against (*See:* USSR)

    Korea Forest Development Co. ... 8473

    Korea Magnesite Development Co. ... 8475

    Korea Mining Development Co. ... 8476

    Korea Rice Exchange Co. ... 8475

Kota Bharu (Malaya), Opening hostilities at ... 10615-17; 10619-20 (*See also:* Malaya)

Kwanganmen (*See:* Atrocities, China)

Kwantung Army:

    Administration, study of, in occupied area ... 37135-62 (*See also:* 31933-34; 36964)
    Asano Unit ... 7705-07
    Chief of General Staff of:
        Koiso (Defendant), aff. and test. ... 32223-31; 32341-90
        Letter to Vice-War Minister ... 2903-11; 2967-71
        Message to War Minister ... 2835-36
        Speech concerning USSR and Mongolia ... 36903-04; 36908-11
        Telegrams:
            Commander-in-Chief of Kwantung Army, from ... 2999-3000; 3002-03
            Vice Chief of General Staff, from ... 4682
            Vice Chief of General Staff, to ... 300-01
            Vice Minister of War, to ... 2838-43; 3004-05
        Umezu (Defendant) instruction vis-a-vis USSR, aff. ... 36893-94
    China, North, problems and Inner Mongolia aff. ... 20747-61
    Commander-in-chief of:
        Concordia Society and, aff. and test. ... 20119-20; 20148-54
        Internal conditions of Manchukuo, aff. and test. ... 20109-54
        Telegram from War Minister ... 2846-47
    Concordia Society (*See:* Japan, Organization)
    Hopei, East, Anti-Communist Autonomous Council and, aff. ... 20757-59
    Hoshino (Defendant), interrogation concerning ... 5120-29; 5139-44; 5159; 5166-67; 5171-72
    Itagaki (Defendant) in, aff. and test. ... 30254-92; 30382-407
    "Kan-Toku-En" (*See:* Japan, Operational plans)
    Koiso (Defendant) as chief of staff of, aff. and test. ... 32223-31; 32341-90
    Manchurian Incident, telegrams concerning ... 32825-26; 32833; 32835-37; 32839-44; 32850-51; 32859-65; 32867-80; 32890-913
    Military preparations against USSR, aff. and test. ... 8093-126; 8138-54; 8167-74
    Military strength, increase of ... 7531-35; 7562-65; 32017-41; 32060-67
    Mongolia, Inner, and, aff. ... 20747-61
    Operational plans against USSR ... 7581-86; 7598-600; 8078-84; 23302-88; 31959-62 (*See also:* Japan, Operational plans)
    Opium and narcotics, sales by, in Kwantung ... 4832-33
    Organization of ... 7536-37
    Plans, 1942, against USSR ... 8128-34
    Propaganda plan ... 2277-79
    Regulations ... 19554-58
    "Special Maneuver of Kwantung Army" (*See:* Japan, Operational plans)
    Technical equipment, increase of, during 1932-45 ... 7537-38
    Testimony concerning ... 1318-98; 1399-438; 1440-518; 1553-2023; 2060-82; 2156-72; 3006-121; 3209-38; 15853-62; 18882-19126; 19275-313; 19320-82; 19393-470; 19474-520; 19773-20107

Korea *(Cont.)*
  Kwantung Army *(Cont.)*
    Tojo (Defendant) in, aff. ... 36751-60
    Umezu (Defendant), instruction vis-a-vis USSR, aff. ... 36893-94
      Commander of ... 37113-18
    US-Japanese negotiations, aff. and test. ... 36895-921
    USSR, against *(See:* USSR)

Kwantung Army's Propaganda Plan ... 2277-79

Kwantung Province *(See:* Atrocities, China)

Kweilin *(See:* Atrocities, China)

Kyowa Kai (The Concordia Society) *(See:* Japan, Organization)

L

Ladybird Incident ... 9452; 9616-20; 15678-79; 28767-81

  Hirota (Defendant):
    Attitude toward ... 29967-68
    Craigie, letter to ... 21367-72

  Indemnity, British government acknowledgement ... 21371-72

  Kido (Defendant), aff. ... 30883-84

  Matsui (Defendant), aff. and test. ... 33833-34; 33908-10 *(See also:* 30883-84)

Lake Khasan Incident *(See:* USSR, Changkufeng Incident)

League of Nations *(See also:* Lytton Report)

  Advisory committee, minutes ... 4667-69; 4712-30; 4751-58; 4853-54; 4865-66

  Anglo-Japanese Alliance, abrogation of, joint declaration ... 17313

  China Incident, report ... 6818-19

  Harada Saionji memoirs ... 37589-92; 37604-05; 37630-33; 37636-37

  Hostilities, outbreak of, agreement designed to prevent ... 9266-67

  Japan, withdrawal from ... 19700-02; 33656-58; 35081-82; 35549-50; 35628-30; 37589-92; 37604-05; 37630-33; 37636-37
    Date of ... 35610-12
    Kido diary ... 30794-97
    Notice of ... 2893-96
    Shiratori (Defendant), test. ... 35081-82
    Togo (Defendant), aff. ... 35549-50; 35628-30

  Manchukuo government, report ... 2847-55

  Manchuria, Japan's action in, report ... 1693-1765; 2855-96

  Marco Polo Bridge Incident, report ... 3297-3312

  Mukden, chaotic conditions in, report ... 2754-80

  Narcotic report and Japanese government ... 4924-25

  Opium and other drugs:
    China ... 4853-54; 4865-66
    China, North ... 4751-58
    Far East, control of smoking in ... 20251-53; 20273-76; 20279-87
    Far East, revenue in stable budgets in ... 20276-79
    Formosa, decreased addiction ... 20271-72
    Manchuria ... 4667-69; 4712-30

  Racial discrimination, abolition of, at Geneva ... 36433

  Shanghai hostilities, report ... 3286-93; 3295-97

Legislation *(See:* Japan, Legislation)

Legislative Power, Allocation of, in Japanese Government ... 645-50

Liaison Bodies ... 679-83

Liaison Committee ... 630-31

Liaison Conference *(See:* Japan, Conferences)

Liaotung, Triple Intervention ... 18777-83

London Naval Conference and Treaty:

  Abrogation of ... 26543-53; 26775-820

  Hirota (Defendant) speech, Japan's withdrawal from ... 15977-79

  Japanese opposition to ratification of ... 9160-9240

  Kaya (Defendant), aff. ... 30574-81; 30597-603; 30619-23

  Kido (Defendant), aff. ... 30721-23

  Oka (Defendant), test. ... 35503-13

  Public opinion ... 9224-25

  Shiratori (Defendant), test. ... 35081-82

  Togo (Defendant), aff. and test. ... 35493-514; 35737-38

Lord Keeper of the Privy Seal (Naidaijin) (*See:* Japan)

Lukuochia Incident (*See:* China, Marco Polo Bridge Incident)

Lytton Report (Report of the Commission of Enquiry Appointed by the League of Nations): ... 1693-765; 1809; 2248-64; 2754-80; 2847-96; 3286-312; 18665-84; 18687-95; 18697-716; 18718-62; 19530-39; 19542-53; 20181-86; 20891-907; 20922-39

    Chinese boycott of Japanese goods, argument concerning admissibility ... 20911-22

M

Malaya:

    Aggression against, test. ... 5351-58

    Atrocities (*See:* Atrocities), test. ... 5624-53; 5671-76; 12883-962

    Chinese activities during Malaya campaign ... 27411-12

    Chinese residents in, Japanese Army operation diary concerning ... 5677-81

    GEACPS and, test. ... 17912-18019; 18032-61; 18064-88

    GEA Ministry ... 35766-67

    Japan, policy toward:
        Economic ... 11944-59; 11974-12007
        Political ... 11961-66; 11974-12007

    Military preparation for war (*See:* Preparation for War)

    Opening hostilities in ... 10615-17; 10619-20; 10623-24; 10643-44; 10707-09

    POW treatment in (*See also:* POW, Prisoners of war, etc., Countries by, Burma, Siam): ... 5492-96; 5506-07; 5510-12; 5515-608; 5627-65; 5799-801; 27397-411; 30215-46; 40188-95; 40224-28; 40259-60; test. ... 5358-610; 5624-846
        Itagaki (Defendant), aff. and test. ... 30215-46 (*See also:* 5418-91; 13913-34)
        Kawamura diary ... 5671-76
        Kimura (Defendant), aff. ... 31818

    Singapore (*See:* Atrocities, Singapore and Malaya):
        Attack on, and Shiratori (Defendant), aff. ... 34964; interrogation ... 34890-91
        (*See also:* 6476-80)

    Chinese residents in, Japanese Army operation diary concerning ... 5677-81
    POW treatment, aff. and test. ... 27397-411

Manchukuo (Post, 1931) (*See also:* Manchuria):

    Airfields, growth of, 1931-45 ... 7549-51

    Anti-Comintern Pact, participation in, Privy Council meeting, minutes concerning ... 6037-45

    Anti-Soviet activities of white guards in ... 7694-7709

    Araki (Defendant):
        Manchukuo and Shanghai Incident, aff. and test. ... 28455-71
        Manchukuo, establishment of, aff. and test. ... 28455-71
        Policy during Manchurian situation, interrogation ... 15843

    Barracks, growth of, 1931-45 ... 7555-57

    Battle, order of, 1943-45, aff. ... 23425-55

    Boundaries:
        Outer Mongolia-Manchukuo, test. ... 35970-73
        USSR-Manchukuo, aff. and test. ... 35630-34

    Conditions, internal, 1936-39, aff. and test. ... 20109-54

    Dohihara (Defendant) (*See:* Manchuria, Aggression against)

    Economic conditions (*See:* Manchuria, Aggression against, economic)

    Establishment of, aff. and test. ... 23425-55; 28455-71; Kido diary ... 31282-84; 32222; 32225-31; 32341-90; 32494-508

    Extraterritoriality, abolition of ... 19717-19; 20473-75

    Fortified districts, construction of, 1934-45 ... 7552-54

    Government, test. ... 32357-72; 32454-58
        Aims of, aff. ... 20181-86
        Structure of, aff. ... 20155-81

    Great East Asia policy, under ... 32578-81; 32689-98; 32704-29; 32730-37; 36773-80; 36807 (*See also:* GEA policy, GEACPS)

    Hoshino (Defendant):
        General Affairs Board in Manchukuo and, aff. ... 29105-11
        Opium in Manchukuo, aff. ... 29115-25

Manchukuo *(Cont.)*
    Itagaki (Defendant) *(See also:* Manchuria, Aggression against):
        Establishment of Manchukuo ... 30063-71; test. ... 31282-84

    Kimura (Defendant), POW, employment of, aff. and test. ... 31699-711

    Koiso (Defendant):
        Establishment of Manchukuo, aff. and test. ... 32222; 32225-31; 32341-90; 32494-508
        Secret fund, disposal of ... 15809-12; 32223-25; 32486-93

    Kwantung Army, stationing in, aff. and test. ... 31824-996 *(See also:* 7330; 7581-86; 7598-6000; 8078-80; 23183; 23278)

    Manchukuo Government National Founding Bonds ... 4683-86

Manchuria *(See also:* Manchukuo):

    Aggression against (Pros. ... 1678-3238; Def. ... 18630-20485; Pros. summation ... 39061-190; Def. summation ... 42515-616)
        Cabinet conferences, minutes of ... 2826-27; 2831-33
        Cabinet decisions concerning ... 2919-43
        Conditions in, 1931 ... 19139-41; 19203-11; 19321-26
            Minami, test. ... 3352-666 *(See also:* 1378; 4356-58; 19916-17; 20054; 20058)
        Conditions in China, 1931 ... 18665-84; 18687-762
        Dohihara (Defendant):
            First trip to Manchuria and assignments thereof, interrogation ... 15713-26
            Lytton, conversation with, aff. ... 28667-69
            Mukden Army Special Service Organization, aff. and test. ... 28602-26
            Policy toward, tel. ... 33605-14
            Pu Y'i, meeting with, in 1931 ... 15726-29; test. ... 30373-81
            Puppet government, tel. ... 30114-15
        Government of ... 1681-88; 2847-55; 32383-84; 32460-63
        Hirota (Defendant):
            Grew, conversation with, concerning Open Door policy in Manchuria, aff. ... 37000-01
            Speech concerning ... 19729-30
        Hoshino (Defendant), appointment of, to Manchurian govt., aff. ... 29099-104
        Incident (September 1931), test. ... 1318-1518; 1553-94; 1964-2023; 2060-82; 2156-72; 3006-121; 3209-38; 15853-62; 18796-19126; 19243-313; 19320-82; 19393-470; 19474-520; 19731-49; 19773-20107; 22098-253
        Araki (Defendant), aff. ... 31824-37; 31911-17
            Attitude toward ... 28580-83
            Speech by ... 28437-44
        Army policy toward ... 30742-43
        Dohihara (Defendant) ... 15921-38
        Emperor, test. ... 31296-322
        Itagaki (Defendant) ... 15735-38; 15853; aff. and test. ... 30255-68; 30323-27; 30338-56; 30523-26; 31276-82; 31299-302
        Kaya (Defendant) ... 30638
        Kido diary ... 30730-31; 30742-43
        Koiso (Defendant), aff. and test. ... 30723; 31404-12; 31475-76; 32215-21; 32300-41; 32365
        Minami (Defendant) ... 1334-35; 1338-39; 13763; 20065-66; aff. ... 32806-07; 32885-89; 33542-52
            Telegrams, identification of, aff. and test. ... 32820-66; 32890-913
        Muto (Defendant), aff. ... 33082-83
        Oka (Defendant), aff. ... 33287-88; 33381-82
        Oshima (Defendant) ... 28029-30; 28032; aff. ... 33760-62; 33983
        Privy Council meeting concerning ... 28580-83
        Public opinion concerning ... 15759-60
        Report ... 19530-39; 19542-53
        Report, Japanese official, concerning, aff. and test. ... 19616-63
        Shigemitsu (Defendant) ... 1372-76; 3037-62; aff. ... 34470-87; 34551-58
        Shiratori (Defendant), aff. and test. ... 35029-31; 35056-84
        Speeches concerning, aff. and test. ... 28437-44; 31824-37; 31911-17
        Suzuki (Defendant), aff. and test. ... 35192-93; 35256
        Telegrams concerning ... 3091; 18779-82; 18813-24; 18890; 18897-901; 18924-25; 18932-35; 18974; 19325-27; 19351; 19413; 19415-19; 19692-99; 19783; 19785; 19787-89; 22140-42; 22231-35; 30058-60; 32217; 32219; 32820-80; 32890-913
    Issues between China and Japan, Lytton report concerning ... 1757-65
    Itagaki (Defendant):
        Connection with Japanese activities in Manchuria ... 15731-32
        Pu Y'i-Dohihara meeting, arrangement for ... 15726-29
        Pu Y'i, establishment of ... 15740-41
    Kwangtung Army regulations ... 19554-58
    League of Nations, Japan's withdrawal from, Imperial rescript concerning ... 19700-02
    League of Nations report concerning Manchurian aggression ... 1693-1765
    Minami (Defendant):
        Duties in Manchuria, interrogation concerning ... 15787-88
        Honjo, authority to take action in Manchuria, interrogation ... 15785-86

Kwangtung Army, command of, interrogation ... 15785
Manchuria and ... 15752-54
Pu Y'i letter to, aff. ... 20207-10; 20212-13
Speech, interrogation ... 15784-85
Population, Lytton report concerning ... 1740
Pu Y'i (See: Manchuria, Pu Y'i)
Questions ... 1372-76; 3037-62; 16939; 34470-81; 35490; 35547-49; 35620-25; 35746-50; 36024-26
Relations with China, Lytton report concerning ... 1742-53
Shigemitsu (Defendant), effort to settle issues ... 1372-76; 3037-62; 34470-81
Telephone and telegraph, Lytton report concerning ... 2919-24
Togo (Defendant), efforts to settle issues, aff. and test. ... 35490; 35547-49; 35620-25; 35746-50; 36024-26 (See also: 16939)
Topography, Lytton report concerning ... 1740-42
Triple Intervention ... 18777-83; 18786-88
Umezu (Defendant):
  Kwantung Army, command in, aff. and test. ... 31885-87; 37113-18
  Kwantung Army policies, aff. and test. ... 23390-424; 23456-77
War crimes, 1931-37, summary of ... 2697-712
Aggression against, economic (Pros. ... 4999-5847; Def. ... 18630-20485; Pros. summation ... 39165-77; Def. summation ... 42591-605)
Chinese regulations against:
  Japanese goods, 1929 ... 19157-58
  Lands:
    Leasing of, to Japanese, 1929 ... 19161-62
    Leasing of, to Koreans, 1929 ... 19168-70
    Sale of, to foreigners, 1929 ... 19165-67
    Unlawful sale of, 1931 ... 19182-86
  Rice field irrigation in Kirin ... 19176-77
Construction (heavy) materials, importation of ... 5339-40
Currency, aff. ... 20459-72
Customs duty, general policy ... 32376-80; 32458-60
Customs and tariffs ... 32377-80; 32458-60
Declaration, Japan-Manchuria-China Joint ... 5332-26
Economic construction programs ... 5003-37; 5052-57; 5114-18
Economic construction, progress of ... 5104-05
Economic exploitation ... 5105-10
Economic Joint Committee, Japan-Manchuria, establishment of ... 8418-35
Financial conditions ... 29115-25
Financial plans ... 5089-99
Hoshino (Defendant):
  Financial conditions in Manchuria and ... 29115-25
  Industrialization and, interrogation ... 29127-31; aff. and test. ... 29137-60
  Manchurian Affairs Board and ... 540; 5113-14; aff. and test. ... 29105-11
  Industrial Development Program ... 5005-06; 5062-99; 5125-28; 5140-41; 5158-59
  Industrialization ... 5005-06; 5052-82; 5099-5101; 5125-28; 5140-41; 5158-59; aff. and test. ... 29137-60; interrogation ... 29127-31
Investment by Japan ... 5347; 19214-15
Law, organic ... 5014-15
Manchurian Affairs Board ... 540; 5113-14; aff. ... 29105-11
Manchurian Development Co. ... 621
  Establishment of ... 5018-20
Manchurian Heavy Industrial Co. ... 5128; 5146
Manchurian Heavy Industrial Development Co. ... 5344; 8277; aff. and test. ... 31824-35
Manchurian Industrial Development Corp. ... 5006; 5129-30; 5171-72; 8471-72
North Manchurian Railway, rights concerning ... 5042-47
Protocol with Japan ... 4257-58; 5034-35
Reports concerning ... 5036-37; 5052-57; 5114-18

Manchurian National Army, aff. and test. ... 31874-83; 32064-67

Manchurian Secret Files of 1933 ... 32990; 32383-84; 32460-62

Manchurian Secret Files of 1938 ... 7560-61

Manchurian State Affairs Information Bureau ... 2969

Military bases, establishment of, aff. ... 7560-61; 7571; 7576; 7679-87
  USSR, against, aff. ... 7501-02; test. ... 32017-41; 32060-67 (See also: 7575; 8816; 27066)

Military dumps, construction of, 1931-45 ... 7554-55

Military, Japanese, service, extension of ... 7562-65

Military, Japanese, settlement in ... 7557-59

Military, Japanese, strength, 1931-45 ... 23555-56

Military police forces, study of ... 32303-05

Military training of Manchurians against USSR, aff. ... 7596-600

Minami (Defendant):
  Duties in Manchukuo government ... 15788-89
  Inspection of Manchukuo, by ... 16213-14
  Party for South Manchurian Railway Co. president ... 15753; 31705; 32315-16; 32809

National Manchukuo Army, right of supreme command ... 37107-18

Manchuria *(Cont.)*

    Opium and narcotics (*See:* Atrocities, Opium and narcotics)

    Policies, Japan (*See:* Japan, Foreign policies)

    Ports, increase of, 1931-45 ... 7559

    POW, employment of, aff. and test. ... 31669-711 (*See also:* POW)

    Proclamation of Manchukuo ... 19704-10

    Protocol, Japan-Manchukuo ... 4257-58; 5034-35

    Protocol, USSR-Manchukuo, final ... 19702

    Pu Y'i, test. ... 3945-4350; 18967-77; 19006-13
        Abduction of, telegrams concerning ... 4376-77; 4379-93; 4398
        Credibility of, test. ... 28075-84
        Dohihara (Defendant), meeting with, 1931 ... 15726-29; 30373-81
        Handwriting of, report on study concerning ... 15543-52
        Independent movement ... 19151-56
        Itagaki (Defendant), and ... 15740-41; aff. and test. ... 23425-55
        Letter by, to Minami, aff. ... 20207-10; 20212-13
        Rescript of, concerning enthronement ... 19696-98
        Signature by, authentication of, aff. ... 20187-206
        Trip to Japan, 1927 ... 19144-50; test. ... 19898-915

    Puppet troops ... 7541-43

    Railroads and highways, growth of, 1931-45 ... 7544-49; 8170-72

    Religion, aff. ... 20230-45

    Secret funds, disposal of ... 15806; 15809-12; 32223-25; 32486-93; 32990

    Sungari River flotilla, growth of, 1931-45 ... 7543-44

    Togo (Defendant):
        Manchukuo-Outer Mongolia boundaries, test. ... 35970-73
        Manchurian Affairs Board and, aff. ... 35748-49

    Tojo (Defendant):
        Kantokuen and ... 31903-11 (*See also:* Japan, Operational plans)
        Military bases, establishment of ... 7560-61
        Relations with GEA policy, test. ... 36773-80; 36807
        Secret funds, disposal of ... 15806; 15811

    Umezu (Defendant):
        Military bases, establishment of ... 7560-61
        Secret funds, disposal of ... 15806; 15811

    US, attitude toward, test. ... 36024-26

March 15 Incident of 1931, aff. and test. ... 19664-85; 22114-17; interrogation ... 1440-61; 1604; 15577-84; 15676-77

    Araki (Defendant), aff. ... 28472

    Kido (Defendant), aff. and test. ... 30728-51; 30769-87; 31235-36

    Koiso (Defendant), aff. and test. ... 32208-14; 32265; 32281-99; 32472-73 (*See also:* 1402-04; 1406-08; 1410-11; 1441-46; 1608; 1627; 32447-82)

    Minami (Defendant), test. ... 31235-36

    Suzuki (Defendant), aff. ... 35228-30 (*See also:* 1927; 1941)

    Umezu (Defendant), aff. ... 36843-45; 36958-61

Marco Polo Bridge Incident or Lukuochia Incident of July 7, 1937 (*See:* China, Marco Polo Bridge Incident)

Mariana Islands (*See also:* Japan, Mandated Islands) ... 8209-10

    Fortification of, aff. ... 9090-111

Marshall Islands (*See also:* Japan, Mandated Islands) ... 8209-10

    Fortification of, aff. ... 9132-39

May 15 Incident of 1932:

    Koiso (Defendant) and, aff. ... 32214-65

    Tojo (Defendant) and, aff. ... 36476-77

    Suzuki (Defendant), and, aff. ... 35230-31 (*See also:* 16215)

"Message to Young Men," Hashimoto (Defendant), article by, excerpts from ... 15648-49; interrogation ... 15700-04

Metropolitan Police Force ... 612

Military:

    Administration between civil and military, Kaya (Defendant), aff. ... 30627-32

    Attache:
        Duties of, aff. ... 33827-28; 33884-90; 33965-66; 33984-86

Oshima (Defendant), appointment of, aff. and
    test. ... 33983-84; 34100-02; 34111-13;
    37055-79

Budgets:
  Army budget, 1931, reduction of, aff.
    ... 32803-07
  Army officers' salary, 1931, reduction of,
    aff. ... 32807-08
  Kaya (Defendant), aff. ... 30582-96; 30599-603
  Koiso (Defendant), aff. ... 32221-22

Clique:
  Tojo (Defendant), aff. ... 36473-80
  Umezu (Defendant), dissatisfaction toward,
    aff. ... 36843-45; 36851-83; 36958-61

Court Martial Law ... 31676-84

Criminal Code ... 31685-86

Criminal Law ... 33283

Discipline:
  Army publication concerning ... 30127-30
  Minami (Defendant), improper conduct of
    young officers ... 32810-12
  Tojo (Defendant), aff. ... 36481-83

Education ... 813-14; 821-914; 936-1007; 1099-
    115; 18438-507; 18536-84

February 26 Incident of 1936, Tojo (Defendant),
    aff. ... 36476-77

Military police (Kempei or Kempeitai):
  Manchuria, in, study of ... 32303-05; 32448-51
  Regulations of ... 31669

Military training ... 589-90 (*See also:* Military,
    Education) Kido (Defendant), aff.
    ... 30833-34

Mitsubishi Trading Co., opium, Iranian,
    purchases of ... 4861

Mitsui Bussan Kaisha ... 8201
  Opium, Iranian, purchase of ... 4861-63

Mongolian People's Republic:
  Army, regulations of strengthening and
    expansion of ... 3689-96
  Border:
    Sino-Mongolian, aff. and test. ...
      22978-23005
    Sino-Mongolian, demarcation of, Japanese
      policy concerning ... 23008; 23085-86
    Inner Mongolia, test. ... 20120-21; 20142-47
    Military preparations, Japan vis-a-vis
      USSR, aff. ... 8087-89
    Political Council ... 1686
    Puppet troops in ... 7541-43
    Special investigation of, message con-
      cerning ... 3675-86

Manchu-Mongolian state, independence
    declaration ... 19688-92
Meteorological organs, establishment of,
    tel. ... 7561-62
New Mongolia, construction of, round table
    of Sino-Japanese notables ... 30063-71
Nomonhan (*See:* USSR, Border incidents)
Occupation army vis-a-vis USSR, test.
    ... 31942-49; 31954-62
Outer Mongolia:
  Itagaki (Defendant), speeches ... 7830-34;
    36903-11
  Manchukuo boundaries with, test.
    ... 35970-73
  Military preparations vis-a-vis USSR,
    report ... 8089-90
  Special investigation of, message concern-
    ing ... 3675-86
  Togo (Defendant), Manchukuo boundaries
    with, test. ... 35970-73
  USSR, Mutual Assistance Pact with ... 1686
Protocol with Manchuria, concerning
    boundary ... 23151-52
Sino-Mongolian border, aff. and test. ...
    22978-23005
  Demarcation of, Japanese policy concerning
    ... 23008; 23085-86
Sino-Russian Basic Treaty, May 1924
    ... 22975-76
War, undeclared, against:
  Article concerning ... 7828-29
  Interrogation ... 7854-56
  Red Army memo ... 7858-60

Mukden:

  Army Special Organ, aff. and test. ... 28602-26;
    30349-66; 30484-85 (*See also:* 15856;
    19976)

  Chaotic conditions resulting from occupation
    ... 2754-80

  Dohihara (Defendant), policy, tel. ... 33605-19

  Official Japanese report of, aff. and test.
    ... 19616-63

  Peace Preservation Committee, test. ... 30366-69

  Triple intervention concerning possession of
    Mukden by Japanese ... 18786-788

  US Consulate General at, narcotic observation,
    test. ... (Oct. 1936) ... 4701-05

Mukden Incident (*See:* Manchurian Incident)

Murder (*See:* Atrocities; Indictment; Tribunal, Law)

N

Nakamura Incident ... 28627-46; 30347-48; 37315-16

Nanking (*See:* China, Central; Atrocities, China)

Nationalistic Organizations in Manchuria ... 2786-2816

"National Movement for Assisting the Throne," Hashimoto (Defendant), article by ... 15695-99

National Policy Co. ... 8187-92; 8290; 8299; 8322; 8416; 8470-77; 8530-35

National Policy Foreign Trade Co. ... 8484

National Policy Institute (*See:* Japan, Organizations)

National Policy Investigation Association (Kokusaku Kenkyu Kai) (*See:* Japan, Organizations)

National Service Law (*See:* Japan, Legislation)

Naval Affairs Bureau (*See:* Bureaus)

Naval Affairs Dissemination Department ... 599

Naval General Staff Office (*See:* Japan, Constitutional organization)

The Netherlands (Includes: Ambon; Borneo; Celebes; Indonesia; Java)

    Aggression against (Pros. ... 11629-12345; Def. ... 26829-27116; Pros. summation ... 39519-735; Def. summation ... 43050-175)
        Economic policy toward ... 11944-59; 11961-66; 11974-12007
        Espionage and subversive activities ... 9055-56; 11885-91; 11910-15
        Military occupation ... 12043-44; 12047-60; 12130-342 (*See also:* 9010-69$\frac{1}{2}$)
        New Guinea, exploration of ... 11905-07
        Political policies toward, Japanese ... (*See also:* Japan, Foreign policy) ... 11936; 11961-66; 11969-12007; 12022-33; 12038; 12068; 12096-97; 12107-19; 12121-23; 12134-215; 12221-26 (*See also:* 10334; 10367; 10418-20)
        Preparation for war, Japanese ... 11885-12342
        Relations and negotiations with Japan ... 11628-884; 25264-97; 35703-08
        German trade with the Netherlands through Japan ... 11748-50 (*See also:* Collaboration among Germany, Italy and Japan)
        GEA Ambassador Conference ... 34767
        GEA policy, under, aff. and test. ... 36464-67
        GEACPS, under, test. ... 17912-18019; 18032-61; 18064-88
        Great Britain-Japanese relations concerning ... 11676-78
        Japanese demands on the Netherlands ... 11798-812
        Togo (Defendant), aff. ... 35703-08
        Tojo (Defendant) as War Minister, aff. and test. ... 34767; 36246-48; 36262-63; 36273-97; 36338-44; 36401-03; 36407; 36721-28 (*See also:* 5691-92)
        Treaties between Japan and the Netherlands ... 11670-71; 11763-67
        Tripartite relations with the Netherlands ... 11748-50; 11826-28; 11838 (*See also:* Collaboration among Germany, Italy and Japan)
        US-Great Britain cooperation with the Netherlands ... 11857-58; 11861-63; 11875-78 (*See also:* US, Foreign policy)
        US-Japanese relations with the Netherlands ... 11679-87; 11702-13 (*See also:* US, Negotiations with Japan)
        Southern advance into, Japanese ... 7032-33; 7138-39; 35244-46 (*See also:* 11943-47)
        War, conduct of ... 12062-64

    Allied occupation of Timor ... 1768-52

    Atrocities (*See:* Atrocities)

    Economic blockade of ABD against Japan: Shimada (Defendant), aff. ... 34678-82
        Togo (Defendant), aff. and test. ... 35691-92; 36250-51
        Tojo (Defendant), aff. ... 36338-44

    Hospital ships, sinking of (*See:* Atrocities)

    Independence of the Netherlands, Koiso (Defendant), aff. and test. ... 32250-51; 32428-29

    Military encirclement by ABD, Tojo (Defendant), aff. and test. ... 36246-48; 36262-63; 36273-77; 36338-44; 36723-28

    Offenses against survivors of torpedoed ships (*See:* Atrocities)

    POW (*See:* POW)

    US policy toward the Netherlands (*See:* US, Foreign policy)

    War against Japan, the Netherlands declaration of, Togo (Defendant), aff. ... 35752

New Britain (*See:* the Netherlands)

New Guinea (*See:* the Netherlands)

Nicobar (*See also:* Free Indies):

    Atrocities (*See:* Atrocities)

    POW (*See:* POW)

Nippon Substitute Fuel Producer Co. ... 8293-94

Nomonhan (*See:* USSR, Border incident)

"No More Compromise," Hashimoto (Defendant), article by ... 15662-63

North Manchurian Railway, purchase of ... 5042-47

No Separate Treaty (*See:* Collaboration among Germany, Italy and Japan)

NYK (Nippon Yusen Kaisha):

Policy adopted by, refusal to carry foreigners to mandated islands ... 9142-53

O

October Incident ... 15584-88; 15676-77; 18950-52; 19664-85; 22117

Araki (Defendant), aff. ... 28472

Kido (Defendant), aff. and test. ... 30735-42; 31235-36

Koiso (Defendant), aff. ... 32213-14; 32265 (*See also:* 15676-77)

Minami (Defendant), test. ... 31235-36

Offenses Against Survivors of Torpedoed Ships (*See:* Atrocities)

Ogikubo Conference ... 36178-81

Oka, Kenryo (Defendant) (*See:* Defendants)

Okawa, Shumei (Defendant) (*See:* Defendants)

Okawa Trial, Tokyo Court of Appeals ... 15555-602

Open Door in China (*See also:* US, Foreign policy), letter, US Ambassador in Japan to Japanese Government ... 5209-222; 5233-46

Operational Plan (*See:* Japan, Operational plans)

Opium and Narcotics (*See:* Atrocities)

Opium Committee ... 30623-26

Opium Control Board ... 15921-39

Opium Suppression Board ... 4876-77; 4955-58

Opium Suppression Laws ... 4408

Ordinance ... 5018-20

Ordinance Bureau ... 585

"Ordinance Power of the Emperor," article entitled ... 586

Organic Law of Manchukuo (*See:* Manchuria)

"Organize a Class A War-time Cabinet that Has No Fear of England and Soviet Union," Hashimoto (Defendant), article by ... 15661

Oriental Development Co. ... 618; 8472; 8515

Oshima, Hiroshi (Defendant) (*See:* Defendants)

"Our Great East Asia Principle," Hashimoto (Defendant), article by ... 32733-37

The Outline of the Establishment of Heavy Industry in Manchukuo ... 2962-67

The Outline of the First Period of the Total War for the Establishment of East Asia ... 7431-34; 7992

The Outline for Guiding Manchukuo ... 2903-11

"Outline of Policy for Establishment of a New China," article entitled ... 7839

Overall War Strength Experimental Station ... 8199 (*See also:* Japan, Operational plans)

P

Pacific Ocean Areas ... 6992 (*See also:* Southern Advance; Southern Regions)

Atrocities (*See:* Atrocities)

Hostility, opening of ... 10621-23; 10635-72; 10706-09

POW (*See:* POW)

US, policies toward (*See:* US, Foreign policies)

Pact of Paris (*See:* Treaties and Agreements; Tribunal, Law)

Panay Incident ... 3466-67; 9282-83; 9452; 15678; 17693-95; 21362-66; 21382-87; 28767-81; 30083-84; 33834-35; 33908-10; 34734-38

Grew diary ... 29964-65

Indemnity paid ... 21361

Japanese Foreign Office announcement concerning preventive measures ... 21350-52

US Navy Board of Inquiry ... 3517-30; 9478-80

Paper Theatre Production (Kamishibai) (*See:* Preparation for War, Propaganda censorship and control of press and publication)

Parliamentary Councillor ... 579

Parliamentary Vice Minister ... 578-79

Peace Preservation Section ... 610; 18509-35

Pearl Harbor Attack (*See:* US)

Peiping (*See:* Atrocities, China; China; POW)

Pension Arbitration Committee ... 545

Permanent Central Opium Board at Geneva ... 4921

Permanent Vice Minister ... 578

Personnel Affairs Bureau (of the Army) ... 3493-96

Personnel Bureau ... 581-82; 598

Petroleum Distributing Co. ... 8284

Philippine Islands (*See also:* Preparation for War; Southern Advance; Southern Regions):

    Alliance Pact with Japan ... 36455

    Atrocities (*See:* Atrocities)

    Campaign, aff. and test. ... 33134-40; 33209-17

    Constitution ... 36354

    Espionage in ... 9058

    GEA Conference, test. ... 17912-18019; 18032-61; 18064-88 (*See also:* Japan, Conferences)

    GEA Conference, speeches ... 18091-93; 36471 (*See also:* Japan, Conferences)

    GEA Ministry ... 35766

    Independence ... 35751-52

    Japanese economic and political policies toward (*See:* Japan, Foreign policies)

    Opening hostilities ... 10635-72; 10707-09

    POW (*See:* Prisoners of war)

    Tojo (Defendant), relations with ... 36454-56 (*See also:* Japan, Conferences, GEA Conference)

    US policies toward (*See:* US, Foreign policies)

    War crimes in ... 12384; 12561-63

"Plan for Carrying Out the Training of White Russian Youths in the Special Immigration Settlements" ... 7669-70

Planning, Board of (*See:* Boards)

Plea (*See:* Defendants)

Police:

    Administration ... 1259-1314; 18509-35

    Coercion ... 814; 1259-314 (*See also:* 18509-35)

    Stations ... 608

    Training School ... 612

Political Organizations (*See:* Japan, Organizations)

Political Parties (*See:* Japan, Organizations)

"Positive Policy toward Manchuria" ... 1680; 1764-70

Potsdam Declaration (*See also:* Treaties and Agreements):

    Acceptance of ... 35593-94; 35785-90

    Togo (Defendant), aff. ... 35468; 35593-94

    Tojo (Defendant), aff. ... 35785

POW (*See:* Prisoners of War)

"Powers are Desperately Building Up Air Forces — Build up an Invincible Air Force," Hashimoto (Defendant), article by ... 15651-52

Preparation for War:

    Army preparation (Pros. 8196-8208; 8789-9076; Def. ... 26822-27116; Pros. summation ... 39366-95; Def. summation ... 43224-63)
    Army, expansion of ... 8196-98
    Chain of command, Tojo (Defendant), test. ... 27083-91 (*See also:* 14552-57)
    Collaboration with Germany (*See:* Collaboration among Germany, Italy and Japan)
    FIC ... 8984-85; 26829-62; 26869-75; 26879-87; 26908-33; 26936-41 (*See also:* 6191-6212; 6262-63; 6250; 6476; 6795; 6844; 7033; 7037; 7043; 7046; 7052; 7055; 7059)
    Hainan, occupation of ... 26863-68
    Hong Kong, military preparation for capture of ... 8973-83
    Mandated Islands (*See:* Japan, Mandated Islands)
    Military administrative measures in event of war ... 8986-92; Tojo (Defendant) ... 36400-04
    Military currency in southern regions, use of ... 8652; 8993-98; 26971-80
    Military preparation, chronology ... 9010-69½
    Military Service Law, revision of ... 8802-06 (*See also:* Japan, Legislation)
    National General Mobilization Law ... 8207-08 (*See also:* Japan, Legislation)

Operational plans ... 26982-27039; 27061-65
  Oshima (Defendant), aff. ... 33958-64
  Tojo (Defendant), test. ... 36283-89; 36317; 36321-26; 36329-35; 36345; 36357-59; 36371-83; 36388-410; 36721-28; 36797-98; 36807-08; 36820-23
Prosecution document, authenticity of, "Outline of Foreign Policy of Japanese Empire" ... 26893-906
Scientific Research Institute for Total War (Overall War Strength Experiment Station; Total War Investigation Laboratory; Total War Research Institute) ... 8198-202; 8820-87; 27066-77 *(See also:* Japan, Organizations)
Shanghai, opening of hostilities in ... 3255; 10544; 10608; 10613; 27098-111 *(See also:* China, Shanghai)
Table Top Maneuvers ... 8202-04; 8891-925; 8941-47
Thai-Japanese Alliance ... 27059-97
War Ministry, Great Diary of, fate of ... 27040-60; 27112-16
War, preparation for:
  Date of ... 26947-48
  Lack of ... 26949-70 *(See also:* 24853-900)
Yunnan railway, construction of ... 20876-77

Financial and industrial preparation ... (Pros. ... 8182-9262; Def. ... 24778-25647; 26964-78; Pros. summation ... 39328-65; Def. summation ... 43050-175)
  Financial preparation ... 8189-95; 8415-8789; 24837-39; 24850-51; 24934-39; 24950-58; 25000-02; 25009-11 *(See also:* 18198-242; 18271-341; 18357-79; 36965-68)
    Foreign trade and exchange ... 8139-95; 8477-522; 24837-39; 24850-51; 25000-02; 25009-11 *(See also:* 36965-68)
    Banks ... 8515
    Companies ... 8471-72; 8484; 8515; 8532-34
    Gold embargo ... 24950-58
    Planning ... 8446-62; 8498-507; 8523-67; 18271-341
    Integration of territories ... 8416-477
    Banks ... 8416; 8435-36; 8443-44; 20468-69
    Companies ... 8478; 8475-76
    National debt, 1940 ... 24940-41
    Planning ... 8191-93; 8442-43; 8457-63; 24934-39
  Industrial preparation ... 8182-89; 8245-415; 24908-32; 24956-63; 24979-94; 25005-06; 25016-23; 25042-44; 25047; 25303-05; 25352-58; 25394-95
    Companies ... 8187-92; 8277; 8290-94; 8299; 8321-22; 8395-401; 8416; 8470-77
    Development ... 25005-06
    Legislation *(See:* Japan, Legislation)
    Oil situation ... 25305-07
    Petroleum problem ... 25016-23
    Plans ... 8183-89; 8261-77; 8288; 8297; 8317-22; 8326; 8336; 8348; 8351-52½; 8360-79; 8382-90; 8414; 8436-44; 8513; 8518-29; 8545-46; 18271-341; 18357-59; 24956-63; 30547-49
    Raw materials ... 25394-95
    Rubber ... 35352-58
    Shipbuilding ... 24908-32
    Shipping ... 18342-55; 25042-44; 25047; 25303-05
    Steel ... 24979-94

Naval preparation (Pros. ... 9159-9262; Def. ... 26397-820; 27245-385; Pros. summation ... 39395-445; Def. summation ... 43177-222)
  Expansion of Japanese navy after 1937 ... 9240-62; 26610-52
    Construction ... 9250-51; 26652-774 *(See also:* 10067-68; 11176-87; 11238-81; 11298-302)
    Number of naval personnel ... 9249; 26651
    US navy budget ... 26651-52
    US navy construction ... 26610-12
  Mandated Islands, fortification of *(See:* Japan, Mandated Islands)
  Naval collaboration between Japan and Germany ... 26654-609
  Naval Limitation Treaties (Washington Naval Treaty, London Naval Limitation Treaty and London Naval Conference):
    Abrogation of ... 26543-53; 26775-820
    Japanese opposition to adherence ... 9160-240
  Navy, organization of ... 26413-66
  Operational plan ... 9161-62; 26654-769

Propaganda, censorship and control of press and publication (Pros. ... 806-1677; Def. ... 17137-41; 18379-629; Pros. summation ... 39419-45; Def. summation ... (unable to include in index):
  Censorship ... 812-13
    High police ... 1264-65
  Control, various means of ... 813-14
    Police administration ... 18509-36
    Police coercion ... 814; 1259-314
  Education ... 813-14; 821-914; 936-1007; 1099-115; 18438-507; 18536-84
  Political organizations, use of ... 815-20; 17708-865; 18140-63
  Press and publication control, newspapers and cultural activities ... 1024-77; 1148-56; 1217-37; 18614-27
  Propaganda ... 810-12; 18598-627
    Film ... 1156-209; 18598-613; 18614-28
    GEACPS ... 17912-18005; 18009-19; 18032-88
    Hakko Ichiu ... 17890-911; 18101-15
    Imperial Way (Kodo) ... 17028-29; 18101-15; 18168-71; 23947-51; 23955
    Information, Board of ... 6047-48; 6668-70; 8055-56; 17482-83
    Paper theatre production (Kamishibai) ... 1115-47
    "Emergency Japan" ... 28229-32

Preparation for War *(Cont.)*
  Propaganda, censorship and control of press and publication *(Cont.)*
    Propaganda *(Cont.)*
      Planning, Board of ... 8290; 8403; 8476; 10204-05; 10228; 15963
      Radio ... 1099-115
      "The Way of a Subject," translation ... 1047-65

President of Tribunal (*See also:* Tribunal Ruling):

  Arguments:
    Defense applications and motions:
      Affiant, production of, for cross-ex. ... 11338
      Affidavit, Mrs. Okawa, by, leave to file as exhibit for med. condition of Okawa (Defendant) ... 16994-95
      Cross-examination:
        Scope of ... 2664-67
        Witness, production of, for ... 11338
      Documents:
        Production of ... 4114
        Service of ... 8243
      Evidence, in mitigation ... 37367
      Exhibits:
        Koiso (Defendant), speech by, be stricken ... 3718
        Presentation of, in original words ... 2997
      Interrogation of pros. wit., submission of ... 1567
      Kido, evidence in mitigation ... 37367
      Koiso (Defendant), speech by, be stricken ... 3718-21
      Leading question, answer of, be stricken ... 3984-85
      Okawa (Defendant), med. condition of, leave to file aff. by Mrs. Okawa ... 16994-95
      Pu Y'i, custody of, in Tokyo for further ex. ... 4351-53
      Tribunal member, challenging participation of ... 2347-49
      Witnesses:
        Answer of, be stricken ... 861; 3984-85; 4037
        Custody of, in Tokyo for further ex. ... 4351-53
    Defense argument:
      Order of proof ... 28571-72; 28574
      Probative value, tribunal ruling re ... 20811-12
    Defense objection to Pres. Webb, absence of ... 32662-65; 32669-72
    Defense objections to pros.:
      Affidavit, form of ... 930-38
      Chao Seng letter, presentation of ... 4910-11
      Documents:
        Paraphrasing of, without reading ... 1014-17
        Presentation of ... 11783-86; 12065-67; 12126-28
        Service of ... 1043-46; 1066-77; 1119-24; 1131-32; 1174-87; 1284-85; 1453-55; 1496-1515; 1598-1603; 1724-25; 1728-34; 1766-67; 2199-2208; 2264-67; 2695-2701; 2715; 2746
        Source of ... 2823-24
        Translation of ... 3573
        Typographical error in ... 2912-16
      Evidence, identical, in different doc. ... 3578-80
      Interrogation of wit., method of ... 4773-75
      Opening statement:
        Class B offenses ... 12853-54
        Part of ... 8243
        Philippine case ... 12345-48
      Witness, speeches by ... 5647
    Prosecution applications and motions:
      Affidavit, evidence in lieu of ... 915-28
      Cross-ex. of wit., scope of, be limited to matters raised in direct-ex. ... 1358-60
      Document, service of, rule be amended ... 1291-1303
      Evidence, aff. in lieu of ... 915-28
      Powell, pros. wit., permission to testify in cases other than for which summoned ... 3202-07
      Pu Y'i, note by, inspection of ... 4225-49
      Rule 6 b (1):
        Amendment of ... 1291-1303
        Exemption from compliance with ... 1846-57; 1869-71
      Testimony of wit. without presenting more than aff. ... 2524-26
      Witnesses:
        Note by, inspection of ... 4225-49
        Testimony of, without presenting doc. other than aff. ... 2524-26

  Objections to defense:
    Opening statement, Japanese constitution, concerning ... 17544-46
    Re-direct ex. of def. wit., method of ... 22072-73; 22968; 23259-61; 23848; 24135; 26603; 26701-02; 28501-02; 34817; 35140; 35149; 36833
    Witnesses:
      Answer of ... 24081; 24095; 24101; 24117; 34785; 34811
      Interrogation of def. wit., method of ... 17858-59; 17880-81; 17905; 17926; 18516-17; 18519; 18531; 18583; 18622; 18801-03; 18805-06; 18811-12; 18877; 18881; 19017; 19296; 20052; 20071; 20076-77; 20096; 21157-58; 21331-33; 21464; 22147-48; 24464-65; 24467; 26120; 26123; 26897-98; 26916; 27052; 27329-31; 31226; 31263; 31710; 33160; 33166; 35336; 35866; 36514-15; 36812-14; 37032
      Interrogation of pros. wit., method of ... 854; 857-58; 870; 876-78; 904-07; 909; 949; 956; 973; 983; 987; 1006; 1110; 1145-46; 1151; 1210; 1222; 1225-26; 1280; 1282; 1314; 1329; 1345; 1390; 1410-11; 1430-31; 1437; 1457; 1461; 1485-86; 1488; 1518; 1523-25; 1565; 1635; 1648; 1654-56; 1662; 1673; 1859; 1866; 1873-75; 1880-82; 2000; 2024; 2081-82; 2085; 2096-97; 2101;

2106-07; 2136; 2144-45; 2375; 2402-03;
2415; 2426; 2432; 2435; 2465; 2467; 2469-
70; 2486-89; 2493; 2497-98; 2501; 2509;
2513; 2595-96; 2614; 2663; 2668; 2672;
2674; 2803; 2806; 2814-15; 3027; 3030-31;
3036; 3058-59; 3082-83; 3086; 3088-91;
3095; 3099; 3108-09; 3118; 3195; 3788;
3790; 3942; 4074; 4218; 4272; 4282-83;
4332; 4348; 4443; 4623; 4965; 10880;
10885; 10944-45; 10961; 11002; 11004;
11006; 11016-17; 11021; 11052; 11059;
11064-66; 11069; 11081-86; 11088-90;
11092; 11095; 11104; 11272-73; 11298;
11486; 11488; 11492-93; 11495; 11497-98;
11500-01; 11516; 11567; 11600; 11612-14;
11622-23; 12315; 12631-36; 12639-41;
12663-64; 12712; 13779; 14008; 14038;
14049; 14288; 14321; 14323; 31894-95;
31935; 31962-64; 31983; 31986-87; 31989-
90; 32020; 32022; 32025-27; 32123; 32125;
32161; 32190

Objections to prosecution:
  Documents, admission of, into evidence ...
    12015; 15806-07; 16000; 16174-75
  Opening statement, nature of ... 3242-43;
    3248-49
  Witnesses:
    Interrogation of def. wit., method of ...
      17864-65; 18057; 18501-02; 19440;
      19453-54; 19611; 19672; 19950; 20541-42;
      20651; 20657; 20661; 20663; 20708; 20713;
      20835; 20949; 20953; 20956; 21208; 21213-
      15; 21227; 21238; 21571-72; 21709-10;
      21715-16; 21928; 22175-76; 22182; 22187;
      22193-94; 22197-98; 22206-07; 22230;
      22646; 22947; 22958; 23039; 23052-54;
      23069-70; 23108-09; 23113; 23361; 23421;
      23423; 23711; 24012; 24059; 24071; 24075;
      24078; 24119-20; 24122; 24129-30; 24132;
      24627; 27264-65; 27268; 27869; 28394-95;
      28499; 28663; 28903; 28935; 30350; 30354-
      55; 30432; 31331; 31343-44; 34771-72;
      34778-79; 36613; 36740; 36783-84;
      36953-54
    Re-direct ex. of pros. wit., method of ...
      31922-23; 31929; 32148

Rebukes and warnings:
  Cross-ex., improper by, def. counsel ... 4976
  Defense counsel:
    Cross-ex., improper ... 4976
    Defense counsel, no right of debate ...
      3116; 3207
    Defense counsel, no right to indulge in
      propaganda ... 20479-84
    Exclusion of, from proceedings ... 17777
    Improper conduct of ... 17777; 19928-29;
      20962
    Objection to USSR pros. presenting case
      in Russian ... 7085-86
    Observations out of order ... 2155
    Offensive language used by ... 17777
    Slur on USSR ... 21869-73; 34366-69

Documents, pros. mispresentation of
  ... 6435-37
Language arbiter, observation of ... 4298-4302
Leading question by pros. ... 4034-35; 4081
Newspaper editor, article concerning IMTFE
  ... 17000-02; 17029-32; 20573-74;
  21933-34
Offensive language used by def. counsel
  ... 17777; 42514; 42692-96; 43469-71
Opening statement, def., in USSR case should
  not insult USSR ... 21869-73
Press interview, pros. ... 10579-80
Prosecution:
  Interview with press ... 10579-80
  Leading question by ... 4034-35; 4081
  Mispresentation of doc. ... 6435-37
Summation, def. not to use offensive language
  in ... 42514

Refusal (to hear):
  Defense, cross-ex. of ... 2443; 2484; 2597;
    3034; 3098; 3145-46; 3199; 3335; 3375;
    3409-10; 3415; 3830; 3878; 4185; 4210;
    4246; 4309; 4328-29; 4623; 4646; 5823;
    12254-56; 12278; 12289; 12296-97; 12313-
    15; 12321; 12323-25; 12334; 12336-37;
    12340-41; 13157; 13561; 14367; 14371;
    14392; 14403; 14421; 14625; 14651; 14939;
    14946; 15131-32
  Defense counsel ... 1151; 1401; 1577; 2236;
    2493; 2738; 3066; 3116; 3207
  Defense objection to pros. introduction of
    Japanese-German cultural agreement
    ... 6572
  Prosecution, cross-ex. of ... 916; 918; 920
  Prosecutors, two, on same question ... 6842
  Witnesses, answers of ... 1548-49; 1669;
    2576; 2615; 3145

Requests:
  Defendants be linked in atrocities case to
    conventional war crimes ... 11759-61
  Movie, procurement of ... 1167
  Prosecution doc., paraphrasing of ... 1010-13
  Prosecution to furnish address of pros. wit.
    to def. ... 4814-15
  USSR witnesses, possibility of production of
    ... 32566-67

Statements (See also: President of Tribunal,
  Arguments; President of Tribunal,
  Rebukes and warnings):
  Affidavits:
    Form of ... 930-38
    Length of def. ... 21646
  Air conditioning, installation of ... 722; 1087;
    2262; 2287; 2294
  Cross-ex., defendants, by second counsel on
    behalf of ... 380-81
  Defense case, length of ... 18978-79
  Defense counsel, manner of making objections
    ... 1391; 1401; 6827; 9505
  Defense individual case, admissibility of
    evidence in ... 19172-74

President of Tribunal *(Cont.)*
  Statements *(Cont.)*
    Document:
      Authenticity of ... 37231
      Non-availability of ... 21651
    Evidence:
      Harada-Saionji memoirs, authenticity of ... 38741
      Probative value of private books introduced by USSR pros. ... 7351-53
      Rebuttal, admissibility of ... 37176-77; 37188-97
      Relevancy of, on opium and narcotics ... 2540-45
      USSR pros., map of Nomonhan, authenticity of ... 38348-51; 38354; 38356-57
    Indictment, mistranslation of ... 9092
    Interrogation of defendants, translation of, in prison ... 2213-17
    Mongolian language, question of interpretation of ... 38399-401
    President, absence of ... 32660-61
    Prosecution:
      Case, length of ... 10110
      Document, inconsistent order in presenting ... 1928-30
      Summing up before conclusion of case ... 1240-45; 1252-53
      USSR wit., appearance of, for cross-ex. ... 31212-15; 31706; 32240-43; 32311-13; 32321
      What can be proved by ... 7300-01
    Siberian Intervention ... 38215-17; 38219; 38221-22
    Summation procedure ... 38592-93; 38742-45
    Togo (Defendant), limitation of charges vs. ... 35357; 35952-53; 35955
    Translation, of proceedings, into Japanese ... 18307-08
    Tribunal ... 1287-88; 2365
    Witnesses:
      Answers of ... 3085; 3785; 3810; 3934; 4241; 4285; 4322
      Notes, original, location of ... 4222-25
      USSR pros. case, possibility of calling of ... 32566-67

"The Principles of the Japanese Propaganda Campaign against Outer Mongolia" ... 7670-71

Prisoners of War (POW) (Pros. ... not divided separately by pros. [*See:* Atrocities]; Def. ... 27117-963; 28085-88; Pros. summation [*See:* Atrocities]; Def. summation ... 42618-91):

Prisoners of war and civilian internees, treatment of:
  Administration:
    Foreign Ministry, aff. and test. ... 17752; 27147; 35667-69; 35768-76
    Navy Ministry, aff. and test. ... 27282-309; 27315-48; 27354-85; 33294-96; 33311-12; 33371-74; 33416; 33418-22; 33424-26; 33504-22
    War Ministry ... 594-96; 27433; 27693-722; 27863; 31687-98; 26412-20; 36825-34; 36837-39
  Camps ... 596; aff. and test. ... 14197-261; 14270-80; 14901-09; 27803-78
    Censorship of news received ... 14539-42
    Imperial ordinance concerning establishment of ... 17530-31
    Improvement of:
      Investigations of undernourishment ... 27837-41
      Regulations ... 27806-07
      Study of ... 27809; 27811-12
    Inspection, test. ... 12873-74; 31790-800
    Japan ... 14270-80
      Fukuoka ... 27880-83
      Tokyo ... 27878-80; 27938-40
      Zentsuji ... 27883-84
    Korea, aff. and test. ... 30159-73; 30175-94; 30320-21; 32175-94
    Living conditions, difference in ... 27128
    Manchuria ... 27680-88; 27918-21
    Religious services, aff. ... 27918
    Supplies ... 27797; aff. ... 27788-96
  Organizations ... 14440-43; 27129-43
    Military Affairs Bureau ... 585; 16966; 32959-63; 33126-29; 33160-61
    POW Affairs Central Investigation Committee:
      Investigation ... 5653-65; 5799-801
      Protests, handling, test. ... 15506-53
  Treatment ... 14426-28; 14558-91; 14597-604; 27435-37; 35162-64; 35247; 35319-22; 35553; 35585-89; 35768-76
    Bataan Death March ... 12610-39; 12668; 12673-724; 12738-75; 12821-27
    Captured air crews ... 14599-604; 14607; 15041-42; test. ... 15026-40
    Court martial ... 27908; 27917; aff. and test. ... 28867-915; 29038-58 (*See also:* 14613-29; 14662-80)
    Execution, aff. and test. ... 14599-606; 27905-07; 27912-17; 29038-58; 32960-61; 34447-49; 34462-64
    Investigation, report ... 27903-04
    Regulations for punishment ... 14662-05; 27908; aff. and test. ... 36419-20; 36490-91; 36820
    Verdict ... 27904-05
  Court martial, list of POWs tried by ... 14867-99
  Doolittle fliers:
    Court martial, aff. and test. ... 14613-29; 27908; 27917; 28867-915; 29038-58
    Execution, aff. and test. ... 27905-06; 27912-17; 29038-58; 32960-61; 34447-49; 34462-64; 38059-60; 38616-17; 38621-22

Investigation, report ... 27903-04
Regulations for punishment, aff.
  and test. ... 14662-65; 27908;
  36419-20; 36490-91; 36820
Verdict ... 27904-05; 38059-60
Gratitude for, expression of ... 27689-
  92; 27820-21; 27844-47; 27941-48
Military education, aff. ... 27751-60
Punishment ... 12871-72; 14477-84;
  27823; 27826-27; 27894-900;
  27909-10; 36419-20
Conventions:
  Geneva Convention of 1929 ... 17191-92;
    27124-27; aff. and test. ... 36415-17
    Application to POW and civilian internees:
      Great Britain-Japanese negotiations
        ... 14754-90; 14846-83
      US-Japanese negotiations ... 14728-32;
        14734-53; 14792-822; 14826-36;
        15001-17
    Ratification:
      Army, Japanese, reply to government ... 27181
      Navy, Japanese, reply to government ... 27178-80
  Hague Convention of 1899, Pacific Settlement of International Disputes ... 9265
  Hague Convention of 1907 ... 9266; 11315-
    17; 17185-89; 27122-23
Countries, by:
  Andaman, aff. and test. ... 13193-200;
    30195-213; 30239-46
  Borneo, aff. and test. ... 27599-619; 30195-
    213; 30247-50 (See also: 12043-44;
    12047-53; 13312-16; 13344; 13420-49;
    13492-95; 13499-504; 13505-28; 40168-
    72; 40203-06; 40236-39; 40267-69; 40294-
    95; 40316-18; 40340-46)
  Burma, aff. and test. ... 27536-95; 27599-
    619; 31722-48; 35772-73 (See also:
    5492-96; 5506-07; 5510-12; 5515-608;
    12966-13012; 14629-50; 14658-61; 14754)
  Burma-Thailand, aff. and test. ... 27438-42;
    27536-56; 27743-50; 30195-213; 31722-48;
    34466; 35772-73; 36421-22 (See also:
    5492-96; 5506-07; 5510-12; 5515-608;
    11403-526; 12963-13111; 15500-02;
    40206-08; 40239-44; 40269-73; 40298-
    300; 40318-19; 40346-49; 42658-61;
    43664-66)
    Administrative responsibility for, aff.
      ... 36421-22
    Report concerning ... 27413-28
  FIC ... 7176; 7181-82; 7193-94; 15291-472;
    40303-04; 40324-25; 40356-61
  Hainan ... 13201-07; 26863-68; 40213-14;
    40249-50; 40277-78; 40304; 40325; 40361
  Hong Kong, aff. and test. ... 27471-73;
    27513-33; 35771-72 (See also: 4648-49;
    13112-84; 13304-11; 40177-83; 40214-17;
    40250-51; 40278-79; 40304-05; 40325-26)
  Japan ... 14197-261; 14270-80; 16258;
    40217-20; 40251-55; 40279-83; 40305-
    07; 40326-29; 40362-72; 42669-72
    Civilian internees, aff. and test. ...
      27169-74; 36413-15; 36419-20;
      36837-39
    POW, aff. and test. ... 27201-28; 27391-
      95; 27803-78; 27927-37; 28750-55;
      28867-915; 29038-58
  Java, aff. and test. ... 30183-88; 30195-213;
    30215-38 (See also: 13291-97; 13476-
    91; 13537; 13629; 13644-47; 13700; 40220-
    22; 40255-57; 40283-84; 40307; 40329-
    32; 40372-75)
  Manchuria:
    Camp reports ... 27680-88; 27918-21
    Civilian internees, aff. and test. ...
      28085-88 (See also: 4655)
    Employment, aff. and test. ... 27533-35;
      31698-711
  New Britain ... 14104-30; 40188; 40208;
    40257-58; 40284-86; 40332-33; 40375
  New Guinea ... 14066-103; 40188; 40222-24;
    40258-59; 40286-87; 40308-09; 40333-34;
    40375-76
  Pacific Islands, aff. and test. ... 27176;
    27354-85; 33515-22 (See also: 14911-
    15047; 40201-02; 40231; 40293; 40314;
    40382-83)
  Philippines, aff. and test. ... 27324-34;
    27625-54; 27723-42; 27761-85; 27820-
    21; 32936-38; 33075; 33141-50; 35772-74
    (See also: 12442-52; 12501-07; 12520-
    36; 12566-76; 12592; 12595-96; 12801;
    15196-281; 40384-481; 42662-64)
  Singapore and Malaya, aff. and test. ...
    27397-411; 30215 (See also: 5624-53;
    5671-76; 5942-93; 12883-962; 13454-76;
    40309-11; 40334; 40376-79; 43657-58)
  Southern regions ... 27565; 28722-33;
    30195-213; 30215-20 (See also: 1319;
    5418-19; 13193-200; 13212-16; 13344;
    13504; 13537; 13573; 13629; 13644-47;
    13700; 13750; 13784; 13820; 13913-34)
  Sumatra, aff. and test. ... 27431-34; 27532;
    27655-79; 30195-246; 32935; 33061-65;
    33121-33; 33195-98 (See also: 13297-
    303; 13554-604; 13733-820; 40264-65;
    40292-93; 40313-14; 40337-38; 40382)
  Thailand, test. ... 34466 (See also:
    Burma-Thailand)
Individual responsibility for treatment of:
  Dohihara (Defendant):
    Japan, Eastern, aff. ... 14270-80;
      16258; 28750-55
    Southern regions, aff. and test. ...
      27565; 28722-23
  Hata (Defendant):
    Doolittle fliers:
      Court martial, aff. and test. ... 14613-
        29; 28867-915; 29038-58; 38030-
        57; 38059-60 (See also: 27452;
        27901-02)
      Military regulations for punishment
        ... 14662-65
  Hirota (Defendant), Nanking, rape of, aff.
    and test. ... 29969-30000

Prisoners of War *(Cont.)*
  Prisoners of war and civilian internees *(Cont.)*
    Individual responsibility *(Cont.)*
      Itagaki (Defendant):
        Korea:
          Camps in, reports, 1942-44
            ... 30175-94
          Internment, aff. and test. ... 30159-73
            (See also: 14512-17)
          Responsibility for breaches of laws
            of war ... 12876
          Southern regions, 1945, aff. and test.
            ... 30195-250 *(See also:* 1319; 5418-
            91; 13193-200; 13312-16; 13344;
            13420-49; 13471; 13537; 13629; 13644-
            47; 13700; 13756; 13784; 13820;
            13913-34)
      Kaya (Defendant), aff. ... 30658-59
      Kido (Defendant), aff. ... 31059-60;
        31062; 31067
      Kimura (Defendant):
        Burma, aff. and test. ... 31722-48
        Court, military, martial law ... 31676-84
        Criminal, military, law ... 31685-86
        Doolittle fliers, investigation of,
          report concerning ... 16177-78
        Employment in Manchuria, aff. and
          test. ... 31669-711
        Manchuria, aff. ... 31699-711
        Regulations concerning employment,
          aff. and test. ... 31712-14
        Responsibility:
          Area of, test. ... 14285-94 *(See also:*
            12966-99; 13102; 14754; 27536-619)
          Mistreatment ... 12875
          Punishment Act, promulgation of
            ... 12871-72; 14477-84
          Vice War Minister, responsibility of,
            aff. and test. ... 31715-21; 31749-
            808; 31815-23
          War Ministry and administration, aff.
            and test. ... 31687-98
      Koiso (Defendant), aff. ... 32246-48;
        32543-44
      Matsui (Defendant), Nanking, rape of ...
        32583-93; 32595-601; 32603-58; 32673-88;
        32738-63; 33821-25; 33826; 33849-83;
        33919-20
      Minami (Defendant):
        Discipline concerning improper conduct
          of young officers ... 32810-12
        Korea, aff. ... 32919-21
      Muto (Defendant):
        Administration ... 3436-39
        Nanking, rape of ... 16130-36
        Philippines (1945), aff. ... 27625-54;
          27723-42; 27761; 33069-76 *(See
          also:* 16130-36)
        Sumatra, aff. ... 36061-65
      Oka (Defendant), administration ... 12874-
        75; test. ... 33294-96; 33311-13;
        33418-22; 33504-22
      Oshima (Defendant), treatment, aff.
        ... 34050
      Sato (Defendant):
        Doolittle fliers, execution of, aff. and
          test. ... 29038-58; 32960-61; 34447-
          49; 34462-64
        Protest, US and British, concerning
          mistreatment, aff. and test. ... 34411-
          37 *(See also:* 14287; 32960)
        Thailand, aff. ... 34466
      Shigemitsu (Defendant):
        Camp inspection ... 12873-74
        Malaya ... 5492-93
        Protests, US and British, concerning
          mistreatment ... 14736-44; 14747-50;
          14779-836
      Shimada (Defendant):
        Administration, aff. ... 34669-71;
          34813-17
        Protests concerning mistreatment
          ... 12874-75
      Suzuki (Defendant):
        Administration, aff. ... 35162-64
        Protests concerning mistreatment
          ... 12874-75
        Treatment, aff. and test. ... 35162-64;
          35247; 35319-22
      Togo (Defendant):
        Camp inspection ... 12873-84
        Protests, US and British, concerning
          mistreatment ... 14728-32; 14744-45;
          14754-57
        Treatment, aff. ... 35553; 35585-89;
          35768-76
      Tojo (Defendant), aff. and test. ... 35553;
        35585-89; 35768-76; 36412-26; 36490-91;
        36804; 36818-34; 36837-39
        Administration:
          Camp inspection ... 12875-76
          Conditions, report of, test. ...
            14605-06
          Control and supervision, aff. and test.
            ... 27433; 27863; 36412-20; 36825-
            34; 36837-39
          Employment ... 12875-76
        Burma, aff. ... 35772-73
        Burma-Thailand railway, administrative
          responsibility for, aff. ... 36421-22
        Camps, instruction to commander of
          ... 14424-26; 14428-30; 36423-24
        Chain of command ... 14552-57; 27083-91
        Civilian internees, treatment of, aff. and
          test. ... 36413-15; 36419-20; 36837-39
        Disciplinary law, aff. ... 36417-18;
          36481-83
        Doolittle fliers:
          Execution of, test. ... 14599-606
          Military regulations for punishment
            of, aff. and test. ... 36419-20;
            36490-91
        Execution, aff. ... 36422-23
        Foreign Ministry, responsibility of,
          aff. ... 35768-76
        Geneva Convention of 1929, aff. and
          test. ... 36415-17
        Hong Kong, aff. ... 35771-72

INDEX TO MILITARY TRIBUNAL PROCEEDINGS

Philippines, aff. ... 35772-74
POW Bureau ... 14558-60
POW Information Bureau, test. ... 14591-96
Regulations, aff. ... 36419-20; 36423-24
Speech concerning treatment ... 14426-28
Treatment ... 12871; test. ... 4426-28; 4558-91; 14597-604
Umezu (Defendant), aff. and test. ... 36926-27
  Administration:
    Employment ... 12875-76
  Atrocity report, 1944-45, received, aff. and test. ... 36921-31
  Captured air crews, execution of, attitude toward, aff. and test. ... 36932-37
  Execution ... 36891; 36932-37
Protests about treatment of ... 576-77; 15506-53
  Great Britain, by ... 14728-32; 14736-50; 14754-57; 14779-836; 32960; 34411-37
    Offenses against survivors of torpedoed merchant ships ... 15154; 15158-68; 15182-83
  Netherlands, by:
    Offenses against survivors of torpedoed merchant ships ... 15155; 15169-75
    Violations of treaty provisions concerning hospital ship 'Op ten Noort' ... 15065-87
  United States, by ... 14728-32; 14736-50; 14754-57; 14779-836; 32960; 34411-37
    Offenses against survivors of torpedoed merchant ships ... 15088-106; aff. and test. ... 15109-48
    Treatment, test. ... 15506-33; 34420; 34422-23; 34426
    Violations of treaty provisions concerning hospital ships ... 15049-64
Regulations ... 595-96; 27238-39; 27242-44; 27387-89; 27806-07; 31669; 31769-84
  Captured air crews, punishment of ... 14662-65
  Court martial law ... 31676-84
  Criminal code ... 31615-86
  Disciplinary law, aff. ... 36417-18; 36481-83
  Employment, aff. and test. ... 31712-14; 36423-24
  Handling of documents ... 31658-62
  POW Information Bureau ... 27182-90
  Vice War Minister, organization ... 31665-67
Responsibility:
  Area of, test. ... 12966-99; 13102; 14285-94; 14754; 27536-619
  Chain of command, aff. and test. ... 14552-57; 27083-91
  Foreign Minister, aff. and test. ... 27147-67; 35768-76; 35667-69
  Laws and customs of war, violation of ... 12875-76
  Navy Minister, aff. and test. ... 33294-96; 33311-12; 33371-74; 33416; 33420-21; 33424-26; 33504-22; 34813-17
  Punishment Act, promulgation of ... 12871-72; 27863; 36837-39; 36809-11
  Vice War Minister, aff. and test. ... 31715-21; 31749-823; 32223; 32277-80; 32443-52
  War Minister, aff. and test. ... 27433; 27863; 30296-317; 30330-36; 30407-43; 36413-15; 36419-20; 36804-07; 36809-11; 36818-25; 36837-39

Sea, aff. and test. ... 33295-96; 33420-22; 34670-89 (*See also:* 15088-196; 27282-309; 27315-48; 27354-85; 40491-97; 42673-75)

Sea transportation, aff. and test. ... 27282-309; 27315-48; 27354-85; 33294-96; 33311-12; 33371-74; 33416; 33418-22; 33424-26; 33504-22 (*See also:* 13228-311; 40482-90; 42673-75)

Privy Council (*See:* Japan, Constitutional organization)

Propaganda, Censorship and Control of Press and Publication (*See:* Preparation for War, Propaganda, censorship and control of press and publication)

Prosecution:

  Applications and motions (*See:* Applications and Motions, Prosecution; Tribunal Ruling, Applications and motions, pros., denied; pros., granted)

  Arguments vs. def. applications and motions:
    Affiants, production of, by USSR, for cross-ex. ... 23791-92; 23795-98; 38350-51
    Affidavits:
      Interrogation of defendants in lieu of ... 26273
      Presentation of, without presenting more than aff. ... 2518-26
    Defendants:
      Evidence, death of Nagano ... 14306-07
      Interrogation of defendants in lieu of aff. ... 26273
      Judicial hearing vs. prisoner of war ... 293-301
      Lack of jurisdiction by tribunal ... 132-33; 137-80; 234-47; 249-77
      Opening statement, individual defendants, permission to object to ... 18661-62
      Shimada, recall of ... 35859; 37022-24
    Dismissal of indictment:
      Bill of particulars vs. certain defendants not contained in ... 315-16
      Lack of jurisdiction by tribunal ... 132-33; 137-80; 234-47; 249-77
    Documents:
      Authenticity of, information concerning ... 11892
      Reading of additional paragraph ... 9353-54
      Service of ... 690-92; 1044; 1066-76; 1119-24; 1130-32; 1173-86; 1193-94; 1283-85; 1454-55; 1496-515; 1595-98; 1600; 1722-25; 1728-34; 1766-67; 2199-2208; 2254-55; 2279-82; 2694-701; 2714-15; 15553

Prosecution *(Cont.)*
  Arguments vs. def. applications and motions *(Cont.)*
    Evidence:
      Evidence in def. gen. case be stricken from record ... 983; 23857-58
      Harada-Saionji memoirs, production of three versions of ... 37529-30
      Hiranuma (Defendant), dismissal of indictment ... 315-16
      Interrogation of defendants, aff., in lieu of ... 26273
      Itagaki (Defendant), judicial hearing vs. prisoner of war ... 293-301
      Judicial hearing vs. prisoner of war ... 293-301
      Judicial notice for def. doc. ... 36973; 36976
      Kimura (Defendant), judicial hearing vs. prisoner of war ... 293-301
      Litvinov diary, entire text, production of ... 22871; 22873
      Matsuoka (Defendant):
        Confinement in sanatarium, and name stricken from indictment ... 328
        Dismissal of indictment ... 315-16
      Muto (Defendant), judicial hearing vs. prisoner of war ... 293-301
      Nagano (Defendant), death, evidence of ... 14306-07
      Okawa (Defendant), name be stricken from indictment ... 330-31
      Opening statements:
        Copies of, in English and Japanese, presented to def. ... 8180-81
        Def., individual defendants be permitted to object to ... 18661-62
        Presentation of ... 9335
        Order re time for making ... 338-39
      Recess ... 334-37; 13892
      Sato (Defendant), judicial hearing vs. prisoner of war ... 293-301
      Shigemitsu (Defendant), dismissal of indictment ... 315-16
      Shimada (Defendant), dismissal of indictment ... 315-16
      Togo (Defendant), dismissal of indictment ... 315-16
      Tribunal:
        Member, challenging participation of ... 94-97; 2346-47
      USSR pros., what can be proved by ... 7298-300
      USSR gen. case, reopening for additional evidence ... 31853-54
      USSR prosecution *(See:* Prosecution, USSR prosecution)
      Witnesses:
        Calling of, without presentation of certificate of illness ... 7577
        Presentation of, without presentation of more than aff. ... 2518-26
        Recalling of defendant ... 35859-60
        USSR case, production of pros. wit. in ... 31853

  Arguments vs. def. objections:
    Affidavits:
      Ballantine, by ... 10715-16
      Commission, taken by ... 33532-33; 33535-37; 33558-87
      Correction of ... 31828-30
      Excerpts from, use of ... 11418-24
      Fitch, by, substitution for cross-ex. ... 4460
      Form of ... 933-38; 1036; 1152
      Murakami, by ... 7573-74
      Presentation of, after close of case ... 32004-06; 32388
      Presentation of, for rebuttal ... 38132-34
      Presentation of, without production of wit. for cross-ex. ... 4459-60; 4851-52; 10066-67
      POW case in, presentation of ... 2287-89
      Smythe, by, substitution for cross-ex. ... 4459
      Testimony by ... 10066-67
      Typographical errors in ... 1032
    Ballantine aff., presentation of ... 10715-16
    Chao Seng letter, presentation of ... 4910-11
    Ciano diary, authentication of ... 6086-87
    Cross-examination:
      Affidavit, by ... 4851-52
      Document, not presented, cross-ex. of def. wit. on ... 19363; 19365-67
      Evidence, citation in lieu of cross-ex. ... 28286-92
      Method of ... 33238-39; 33277-81
    Documents:
      Authentication of ... 2823-24; 4858; 9222-24; 9671-72
      Evidence, doc., not read ... 29718-25; 29728
      Extra-comment on ... 10296; 11762-63; 15980-81
      Manner of presentation of excerpts from ... 7942; 7950; 7952
      Official doc., certificate of ... 6897-907
      Order in presenting ... 1929-30
      Photostatic copies ... 6086-87
      Presentation of ... 7340; 7343; 7456; 7507-08; 7522-23; 7716-17; 7866; 7901; 7921; 7924-25; 9486; 9776; 10110; 11775-76; 11784; 11820; 11968; 12650-51; 12751; 15427-28; 29158; 30399; 30672; 31499-50; 31505; 34116; 34241-42; 34246; 34292; 34309; 34315-16; 34372; 34707; 35261; 36702; 36880; 36916-17
      Presentation of, for rebuttal ... 37234-35; 37244; 37248; 37259-60; 37277-80; 37282; 37284; 37305; 37318-19; 37322; 37324; 37342-44; 37369-71; 37381; 37384-85; 37393; 37396; 37404-05; 37416-17; 37421-22; 37428; 37430-31; 37437-38; 37441; 37547-48; 37557; 37577; 37586; 37588-89; 37593-94; 37596-98; 37602-03; 37608-09; 37623-26; 37639; 37644-45; 37658-60; 37664-65; 37669-72; 37676-79; 37683-84; 37688-89; 37691; 37702-03; 37708-09; 37713-14; 37717; 37740-42;

INDEX TO MILITARY TRIBUNAL PROCEEDINGS

37751-53; 37763-64; 37766; 37770; 37772; 37775; 37780-81; 37787-88; 37795; 37798-801; 37804; 37806-07; 37810; 37814; 37828; 37835-36; 37845; 37849-50; 37852-53; 37855; 37858; 37860; 37870-73; 37877; 37929; 37955; 37970-71; 38005; 38010; 38012-13; 38077; 38104-05; 38126; 38158-59; 38161; 38165; 38173; 38178; 38187-88
    Reading of excerpts from ... 14437-39
    Service of ... 721-22; 5615-17; 6282-83; 7305-06; 7322; 7325; 7335; 15642; 15994-96; 19381-82
    Typographical errors in ... 803-05; 2254; 2912-16
Evidence:
    Applicability of, in gen. case to all defendants ... 25875; 25887-89
    Chao Seng letter, presentation of ... 4910-11
    Citation in lieu of cross-ex. of def. wit. ... 28286-92
    Document not read in evidence ... 29718-24; 29725; 29728
    German decorations to defendants, presentation of ... 11347-48
    Harada-Saionji memoirs (*See:* Harada-Saionji Memoirs)
    Hearsay evidence, admission of ... 29709-11
    Maps (*See:* Maps)
    Presentation of, after close of case ... 16991-92
    Tripartite Pact in USSR case, presentation of ... 7907
Extra-comments on doc. ... 10296; 11762-63; 15980-81
Fitch aff. ... 4460
Harada-Saionji memoirs, authentication of ... 37519-24
Harada-Saionji memoirs, presentation of ... 37507-09; 37547-48; 37557; 37577; 37586; 37588-89; 37593-94; 37596-98; 37602-03; 37608-09; 37623-26; 37639; 37644; 37658-60; 37664-65; 37669-72; 37676-79; 37683-84; 37688-703; 37708-09; 37713-14; 37717; 37740-42; 37751-53; 37763-64; 37766; 37770; 37772; 37775; 37780-81; 37787-88; 37795; 37798-801; 37804; 37806-07; 37810; 37814; 37828; 37835-36; 37845; 37849-50; 37852-53; 37855; 37858; 37860; 37870-73; 37877
Interrogation of defendants:
    Oshima, excerpts from ... 5908-10; 5923
    Translation of, in prison ... 2214
Interrogation of witnesses:
    Document, presentation of, during interrogation of def. wit ... 26329-30
    Judicial notice, Japanese aggression, Lake Khasan ... 7896-97
    Maps, presentation of, during test. in def. wit. ... 23701; 23714-17
    Soviet Far East, presentation of ... 7302-03
    World, presentation of ... 7356
Murakami aff. ... 7573-74
Re-direct ex. of pros. wit. ... 14964; 31924; 31926-27; 32149; 32193-95

Smythe, aff. substitution for cross-ex. ... 4459
Stimson, test. by aff. ... 10066-67
Summing-up before conclusion of case ... 1239-45; 1252
Tamura, recalling of ... 15852
Translation:
    Interrogation of defendants in prison ... 2214
    Pros. translation ... 4015-16
Witnesses:
    Answers not responsive to question ... 4004
    Interrogation of def. wit., for surrebuttal, method of ... 38894-95
    Interrogation of pros. wit., method of ... 2011; 2018; 2540-45; 3752; 3961; 4421; 4432-33; 4439; 4774-76; 4979-80; 4993-94; 5357; 7768; 17828-29; 17943; 17987; 18018-19; 18332; 18476; 18865-66; 19365; 19446-47; 19451; 19455; 19641-42; 19854; 19890-92; 19905; 19910-11; 20640; 20650; 21945; 22034; 22192; 22224; 22772; 22776-77; 22788; 22965; 23043; 23074; 23214-16; 23242-43; 23411-12; 23681; 26687; 26697; 27195-96; 27266-67; 28317-18; 28327-28; 28354; 28367; 28379; 28390; 28393-94; 28402; 28642-43; 28653; 28662; 28719; 28953-55; 28970-72; 28989; 29092; 29281-82; 29287-89; 29293-94; 29298-99; 29546; 29550; 29796; 30396; 30404; 31304; 31325-27; 31387-88; 31399-400; 31469; 31534-35; 31558-60; 31603; 32277; 32279; 33185-86; 33373; 34101; 34108; 34229; 34578-80; 34596; 34599-600; 34615; 34721; 34731-32; 34742; 34746; 34748-49; 34753; 34766-69; 34981-82; 35111; 35125; 35886-87; 35911; 36089-90; 36536; 36570-71; 36873-74; 36876-77; 36952-53; 36955; 37041
    Interruption of def. wit. during answer ... 31357-59; 34730-31
    Recalling of ... 14283; 15852
    Scope of test. ... 4006-07

Argument vs. president of tribunal:
    Application, defendants, joining of atrocities case with conventional war crimes ... 11760
Objections:
    Documents, presentation of ... 12015; 16000; 16071-72; 16075; 16078-79; 16175
    Leading question ... 4034
    Press interview ... 10579-80
    Witnesses:
        Interrogation of def. wit., method of ... 17865; 18057; 18501; 18503; 21571; 21710; 22175-76; 22207; 22947-48; 23052-54; 23711; 27264; 28394; 28499; 28663; 30354-55; 31443-44; 34771-72; 34778-79; 36783-84; 36954
        Interrogation of pros. wit., method of ... 4056-57; 12641

Argument vs. tribunal ruling:
    Affidavit, evidence of def. wit. be given on ... 19100-01

Prosecution *(Cont.)*
  Argument vs. tribunal ruling *(Cont.)*
    Defendants, evidence of, may be given once in ind. case ... 19731-33; 19744-47; 19756-58
    Defendants, interrogation of, admissibility against other defendants ... 10105-07
    Documents, reading of excerpts from ... 10728-33; 12408; 12454-55; 15144-45
    Evidence:
      Cumulative ... 12088-93
      Defendants, of, may be given once in ind. case ... 19731-33; 19744-47; 19756-58
      Defense wit., of, be given on aff. ... 19100-01
    Individual case, presentation of evidence of defendants in, procedure concerning ... 19731-33; 19744-47; 19756-58
    Interrogation of defendants, admissibility of, against other defendants ... 10105-07

  French prosecution:
    Argument against def. objection to introduction of doc. into evidence in rebuttal ... 38187-88
    French language, use of ... 6700-07; 6736-91

  Objections to def. (*See also:* Tribunal Rulings):
    Affidavits, presentation of entire def. aff. ... 21744; 22082-84; 22087; 22295; 22432-35; 22551-55; 22880-81; 22886-91; 23089-91; 23294-95; 23297; 23565-68; 23611-15; 23629-32; 23653; 23655; 23681; 23865; 23932-33; 23947-48; 24240-45; 24252-53; 24264-66; 25047-48; 25242-46; 25413-15; 26233-34; 26461; 26463-64; 26543-46; 26982; 27040-41; 27043; 27893; 27949-52; 28049-50; 28066-68; 28072-74; 28477; 28479-83; 28517; 28533-35; 28541; 28560-61; 28563; 29236-37; 29246; 29320; 29375-77; 29388-90; 29404-05; 29688-71; 29673; 30051-52; 30138-39; 30141-42; 30147-48; 30535; 30540-41; 30545-46; 32478; 32519-21; 32687-88; 32800; 32882-83; 32944-45; 32974-75; 33058; 33066-68; 34534-35; 34548-49; 36932-33; 36999; 37002-05; 37008; 37011
    Affidavits, presentation of entire def. aff. for surrebuttal ... 38615-16; 38709; 38712; 38714; 38724; 38727-28; 38775-77; 38804-07; 38833-34; 38842-43; 38865; 38867-68
    Affidavits, presentation of part of def. aff. ... 20749-50; 20756; 20773; 21144-48; 21158; 21164; 21244-45; 21436; 21438-41; 21497-98; 21560; 21636; 21638; 21648-49; 21695-96; 21764-65; 21970-73; 22100; 22102-04; 22106; 22255-56; 22714; 23012-14; 23026-27; 23494-95; 23503; 23973-74; 24281-87; 24395; 25264-66; 25268-69; 25902-05; 25907; 25910-11; 26508-09; 26551-53; 26559-60; 26613-14; 26654-55; 26707-09; 26742-43; 26777-78; 26869-70; 26879; 27102; 27129-31; 27246-47; 27250; 27486-87; 27618-19; 27653-54; 27762-63; 27803; 27818-19; 27827-28; 27831-32; 28018; 28522; 28553-55; 28672-74; 28864-65; 28868; 29006-07; 29031-32; 29038; 29137-38; 29230; 29242; 29255-57; 29406-07; 29476-80; 29645-47; 29657-58; 29680-81; 29899; 29915; 30003-04; 30021-22; 30028-30; 30075-76; 30078-79; 30099-100; 30215; 30252; 30566; 30575; 30583; 30711-14; 31616-18; 31622-26; 31633-35; 31653-54; 31688; 31690; 31745-46; 31749-50; 32487; 32494-97; 32544-45; 32619-20; 32801; 32871-72; 32890-91; 32940-41; 32977-78; 33015; 33303-04; 34397-402; 34833; 34951-53; 34991-94; 35179-80; 35375; 35459-60; 35589-90; 35594; 36840-41; 36845-47; 36850; 36891; 36990-91; 37013-14; 37026-27
    Affidavits, service of def. aff. ... 22979-80; 22983-86; 23022; 23280; 23425; 23427; 23651; 24233; 24379
    Applications and motions:
      Documents, copies of, processing of, relaxation of tribunal ruling concerning ... 22560-61; 22563-66
      Harada-Saionji memoirs, production of three versions of ... 37529-30
      Judicial notice for def. doc. ... 36976; 37168-73
      Recess, preparation def. case ... 18958-63
      Witnesses:
        Answers of, be stricken from record ... 14314
        Direct ex. of, before presentation of case ... 1354-55
        Qualification of def. wit. (Tamura) as expert ... 17888
    Cross-examination:
      Evidence, presentation of, during cross-ex. ... 3048-49
      Second counsel, by, on behalf of defendant ... 1380
    Defense counsel:
      Cross-ex. by second counsel on behalf of defendant ... 1380
      Statement of, introduction of evidence based on ... 4263
    Documents:
      Affidavit without annexed doc. ... 21695-96
      Authenticity of ... 17287-88; 19785-86; 20220; 21388; 21805; 24565-67; 24569; 24788; 24799-800; 24802-04; 24808-11; 24818-19; 24824; 24826-30; 24833; 24836-37; 26843-44; 26961-62; 28590-91
      Certificate of doc., introduction of ... 21960-61; 21964-65
      Presentation of ... 17274; 17277; 17282; 17287-88; 17298-301; 17305; 17336-37; 17342; 17344; 17356; 17359-60; 17392-96; 17410-11; 17419-21; 17432; 17450; 17454; 17459; 17462-64; 17601; 17622-29; 17644-45; 17655-57; 17660; 17666-67; 17672; 17685; 17689; 17691; 17866-67; 17901; 18022-23; 18027-29; 18099; 18172; 18174; 18382; 18386; 18401; 18403-05; 18410; 18414; 18416; 18418; 18422; 18424-26;

18428; 18430-34; 18436-37; 18439-40; 18585-87; 18589; 18594-95; 18597; 18628; 18696; 18762-63; 18772; 18774-76; 18780-81; 18789-90; 18792-95; 19137; 19141-44; 19159; 19178-79; 19181; 19187-88; 19190; 19194; 19199; 19204; 19215; 19318; 19398-99; 19404; 19476-77; 19488-89; 19520; 19539; 19597; 19613-14; 19619-20; 19686; 19692; 19694; 19699; 19715-16; 19720-22; 19725-26; 20214; 20218-19; 20235-36; 20241; 20261-62; 20266-67; 20455-58; 20508-09; 20511-12; 20514-15; 20549; 20589; 20606-08; 20795; 20797; 20801; 20804; 20807-08; 20815; 20825-26; 20828-29; 20859-62; 20865-67; 20871; 20873; 20881-85; 20887-90; 20911-22; 20939-40; 20960-64; 20966; 20994; 21007; 21011-12; 21014-22; 21033-35; 21037-39; 21042; 21045-51; 21054-57; 21064; 21067; 21069-74; 21079-80; 21083-95; 21097-100; 21102-03; 21106-09; 21111; 21113-16; 21118-32; 21135-37; 21140-43; 21342-44; 21348; 21357-61; 21368-69; 21377; 21388-89; 21392-95; 21403-06; 21409-10; 21417; 21419-20; 21422-23; 21427-28; 21431-34; 21494; 21496; 21506; 21544-48; 21726-28; 21732; 21805; 21812; 21814-21; 21824; 22297-99; 22302; 22372-73; 22377-81; 22449-52; 22458-60; 22462; 22464-66; 22474; 22476; 22496-99; 22503-04; 22511-13; 22535; 22538-39; 22556; 22568; 22570; 22693-94; 22702-04; 22706-07; 22709; 22800-02; 22819-21; 22836-39; 22847; 22849-50; 22863-65; 22867-77; 22919-20; 22970; 22973; 23084; 23144-45; 23177; 23182; 23186-87; 23480-81; 23483; 23546-47; 23584-87; 23645; 23649-50; 23722-23; 23726-27; 23729-31; 23733-40; 23742; 23745; 23747; 23749; 23751-56; 23758-60; 23762; 23769-73; 23779; 23783; 23954; 24201; 24220-22; 24224-25; 24257-58; 24270-71; 24273-76; 24281-83; 24311; 24340; 24342; 24345-46; 24367-69; 24372; 24571; 24574; 24588-89; 24601; 24607; 24609; 24668-69; 24671-73; 24677-79; 24683; 24686; 24689-90; 24730-31; 24735-36; 24747-49; 24798-800; 24802-04; 24808-11; 24818-19; 24824; 24826-29; 24839-42; 24845-46; 24848-49; 24851-52; 24903-06; 24942; 24944; 24947-48; 24964; 24967; 25083-85; 25087-88; 25101-04; 25108-12; 25115; 25118-24; 25128-32; 25134-39; 25141; 25146-49; 25153; 25160; 25164-66; 25170-72; 25175; 25182; 25188-89; 25194-95; 25216-18; 25221; 25223; 25225-27; 25231; 25233-34; 25237; 25241; 25249-50; 25298; 25302-03; 25313-14; 25318-19; 25328-31; 25333-34; 25350; 25358; 25366-67; 25374; 25389-90; 25393; 25396-98; 25402-08; 25433-34; 25437-40; 25445-46; 25455-56; 25458-61; 25464-68; 25474-81; 25483-89; 25491-92; 25494; 25500-02; 25504-05; 25514-17; 25520-22; 25525-31; 25541-42; 25544-45; 25551-52; 25556; 25558; 25560-62; 25568-69; 25571-72; 25574-75; 25577-78; 25580-82; 25587-94; 25596-98; 25600-04; 25606-07; 25610-11; 25613-14; 25616-17; 25623; 25627-29; 25633-38; 25641-43; 25646; 25662-63; 25665-66; 25736-37; 26215-16; 26227-28; 26253; 26358; 26360; 26381-83; 26387-88; 26431; 26450; 26452; 26604; 26606-08; 26617-18; 26770-71; 26777-78; 26961-62; 27078-80; 27238; 27835; 27845; 27849; 27959-60; 28023-25; 28037-43; 28100; 28239-42; 28247; 28271-72; 28415-16; 28418; 28421-23; 28425; 28430-31; 28436; 28445; 28471; 28474; 28513-16; 28520-21; 28537-39; 28551-52; 28566-68; 28575-78; 28587-90; 28696-98; 29248; 29251; 29379; 29385-86; 29434; 29445; 29447-50; 29462; 29464; 29466-67; 29471-72; 29566-68; 29578; 29589; 29605; 29607; 29609-10; 29620; 29624; 29629; 29632; 29638; 29642-43; 29654-55; 29664; 29883-84; 29894-96; 29933; 29947; 29949; 29953-54; 29961-63; 29966; 30034-35; 30047-50; 30057-58; 30060-61; 30072-74; 30144-45; 30544; 30616; 32550; 32699-700; 32771-72; 32807; 32837-38; 32853; 32917; 33059; 33282; 33953-54; 34031-32; 34334-35; 34344-46; 34348; 34350-51; 34355-57; 34491; 34493; 34501-03; 34526-27; 34539; 34680-81; 34846; 34856-57; 34859; 34868; 34870-71; 34880-82; 34884-85; 34889; 34895-96; 34898; 34995; 35136-37; 35350-52; 35357-60; 36886-87; 36979-80; 37018

Presentation of def. doc. for surrebuttal ... 38594-95; 38597; 38601-02; 38604-05; 38608; 38611; 38613; 38620; 38622; 38625-33; 38638-41; 38647; 38650; 38652-53; 38657; 38661-63; 38667-69; 38674-76; 38684; 38693; 38695-98; 38705; 38748; 38753-54; 38757-61

Reading of def. doc. not in evidence ... 1643-45

Service of ... 18918-19; 19486; 19540-41; 19553-54; 19620; 19801-05; 21428; 24332-33; 26607-08; 26773-74; 26961-62; 27271

Evidence:
Admission of, for surrebuttal ... 38586-89; 38594-95
Defense surrebuttal ... 38586-89; 38594-95
Harada-Saionji memoirs, introduction of, not accepted during pros. rebuttal ... 38632-33
Harada-Saionji memoirs, presentation of, for def. surrebuttal ... 38632-33; 38638; 38639-41; 38647; 38652-53; 38657; 38661-63; 38667-69; 38674-76; 38693; 38695-96
International law and ambassadorial immunity, facts of, introduction of ... 34355-57
Introduction of, during pros. case ... 10916-18
Johnston, book by, introduction of ... 4180-81
Map, introduction of, during def. test. of def. wit. ... 23837-38; 23851

Prosecution *(Cont.)*
  Objections to def. *(Cont.)*
    Evidence *(Cont.)*
      US President, proclamation of, introduction of ... 25170-72; 25182; 25188-89
      Extra-comment ... 17249; 22691; 24193; 29465; 33672-73; 33715; 34848
      Harada-Saionji memoirs:
        Authenticity of, def. statement concerning ... 38740-41
        Introduction of, not accepted during pros. rebuttal ... 38632-33
      International law and ambassadorial immunity, facts of, introduction of ... 34355-57
      Johnston, book by, introduction of ... 4180-81
      Opening statements:
        Defense general opening statement, introduction of part of ... 17103-04
        Defense opening statement, introduction of events prior to 1904-05 ... 18633
        Defense opening statement, introduction of part of ... 17116-18; 18633; 20476-77; 22411
      Re-direct ex. of def. as wit. on behalf of other def. ... 20090-94; 20096-97; 20104
      Re-direct ex. of defendants as wit., method of ... 21320-21; 21323-27; 21329-30; 21334; 21465-66; 21580; 21692; 22069-71; 22756; 22967; 23140; 23257; 23846-48; 23901; 23903; 24147-48; 24552; 24555; 24559; 24658-59; 24661-62; 26906; 27226; 29316-17; 29562-65; 29995-97; 30010; 30134; 30137; 31799; 31823; 32456; 32469; 33046-47; 33798; 33803; 33805; 33807; 33809; 34621; 34804; 35151; 36117; 36119-21; 36125; 36827-29; 36831; 36833; 37158-59
     Statements:
      Harada-Saionji memoirs, authenticity of ... 38740-41
      Oshima (Defendant), references to ... 34334-35
      Prosecution doc., production of ... 2201-02
     Summation:
      Case of, during test. of wit. ... 31244
      China case, insult in part of ... 42692-93; 42695
     Witnesses:
      Answers of ... 21328; 22241; 24451; 24455; 28934; 28939; 36519; 36609; 36744
      Interrogation of def. wit., method of ... 17720; 17736; 17762-63; 17772; 17799; 17856; 17859-60; 17862; 17875; 17882; 17895-96; 17925; 18015-16; 18067; 18070; 18075; 18077; 18084; 18249; 18301-02; 18315-16; 18334; 18505; 18519-21; 18533-34; 18550; 18558; 18605; 18608; 18622; 18626-27; 18805-08; 18816-17; 18827; 18877; 18885; 18898; 18902; 18905; 18914-17; 18987; 19025; 19066-67; 19125; 19297; 19358-59; 20079-80; 20084; 20094; 20096; 20099; 20736; 20738-39; 20741; 22143-45; 22148; 22151; 22944-45; 24451; 24456-64; 24469-70; 24473; 24475-77; 24487-88; 26157; 26159; 26428-29; 26584; 26680-81; 26683; 26703; 26897-99; 27051; 27328-30; 27332-33; 27462; 27716; 27719; 28246; 28254-55; 28277-78; 28281-82; 28856; 29024; 29246; 29430-31; 29662-63; 29743; 29913; 29993; 31219; 31221-27; 31232-33; 31760; 32857-58; 33151; 33157; 33167; 33174; 33347; 33430; 33442; 33658; 33750-51; 34387-89; 34836; 34856-57; 34859; 34868; 34870-71; 34880-82; 34884-85; 34889; 34895-96; 34898; 34969; 34971-72; 35010; 35828; 35831-32; 35836-37; 35842; 35844-46; 35863; 36493; 36510-11; 36513; 36530
      Interrogation of pros. wit., method of ... 845; 873; 901; 906-07; 951; 958; 976; 984; 1006; 1106; 1142; 1207-08; 1269; 1271; 1282; 1307; 1343; 1353; 1368-71; 1374; 1378-79; 1393; 1410; 1428; 1470; 1648; 1874-75; 2058; 2079; 2083; 2136; 2424; 2462; 2468; 2470-71; 2482; 2513; 2660; 2812; 3030; 3035; 3037; 3063-65; 3072; 3076-77; 3079; 3081-83; 3085; 3092; 3095-97; 3099-100; 3102-03; 3105-06; 3109-11; 3113; 3115; 3117-18; 3133; 3136; 3138-39; 3142-43; 3375; 3379; 3382; 3384-86; 3388; 3412; 3414; 3798; 3816-17; 3825; 3832; 3837; 3840; 3845; 3851; 4053; 4065; 4072; 4092-95; 4103-04; 4106; 4123; 4127; 4133; 4138-39; 4145; 4177; 4197; 4204-06; 4211-12; 4304; 4306-08; 4318; 4324; 4326-27; 4330; 4333; 4335-36; 4347; 4349; 4444-45; 4769; 4892; 4957; 4962; 4966; 4969-72; 4974; 5206; 5820; 7464; 7469-70; 7635; 8579; 8639; 8661; 8693-94; 8733; 8829-30; 8841; 8857; 8867; 8871; 10865; 10869-70; 10875; 10877; 10882-83; 10897-98; 10926; 10931-32; 10953; 10968; 10971; 10977-79; 10981; 11009; 11075-76; 11253; 11259; 11261-62; 11270; 11273; 11293-94; 11297-98; 11494; 11499; 11515; 11521; 11581; 11584; 11623; 12247; 12257; 12271; 12279; 12308; 12312; 12315-17; 12322; 12326-29; 12584-86; 12588-89; 12628; 12663; 14316; 14339-40; 14347-48; 14398-99; 14406-07; 14410-11; 14420-21; 14625; 14854-55; 14857-58; 14877-79; 14938; 14946-47; 15449; 15457; 15460-61; 15924; 15930-31; 15944-45; 16153; 16155; 16172; 31845; 31856; 31868; 31877; 31880; 31891; 31911; 31914; 31935; 31938; 31940-41; 31948; 31957; 31971-72; 31974-75; 31976; 31980; 31983-84; 31988-90; 32021; 32025; 32030; 32079-80; 32090-91; 32128-29; 32173; 32176-77; 32186
      Interrogation of pros. wit. for rebuttal, method of ... 37447-48; 37467-68; 37476; 37518
      Summation of case during test. ... 31244

  Objections to president of tribunal:
    Interrogation of def. wit., method of ... 20055
    Interrogation of pros. wit., method of, pres. objection concerning ... 1210

Objection to tribunal ruling, opening statement, nature of ... 7867; 7869

Statements: (See also: Prosecution, Arguments; Prosecution, Objections):
  Affiants in USSR case, production for cross-ex. ... 32554-56
  Cross-ex.:
    More than one counsel, by ... 33237; 36533-34
    Postponement of cross-ex., Muto (Defendant), illness of counsel ... 33231-33
    Replacement of counsel for cross-ex. of Muto ... 33237-38
    Witness in USSR case, appearance of ... 31211-13; 31705-06; 32239-42; 32318-22
  Document, admissibility of official ... 6841-44
  Evidence, admissibility of, for rebuttal ... 37176-77; 37188-97
  Harada-Saionji memoirs, production of part of ... 27143-45
  Hostile witness ... 901-02
  Indictment, mistranslation of ... 87-91
  Press interview, denial of ... 10579-80
  Procedures:
    Mitigation ... 38916-17; 38923
    Pros. case, opening of ... 108
    Summation ... 38592-93; 38942-45
  Recess for preparation for case ... 108
  Togo (Defendant), limitation of charges against ... 35347-48; 35375-58; 35951-56
  Translation, method of, from Chinese to English ... 2300; 2304-05
  Tribunal:
    Member of, participation in ... 2346-47
    Member of, withdrawal of ... 2286
  Witness, appearance of, in USSR case for cross-ex. ... 31705-06; 32211-13; 32239-42; 32318-22

USSR prosecution:
  Applications and motions:
    Cross-ex. of wit., events prior to indictment period ... 7323-24
    Judicial notice (Imperial Rescript, Russo-Japanese War, 1904-05) ... 38200
  Argument vs. def. applications and motions:
    Changkufeng, evidence be stricken ... 7783-84
    Document, production of entirety, if excerpts tendered ... 36922-23
    Statement of what can be proved by USSR pros. ... 7298-300
    USSR general case, reopening for additional evidence ... 31853-54
    Witnesses:
      Production of information, status and location of ... 8091; 8163; 8173
      Production of wit. whose aff. presented 7454; 7525; 7529; 8001-02; 8163; 23166-67; 23791-92; 23806-25; 24560-63; 31853-54; 32795-98; 38350-51
  Argument vs. def. objections:
    Affidavits:
      Admission of, for rebuttal ... 38236-37; 38288
    Affidavit by affiant later executed, admission of ... 7314-15
    Documents:
      Admission of, for rebuttal ... 38199; 38206-07; 38210-11; 38213; 38222-23; 38226-27; 38242-43; 38250; 38255-58; 38262; 38264-65; 38268; 38270-71; 38402-07; 38409; 38511; 38513-14; 38518; 38521; 38524-26
      Authenticity of ... 7721
      Reading of excerpts from ... 7700
    Extra-comment ... 7649; 7731; 7834-35; 7837-38
    Japanese-German collaboration case, reopening of ... 7862-64
    Nomonhan map, authentication of ... 7844
    Siberian Intervention, admission of ... 38210-11; 38213-16; 38222-23
    Statement, admission of part of ... 8136; 8159-60
    USSR case, presentation of, in Russian ... 7083-101
    Witness, interrogation of, method of ... 38433
  Objection to defense:
    Affidavit, presentation of, for surrebuttal ... 38847-48; 38852-53; 38856
    Document, admissibility of, for surrebuttal ... 38883-85; 38887-90
    Witnesses:
      Interrogation of def. wit., method of ... 8106; 8120
      Interrogation of USSR pros. wit. for rebuttal, method of ... 38310; 38339; 38444; 38446; 38449-50; 38452-53; 38457; 38463-65; 38468-69; 38472; 38475-78; 38481-82; 38484-85; 38495-96
  Statements:
    Mongolian, interpretation of ... 38396-97; 38399-400
    Nomonhan map, authentication of ... 38343-44; 38349-54
    Witness, impossibility of production of, (Japanese prisoners of war in USSR) ... 32907

Pu Y'i (See: Manchuria)

R

Rape of Manila (See: Atrocities, Philippines)

Rape of Nanking (See: Atrocities, China)

"Reform of Parliamentary System," Hashimoto (Defendant), article by ... 15649-51

Reform Plan of the Local Administrative System ... 30869-70

Reorganization of Japanese Jurisdiction in Manchuria ... 5714-18

Resources Investigation Committee ... 545

Revolutionary Government in China ... 3589-90

Rice and Cereals Investigation Committee ... 545

"The Road to the Reconstruction of the World," Hashimoto (Defendant), article by ... 15649-51

Russian Fascist Union ... 7701-02

Russian Emigrants Bureau, Harbin ... 7709

S

Sabotage Activities (*See:* Espionage)

Sakura Gate Incident ... 30753

Sakura Kai (*See:* Japan, Organizations)

Salt Monopoly (*See:* Japan, Constitutional organization)

Sato, Kenryo (Defendant) (*See:* Defendants)

"Sato Shinnen's Ideal State," Okawa (Defendant), book by ... 15633

Scientific Research Institute for Total War (Research Institute for Total War) (*See:* Japan, Operational plans)

"The Second Creation," Hashimoto (Defendant), book by ... 15669-73

Secretariat, Ministry of Foreign Affairs (*See:* Japan, Constitutional organization)

"Sekai Saiken no Michi (How to Rebuild the World)," Hashimoto (Defendant), article by ... 15674-75; 15699-700

Self-Government Guidance Organization ... 19075-80; 19218-34; 19879-82; 22245-53

Senior Statesmen Conference (*See:* Japan, Conferences)

Sentence ... 49854-858

Shanghai (*See:* China, Central)

Shanghai City Tatao Government (*See:* China, Central)

Shanghai Concession, International Settlement of (*See:* China, Central)

Shanghai Expeditionary Forces (*See:* China, Central)

Shanghai Incident (*See:* China, Central)

"Sharing Our Fate," book entitled ... 22306-12; 22314-28; 22330-38; 22341-50; 22353-56; 22358-72; 22383-85

Shigemitsu, Mamoru (Defendant) (*See:* Defendants)

Shimada, Shigetaro (Defendant) (*See:* Defendants)

Shinnan, Gunto (*See:* Spratley Islands)

Shiratori, Toshio (Defendant) (*See:* Defendants)

Showa Research Society (*See:* Japan, Organizations)

Siam (*See:* Thailand)

Singapore (*See:* Malaya)

Sino-Japanese Relations (*See:* China)

"Situation in Caucasia and its Strategic Use for the Purpose of Sabotage Activities," Hashimoto (Defendant), report by ... 7647

Society for Study of National Policy or "Kokusaku Kenkyu Kai" (*See:* Japan, Organizations)

"The Solution of the Incident Depends on the Expulsion of England," Hashimoto (Defendant), article by ... 15660-61; 15685-87

Southern Advance (*See also:* US, US-Japanese negotiations)

   Koiso (Defendant) ... 15819-27

   Oshima (Defendant), aff. and test. ... 34022-23; 34198-200; 34284-317 (*See also:* 6459-73; 6552-53)

   Oshima-Ribbentrop conversation ... 6992

   Report, Japanese Foreign Office ... 7138-39

   Shiratori (Defendant), aff. ... 34960; 34964; 35050

   Suzuki (Defendant), aff. and test. ... 35216-20; 35244-46; 35294-96; 35300-01; 35198-99; 35309-12 (*See also:* 11943; 11947)

Southern Regions (Include: Borneo; Burma-Thailand; Celebes; FIC; Hainan; Java; Malaya; New Britain; New Guinea; Lesser Sunda; Philippines; Singapore; Solomon and Gilberts; Sumatra):

   Atrocities (*See:* Atrocities)

   Management of ... 11961-66

   Military currency, use of ... 8446-70

   Policies toward, Tojo (Defendant), test. ... 36231-51; 36398-400; 36764-69; (*See also:* 35754-55)

POW (See: POW)

Problem of, Tojo (Defendant), aff. and test. ... 36187-88; 36197-205; 36230-31; 36636-40; 36709-21

South Manchurian Railway Co. ... 618; 5342-43; 8277; 8292; 8416; 8471; test. ... 18798-881

    Blasting on, report ... 19616-63

    Hoshino (Defendant), interrogation ... 5121-82

    Koiso (Defendant), aff. ... 32214-15

    Minami (Defendant) and party for president of, aff. ... 32809 (See also: 15753; 31705; 32215-16)

    Organization charter ... 5021-28

    Progress in, report ... 5036-37; 5114-18

    Role of, against USSR, tel. ... 7566-68

South Region Affairs Bureau ... 621-22; 5187

South Sea Development Co. ... 8473

    Exploration of New Guinea ... 11905-10

South Sea Islands Under Mandate of Japan (See Japan, Mandated Islands)

Spratley Islands (Shinnan Gunto), administrative jurisdiction over ... 6145-46

Strategic Bombing Survey, Hoshino (Defendant), aff. and test. ... 29072-94

Structure Preparatory Committee, Muto (Defendant), aff. and test. ... 33095-97; 33256-65

Submarine Warfare (See also: Atrocities), aff. and test. ... 27245-69; 27282-309; 27315-23

    General Headquarters directive ... 27270; 27274-75; 27311-14; 27387-89

    Indian Ocean ... 27349-53 (See also: Atrocities)

    Order of, Oshima (Defendant), aff. and test. ... 15187-95; 34057-61; 34259-63

    Pearl Harbor, at ... 11225-37; 11281-95

    Transfer of submarine by Germany ... 15186-95 Oshima (Defendant), aff. and test. ... 33967-73; 34045-48; 34259-60

Sumatra (See also: the Netherlands):

    Atrocities (See: Atrocities)

    GEACPS and, test. ... 17912-18019; 18032-61; 18064-88

    POW treatment (See: POW)

Supreme Command (See: Japan, Constitutional organization)

Supreme Council for the Direction of War or Supreme War Council (See: Japan, Conferences)

Suzuki, Teiichi (Defendant) (See: Defendants)

"Système Representatif au Japon" ... 554

T

Table Top Maneuvers (See: Japan, Operational plans)

Taiwan Development Co ... 8473

Taiwan Electric Power Generation Co. ... 8277; 8473

Tangku Truce (See: Treaties and Agreements)

Temporary Committee ... 545

"Ten Days Report from the Home Ministry of January 11, 1941," report entitled ... 15663-68

Textbook Committee ... 613

Thailand (Siam) (See also: Burma-Thailand):

    Aggression against ... 6718-21; 7117-19

    Atrocities (See: Atrocities)

    Border dispute with FIC:
    Japan, mediation in ... 34295-302
    Report ... 6868-74

    Economic exploitation plan ... 11944-59

    Military preparation against ... 9010-69½

    Neutralization of ... 35703-08 (See: US, US-Japanese negotiations)

    Opening hostilities in ... 10635-76

    Policies toward ... 11719-28; 11738-41; 11744-47; 11751-56 (See also: 12038; 35050; 35703-08)

    Prince Wan Waitayakon speech at GEA Conference, Thai-Japanese Treaty ... 36460-61

    POW (See: POW)

Thailand *(Cont.)*

   Relations with Japan:
      GEA Ambassadors Conference ... 35767
        (*See also:* 18089-91)
      GEACPS under ... 17912-18019; 18032-61; 18064-88
      Shiratori (Defendant), aff. ... 34960; 35050
      Tojo (Defendant), aff. and test. ... 32321-35; 36249-51; 36375-76; 36401-04; 36456-64; 36763-69 (*See also:* 5691-92)

   Treaties and agreements with Japan:
      Alliance Pact ... 36457
      Cultural Agreement ... 36458
      Protocol on Guarantee and Political Undertaking ... 7014-26

Theoretical Maneuvers for Total War (*See:* Japan, Operational plans)

Tientsin (*See:* China, North)

Togo, Shigenori (Defendant) (*See:* Defendants)

Tojo, Hideki (Defendant) (*See:* Defendants)

Total Investigation Laboratory (*See:* Japan, Operational plans)

Total Strength War Research Institute (*See:* Japan, Operational plans)

Transport and Communication Bureau ... 589

Treaties and Agreements:

   Anti-Comintern Pact:
      Accessory Protocol ... 17230-31
      Conclusion ... 5028-29; 5931-32; 5939-40; 5953-54; 5958-72; 5975-82
      Hungary, participation in ... 6037-45
      Japan, official statement ... 5957; 6047-48
      Manchuria, participation in ... 6037-45
      Renewal of ... 501

   Brussels Conference ... 503; 20984-89; 21000-06

   Cairo Declaration ... 17142-43; 17243-48; 17250-53

   China:
      Alliance Pact with Japan ... 5334-36; 36447-49
      Basic Treaty, Nov. 30, 1940 ... 5320-21; 5327-30; 5331; 36206-12; 36220-27; 36540
      Brussels Conference ... 503; 20984-89; 21000-06
      Ho-Umezu Agreement ... 20781-90
      Hunchun Border Protocol ... 7251; 34499-507
      International Agreement, 1902 ... 20594-98
      International Agreement, 1912 ... 20602-04
      Joint Declaration, China-Japan-Manchukuo ... 5322-26
      Joint Treaty between Japan and Occupied China ... 5008-09
      Lansing-Ishii Agreement ... 17388-92
      Li-Lobanov Agreement ... 17287-93
      Shimonoseki Treaty ... 17263-76
      Sino-Japanese Treaty Renouncing Extraterratoriality ... 17245-47; 22387-89
      Tangku Truce ... 2273-74; 20772-81
      US-Japanese letters, protection of commercial rights ... 17293-98
      USSR-Japanese Agreement ... 17325-28
      Wang Ching-wei, Basic Treaty with ... 499; 7245-47

   Court of International Justice, statute of aggression, interpretation of ... 413-14

   France and FIC:
      Accord relative to Customs System, Trade and Forms of Payment ... 7140-46; 7150-54
      Commercial Treaty with Japan ... 501
      Joint communique relative to Japanese stationing in FIC ... 26844-45
      Military Agreement, joint defense of FIC ... 500; 6875-954; 6969-71; 7014-20; 7059-65; 7069-87; 7121-32; 35752
      Peace Treaty with Japan ... 500-01
      Protocol with Japan, joint defense of FIC ... 7104-05; 7148; 7913
      Thailand, Peace Treaty with ... 500-01; 17250
      Treaty of Residence and Navigation ... 7159-60; 17250
      Treaty with Japan, Great Britain and US relative to Insular Possessions and Insular Dominations in the Pacific Ocean and Supplementary Agreement attached thereto ... 497
      Triple Intervention ... 17285-86

   Geneva Convention of 1929, Treatment of POWs:
      Great Britain-Japanese negotiations, application of Convention to POW and Civilian Internees ... 14754-90; 14846-83
      US-Japanese negotiations, application of Convention to POW and Civilian Internees ... 14728-32; 14734-53; 14792-822; 14826-36; 15001-17; 15200-04

   Geneva Convention, Narcotics and Drugs, 1931 ... 496

   Geneva Red Cross Convention, 1929 ... 496

   Great Britain:
      Alliance Pact ... 17305-10; 17206-07; 17313-15
      "Anglo-American Joint Declaration" ... 17465-66
      Treaty with Japan, France and US relative to Insular Possessions and Insular Dominations in the Pacific Ocean and Supplementary Agreement attached thereto ... 497

   Hague Convention of 1899 relative to the Pacific Settlement of International Disputes ... 493; 9265; 17167-74
      Aggression, interpretation of ... 416; 42154-55

Hague Convention I relative to the Pacific Settlement of International Disputes ... 494; 17176

Hague Convention III relative to Opening of Hostilities ... 494; 9266; 17372-85
 Aggression, interpretation of ... 415-16; 42146-51
 "Reports to the Hague Conference of 1899 and 1907" ... 17371-85
 Study ... 11315-37
 War in violation of ... 421; 11315-37

Hague Convention IV relative to the Customs of War on Land ... 494; 17184-89
 Conventional war crimes, interpretation of ... 428
 War in violation of ... 425-27

Hague Convention V relative to the Rights and Duties of Neutral Powers and Persons in War on Land, POW Treatment ... 27122-23

Hague Convention X relative to the Principles of Maritime Warfare ... 495

Hague Convention and Final Protocol for the Suppression of the Abuse of Opium and other Drugs ... 496; 4665-67

Ho-Umezu Agreement ... 3746-49

Hunchun Treaty of 1886 ... 7251

Hungary, Participation in Anti-Comintern Pact ... 6037-45

IMTFE, Special Proclamation, establishment of ... 17159-66

Japan:
 Annexation of Korea ... 17316-20
 Cairo Declaration ... 17142-48; 17250-53
 Convention with Korea ... 17315-16
 Instrument of Surrender ... 17154-57
 Potsdam Declaration ... 17144-47
 Surrender:
  Japan, acceptance ... 17152-54
  Japan, qualified acceptance ... 17148-50
  Japan, qualified acceptance, reply by US ... 17150-52
  Proclamation, Emperor by ... 17157-58

Kellogg-Briand Pact (Pact of Paris):
 Aggression, interpretation of ... 417; 42155-80; 42399
 Japan, declaration concerning Art. I ... 499
 "Treaty for the Renunciation of War" ... 17361-71

League of Nations:
 Aggression, interpretation of, Eighth Assembly ... 416-17
 Agreement, prevention of hostilities ... 9266-67
 Anglo-Japanese Alliance, abrogation of, joint declaration ... 17313
 Assembly, first and second reports ... 502
 Assembly, Japan, notice of withdrawal from ... 503; 17258-61
 China, application of Art. 17 ... 502
 Council, invitation to Japan to sit with ... 502-03
 Covenant, terms of mandate ... 9081-84; 9269-70
 Manchuria, Japan aggressor in ... 502; 1693-765; 2855-96
 Resolution, cessation of hostilities and withdrawal of forces ... 501-02
 Resolution, doctrine of non-recognition or alteration of *status quo* ... 501-02
 Second Opium Convention ... 496; 17197-99; 20247-51
 Social and technical organs, Japan withdrawal from ... 503
 Third Opium Convention ... 17199

London Naval Conference:
 Abrogation ... 26543-53; 26775-820
 Japan, withdrawal from ... 502

London Naval Treaty ... 9161-240; 17221
 Abrogation of ... 26543-53; 26775-820
 Japanese opposition to ratification of ... 9160-68

Manchuria:
 Anti-Comintern Pact, participation in ... 6037-45
 Convention, USSR and Japan ... 17321-25
 League of Nations, declaration of Japan aggressor in ... 502
 Protocol with Japan ... 4257-58; 5034-35
 Shimonoseki Treaty ... 17263-76
 Treaty of Joint Economic Committee with Japan ... 8433-47
 Treaty of Residence, Taxation etc. and supplementary agreement attached ... 2944-59

Mixed Claims Commission, US-Germany, 1922, aggression, interpretation of ... 414-15

Netherlands:
 Insular Possessions and Insular Domination in the Pacific Ocean ... 17208
 Japan, declaration to respect rights of the Netherlands ... 17208
 Thailand, Peace Treaty with ... 501
 Treaty of Arbitration, Japan, notice of abrogation ... 501
 Treaty with Japan, France, Great Britain and US relative to Insular Possessions and Insular Domination in the Pacific Ocean ... 497

Nine Power Treaty ... 498; 3308; 9270-73; 17210-14; 17392-98

Pact of Paris (*See:* Treaties and Agreements, Kellogg-Briand Pact)

Pekin Convention ... 499; 17225-30

Portsmouth, Treaty of ... 496; 17200-03; 17313-15

Treaties and Agreements *(Cont.)*

    Potsdam Declaration ... 17144-47

    Shimonoseki Treaty ... 17263-76

    Tangku Truce ... 2273-74; 20772-81

    Thailand:
        Alliance Pact with Japan ... 36457
        Cultural Agreement with Japan ... 36458
        FIC, Peace Treaty with ... 500-01; 17250
        Japan, treaty with ... 17248-49; 36458
        Netherlands, Peace Treaty with ... 501
        Non-Aggression Pact with Japan ... 500
        Protocol on Guaranteeing Political Undertaking ... 7014-26

    Tripartite Pact ... 500
        General operation plan ... 6682-84
        Military Convention ... 501
        Military cooperation ... 6684-86
        Non-Separate Treaty ... 5889-93
        Tripartite Economic Agreement ... 501
        Tripartite Military Alliance ... 501
        Zones for operation ... 6081-82

    Triple Intervention ... 17285-86

    US:
        Anglo-American Joint Declaration ... 17465-67
        Lansing-Ishii Agreement ... 17388-92
        Treaty with Japan, France, Great Britain relative to Insular Possessions and Insular Domination in the Pacific Ocean and supplementary agreement attached thereto ... 497
        US-Japanese, exchange of letters, commercial rights in China ... 17293-98
        US-Japanese Treaty of Commerce and Navigation ... 501; 17253-55; 17386-88
        Washington Conference Treaty ... 498; 17206-07; 17214-15; 17399-417

    USSR:
        Agreement among China, Outer Mongolia and ... 17325-29
        Agreement with Outer Mongolia ... 17329-33
        Basic Treaty with Japan ... 17225-30; 17347-54; 17357-58
        Convention with Japan ... 17321-25
        Declaration of war on Japan ... 503; 17243-45
        Exchange of notes with Japan ... 17343-46
        Li-Lobanov Agreement ... 17287-93
        Molotov-Togo Agreement ... 23104-43
        Neutrality Pact with Japan ... 501; 17241-43; 17234-41; 17385-88
        Non-Aggression Pact with Germany ... 24185-89
        Protocol A, Basic Treaty with Japan ... 17347-49
        Protocol B, Basic Treaty with Japan ... 17350-53
        Protocol, Manchukuo-Mongolia boundary ... 23151-52

    Sino-Mongolia Border Agreement ... 22978-23005

    Triple Intervention ... 17285-86

    Versailles Conference ... 497

    Washington Conference Treaty ... 498; 17392-98

    Washington Naval Treaty ... 499; 17214-15; 17217-21
        Abrogation of ... 9161-9240; 26543-53; 26775-820
        Japan, notice of withdrawal from ... 502; 17255-58

Tribunal, Law ... 383-475; 17594-697; 38949-39061; 40538-66; 42111-284; 42402-513

    Charter ... 394-400; 38989-98; 42116-35

    Conventional war crimes ... 427-28; 42201-04; 42232-39; 42255-68
        Hague Convention IV, 1907 ... 428

    Crimes against humanity (murder) ... 428-35; 17693-95; 39030-34; 42196-201; 42251-55

    Crimes against peace ... 395; 397-427; 17595-662; 38998-39061; 42135-93; 42224-49
        Aggression, war of ... 404-19; 17595-662; 38998-39030; 42142-89
            Aggression, meaning of ... 419
            Geneva Protocol for the Pacific Settlement of International Disputes, 1924 ... 416; 42154-55
            Hague Convention for the Pacific Settlement of International Disputes, 1899 ... 415; 42146
            Hague Convention III relative to the Opening of Hostilities, 1907 ... 415-16; 42146-51
            International Law ... 405-15
            Kellogg-Briand Pact ... 417; 42155-80; 42239-42
            League of Nations, Eighth Assembly, 1927 ... 416-17
            Mixed Claims Commission, US-Germany, 1922 ... 414-15
            Pan-American Conference, 1928, Havana ... 417
            Permanent Court of International Justice, statute ... 413-14
        Conspiracy ... 397-404; 39034-61; 42135-41; 42242-50
        War in violation of international law, treaties, agreements and assurances ... 419-27; 42189-93
            Hague Convention III, 1907 ... 421
            Hague Convention IV relative to the Customs of War on Land, 1907 ... 425-27

    Individual responsibility ... 435-75; 17662-97; 40538-66; 42204-24; 42268-80

Tribunal Ruling *(See also:* Applications and motions, Defense; Applications and motions, Prosecution; President of Tribunal):

INDEX TO MILITARY TRIBUNAL PROCEEDINGS 79

Affiants:
   Admissibility of certificate of death of ... 8164
   Execution of ... 7316-18
   Production of, for cross-ex. ... 10617-18; 10633; 10678; 11732-34; 13851; 13858; 13864-65
   USSR pros., production by, for cross-ex. ... 23172; 23828; 24517-18; 24564

Affidavits:
   Admissibility of ... 928; 3352-53; 7448; 7500-01; 8127
   Affidavits taken on commission ... 33532; 33537-38; 33541-42
   Ballantine, by ... 10715-16
   Budarin, by, pros. not permitted to read part previously read ... 32571
   Defendants, by ... 37029
   Defendants, interrogation of, in lieu of ... 26274
   Defense wit., by, must be in form of ... 21058-64
   Defense wit., portion not admitted into evidence ... 20751; 20756
   Form of ... 937-38
   Grew, by, addition ... 10207-08
   Presentation of, without cross-ex. ... 4452-56
   Semyonov, by ... 7319
   Service of, exemption from compliance with rule ... 1860-61
   Swearing, method of, in Chinese form ... 2298
   Testimony, admissibility of, by ... 10067; 10088-89; 10620-21
   Use of, as exhibit ... 2530

Anti-Comintern Pact, evidence ... 6049

Applications and motions, def., denied:
   Defense counsel, Blakeney, second counsel for Umezu ... 2153
   Defense, permission to file argument vs. Supreme Commander authority into record ... 16271
   Evidence, Harada-Saionji memoirs, production of three versions of ... 37530
   Exhibits, lack of probative value, be stricken from record ... 15444; 29113; 32915
   Indictment:
      Dismissal of ... 343; 16997
      Dismissal of for lack of jurisdiction by tribunal ... 16267-68
   Interrogation of defendant, suspension of reading ... 3441
   Koiso (Defendant), exhibits of speech by, be stricken from record ... 3721
   Law, leave to file brief of authorities on question of ... 34376
   Muto (Defendant), interrogation of, suspension of reading ... 3441
   Recess ... 19093; 19095
   Re-direct ex. of def. wit. ... 28502
   Umezu (Defendant), Blakeney, second counsel for ... 2153

Applications and motions, def., granted:

Affiants, production of for cross ex. ... 14228; 35598
Affidavits, wit. be stood down until revision of ... 21640; 22090
Defense:
   Cross-ex. of USSR wit. in rebuttal, def. right to postpone until further ex. of doc. ... 38246
   Right to make objection at conclusion of pros. general opening statement ... 382
   Right to make objection to pros. statement re def. ind. motion to dismiss ... 16771
   Defense counsel, Warren for Hiranuma ... 16331
   Document, withdrawal of, and substitution of photostatic copy ... 3072
   Hiranuma (Defendant), Warren, counsel for ... 16331
   Opening statement, separate order authorizing ... 380-81
   Tribunal rulings, exception to:
      Permission to file motion to dismiss re certain defendants ... 16263
      Permission to present argument to dismiss re all defendants ... 16712
      Re-direct ex. of defendant as wit., on behalf of other defendants, rejection ... 20098
   Witness, stood down until further revision of aff. ... 21640; 22090; 22555

Applications and motions, pros., denied:
   Cross-ex., change of counsel to conduct ... 30487
   Document, presentation of, after revision ... 11351
   Judicial notice, schedule A, events set out in ... 379-80
   Witness, recall of ... 29064

Applications and motions, pros., granted:
   Affiants, production of, for cross-ex. ... 18174-75
   Documents:
      Japanese official, presentation of, without authentication ... 379
      Reading excerpts from, provided served to def. ... 14439
   Exhibits, numbered consecutively ... 380-81
   Opening statement, separate, order authorizing ... 380-81

Araki (Defendant):
   Summation, suspension of ... 45714-16
   Witness for, refusal to subpoena ... 27925-26

Atrocities, evidence admissible if conspiracy established later ... 2629

Ballantine, aff. by ... 10715-17

Budarin, aff. by ... 32571

Budarin, cross-ex. of, by tribunal member ... 32557

Tribunal Ruling *(Cont.)*

    Changkufeng Incident, USSR pros. evidence ... 7784-86

    Chao Sen, letter by ... 4910-11

    Chinese Eastern Railway, sale of, not part of indictment ... 29441-45

    Cross-ex. ... 836; 840; 850; 866-67; 873-74; 876-78; 955; 1234; 1329; 1384-87; 1396; 1401; 1487; 1521; 1663; 1892; 1894; 1954; 2005; 2043; 2047-48; 2461; 2467; 2484; 2515; 2657; 2663; 3076-77; 3117; 3193; 3205; 3237-38; 3399; 3507; 3752-53; 3818-20; 3835-36; 3838; 3841; 3844; 3851; 3929; 3939-40; 3986; 4013; 4046; 4074-75; 4106; 4196; 4198; 4212; 4229; 4238; 4263; 4309; 4972; 10879; 11003; 11067; 11076-79; 11097-98; 11102-03; 11147-48; 11152; 11160-61; 11164; 11259; 11262; 12670; 14339-41; 14390-91; 14413; 14855; 14935; 14963; 20048-49; 21291-92; 22220; 23004; 26222-23; 27075-76; 27718; 28382; 30487; 32007; 33241; 33276-80; 35333-36; 35499-501; 35599; 35832; 36534-35; 37032

    Defendant:
        Absence of ... 14654
        Affidavit by ... 37029
        Deceased defendant, name stricken from indictment ... 1452
        Defendant right to cross-ex. if affected by pros. presentation of additional evidence after close of case ... 32007
        Defense counsel, inability to consult with, in prison ... 10599
        Document, rejected, def. right to present on behalf of ind. defendant ... 25555; 25557
        Examination of, offer to def. ... 29336-39
        Interrogation of, in lieu of aff. ... 26274
        Matsuoka, doc. vs. other defendants ... 2185
        Non-applicability of evidence in general case to all ... 25891
        Statement by, use against other defendants ... 24260-63

    Defense *(See also:* Tribunal Ruling, Indictment):
        Defendants', ex. of, offer to def. ... 29336-39
        Document, errors in, def. right to conceal ... 1036-37
        Document, rejected, def. right to present on behalf of ind. defendant ... 25555; 25557
        Individual case, scope of evidence offered in ... 28274
        Individual responsibility ... 36944-45
        Translation question, counsel right to refer directly to language section ... 31231; 32551

    Defense counsel *(See also:* President of Tribunal, Rebukes and warnings):
        Documents:
            Errors in, right to conceal ... 1036-37
            Right to read parts not offered by pros. ... 2734
            Right to receive certificate of ... 6897-908
            Right to receive copies of ... 3470
        Japanese bar, no member of ... 37154-55
        Propaganda, no right to indulge in ... 20479-84
        Prosecution:
            Document, right to comment on ... 3582
            Witness, right to call after pros. case ... 1214
        Translation question, right to refer directly to language section ... 31231; 32551
        Witness:
            Attack, right to ... 4106; 4229
            Credibility of, right to test ... 4623
            Memory, right to test ... 4185
            Note of, right to read ... 2640
            Witness, right to make statement to ... 2484; 3878

    Direct examination:
        Cross-ex., direct ex. be followed by ... 3205
        Presentation of case before, permission for ... 1354-55
        Re-direct ex. ... 14963

    Document:
        Admissibility of ... 3417; 3601-02; 3606; 3700; 4860; 6283; 6844; 6897-908; 7000; 7341-43; 7457; 10139
        Authenticity of ... 9220-21; 37231
        Certificate, reading of ... 3575-76; 3600
        Copies, number of ... 22559-63; 22566-67
        Correction of, during test. ... 31829-32
        Defense counsel, right to receive copies ... 3470
        Document not read ... 29724; 29727-39
        Errors in:
            Defense right to conceal ... 1036-37
            Defense right to consult with language section ... 11776
            Typographical errors ... 2912-16
        Excerpts, reading of ... 1809; 7701; 12408; 12454-55
        Extra-comment on ... 10300; 10477
        Identification of ... 29880-81
        Matsuoka (Defendant), doc. vs. other defendants ... 2185
        Non-availability of ... 21651
        Paraphrasing of ... 1016-17; 7946-49
        Photostatic copies of ... 3072; 6085; 26307
        Probative value of ... 20810; 20812-14; 21343-44; 22505-08; 22928-30; 23027-28; 24243-49
        Reading of additional paragraph ... 9355
        Reading of, already in evidence ... 17167-76; 17181-84; 17514-18; 17535-38
        Reading of excerpts ... 1645; 1809; 7701; 12400; 12454-55
        Rebuttal, in, presentation of ... 34317
        Rejected doc., def. right to present, on behalf of ind. defendant ... 25555; 25557

Rejection of def. doc. ... 17635-36; 17638;
17640-42; 17653-55; 17662; 17682-83;
17689-91; 18027-31; 18385; 18387; 18402;
18410; 18419; 18424-25; 18428; 18430-31;
18433-34; 18437; 18587-88; 18593-95;
18598; 18624; 18628; 18765; 18790-91;
18793; 18795; 19138; 19143; 19179-80;
19182; 19189; 19192; 19478; 19540; 19615;
19694-95; 19700; 19716; 19722; 19727;
20127; 20219; 20266-67; 20457-58; 20510;
20514; 20516; 20550; 20592; 20607-08;
20796-98; 20802; 20807; 20809-10; 20816;
20825-27; 20860-61; 20866-67; 20872;
20882-84; 20886-87; 20940; 20961; 20963;
21012-14; 21016-20; 21022; 21037-38;
21046; 21048-51; 21054-55; 21057; 21065;
21068-69; 21085-91; 21093-95; 21098-101;
21103; 21107; 21109; 21115; 21117-20;
21122-24; 21126-29; 21131-33; 21139;
21141-42; 21144; 21342; 21349; 21362;
21370; 21378; 21388-89; 21393; 21395-96;
21403-05; 21409; 21418; 21420-23; 21427;
21429; 21432-34; 21494; 21496; 21545-47;
21806; 21813-16; 21819; 21822; 22377;
22379; 22381-82; 22457; 22461; 22463;
22477; 22498-99; 22504; 22511; 22535-36;
22538; 22557; 22848; 22850; 22865; 23182;
23188; 23647; 23649-50; 23732; 23734;
23736; 23739; 23741; 23744; 23746-47;
23749-50; 23752; 23754; 23756-59; 23761;
23763; 23781; 23954; 24221; 24226; 24271-
75; 24600; 24671-72; 24678; 24680; 24687;
24690; 24736; 24803; 24809; 24814; 24824;
24826; 24944; 25108; 25117; 25119-22;
25126; 25128; 25130; 25132; 25134-40;
25145-47; 25149; 25151; 25163; 25165;
25170; 25197; 25219; 25221; 25224-25;
25232-33; 25235; 25240-41; 25250; 25301;
25330-33; 25351; 25367; 25390; 25401-02;
25438-39; 25457-61; 25465; 25467-68;
25473; 25475-78; 25480-93; 25500-05;
25509; 25514-16; 25520-21; 25524-30;
25535; 25555; 25557; 25559; 25570; 25572-
73; 25575; 25578; 25581-82; 25588-89;
25591-601; 25603; 25606; 25614; 25627-
30; 25632; 25634-37; 25641-44; 25646;
26359; 26361; 26382; 26385; 26451-52;
26606-07; 26780; 26964; 27082; 27845-46;
27961; 28026; 28045; 28047-49; 28106;
28243; 28250; 28253; 28416; 28422-23;
28426; 28431; 28445; 28472; 28474-75;
28513-16; 28521-22; 28539-40; 28551-52;
28571; 28575-76; 28579; 28588-89;
29380; 29386; 29447; 29465; 29468;
29472-73; 29568-69; 29606; 29609;
29620; 29638; 29643; 29655-56; 29666;
29895; 29897; 29933; 29948; 29962;
30048-50; 30057-58; 30060-61; 30073-
74; 30146; 30544; 32550; 32703; 32772;
32838; 32857; 32918; 33958; 34033;
34336; 34350; 34540; 34858; 34868;
34870; 34872; 34881; 34883; 34890;
34897-98; 34996; 35137; 37018-19
Service of ... 1013; 1043-46; 1186-87; 2293;
5618-20; 6047; 6323; 11730; 21281-82;
23004

Translation ... 7765-66 (See also: Tribunal Ruling, Translation)

Evidence:
Additional evidence, hearing of, at request of tribunal member ... 1538
Admissibility of def. evidence ... 11349; 17635-38; 22305-06
Admissibility of, in def. ind. case ... 19172-74; 28274
Admissibility of, in rebuttal ... 19372; 37205; 37330-31
Admissibility of, in surrebuttal ... 38589-90; 38596
Anti-Comintern Pact evidence be stricken ... 6049
Changkufeng, USSR pros. evidence ... 7784-86
Chinese Eastern Railway ... 29441-45
Cumulative ... 12088-93
Defense counsel right to present, during cross-ex. ... 10916-18
Harada-Saionji memoirs (See: Tribunal ruling, Harada-Saionji memoirs)
Hearsay test., admissibility of ... 1954
Identical evidence in different doc. ... 3578-80
Kido diary, entire text of ... 1932
Limitation of, in summation ... 43222-23; 43228; 43263; 43282; 43433; 43813; 44799; 44820; 45182; 45253; 45473; 45564; 45670-71; 45711-13; 46040-42; 46049
Mitigation, in ... 2154; 38917-18
Non-applicability of evidence in general case to all defendants ... 25891
Oshima (Defendant), admissibility of ... 5894; 5898-99
Pu Y'i (See: Tribunal Ruling, Pu Y'i)
Rebuttal, in ... 19372; 37205; 37330-31; 38222
Relevancy of ... 4549-52; 7304
Rules of, not applicable to tribunal proceedings ... 6441-43
Shimizu, relevancy of ... 1406
Siberian Intervention ... 38215-22
Surrebuttal, in ... 38589-90; 38596
Telegrams and other communications as ... 6093
Type of ... 4549-52

Film to be shown in entirety ... 1194

Flag Incident:
Prosecution right to use ... 4556
War crimes, no evidence of ... 4552

Grew, aff. by, addition to ... 10207-08

Harada-Saionji memoirs (See also: Tribunal Ruling, Overruled, Upheld)
Admissibility only of parts accepted for rebuttal ... 38637
Authenticity of ... 38741
Version, one only, admissible ... 37350

Hiranuma (Defendant):
Transfer of, to Tokyo Imperial Hospital ... 2128-29
Warren, counsel for ... 16331

Tribunal Ruling *(Cont.)*

   Hoshino (Defendant), interrogation of, reading from ... 5153

   Indictment (*See also:* Applications and motions, Defense; Applications and motions, Prosecution; Tribunal Ruling, Applications and motions, def., denied):
     Chinese Eastern Railway, sale of, not part of ... 29441-45
     Deceased defendant, name be stricken from ... 1452
     Motions to dismiss ... 13577-79; 16711-12; 38945; 38947

   Interrogation of defendant:
     Admissibility of ... 16103-04; 24571-72; 25662-63; 25665-66
     Affidavit, in lieu of ... 26274
     Defense, offered for ... 29336-39
     Other defendants, used against ... 24260-63
     Other defendants, used in favor of ... 34348-49
     Reading from ... 5153
     Reading, suspension of ... 3441
     Substitution of counsel, permission due to illness ... 33233-34; 33241

   Interrogatories, commission, by ... 32884; 32976

   Johnston, book by ... 4181-82; 4199-200

   Judicial notice:
     Defense application for ... 36977-78; 37171; 37174
     President Roosevelt, proclamation of ... 25172-91
     Schedule A, events set out in ... 379-80
     Tripartite Military Alliance ... 6120-22; 6144-45

   Kido (Defendant):
     Diary by, entire text of ... 1932
     Diary by, original must remain in possession of tribunal ... 1932
     Evidence in mitigation ... 38917-18

   Koiso (Defendant):
     Exhibits of speech by, be stricken from record ... 3721
     USSR pros. evidence, inaccuracy of ... 7704

   Languages (*See also:* Tribunal Ruling, Translation):
     French, use of ... 6782; 15306
     Mongolian, interpretation of ... 38399-401
     Russian, use of ... 7100

   Leading question ... 834; 890; 892; 895; 1998; 3986; 5431-32

   Maps:
     Defense counsel right to receive ... 3470
     Nomonhan, authenticity of USSR pros. ... 7844

   Matsuoka (Defendant):
     Document vs. other defendants ... 2185
     Interrogation of, in favor of other defendants ... 34348-49

   Minami (Defendant), letter by ... 4199

   Mitigation, evidence in ... 38917-18

   Muto (Defendant), interrogation of, suspension of reading ... 3441

   Offensive language to pros. countries ... 17777; 42692-96; 43469-71 (*See also:* President of Tribunal, Rebukes and warnings)

   Okawa (Defendant):
     Counsel for, withdrawal of ... 1433
     Medical ex. of ... 1537

   Opening statement:
     Defense general opening statement, limitation of ... 17005
     Defense opening statement, pros. right to object to part of ... 17010
     Japanese constitutional organization ... 17544-46
     Law, theory of ... 4009
     Nature of ... 7867-70
     Prosecution, Class A offenses ... 12853-54
     Prosecution, Class B offenses ... 12853-54
     Prosecution, comment on ... 9337-38
     Prosecution, Philippine case ... 12345-48
     Prosecution, USSR case ... 7294
     Prosecution preliminary opening statement ... 2239
     Separate opening statement, order authorizing ... 38081
     Togo (Defendant), limitation of charges against ... 35956

   Oshima (Defendant), evidence, admissibility of ... 5894; 5898-99

   Overruled, def. objection to the Netherlands pros., Netherlands case, presentation of ... 11631

   Overruled, def. objections to pros.:
     Affidavit:
       Cross-ex., provision for in USSR case ... 32557
       Presentation of ... 1158; 1322; 10088; 10621
       Presentation of, after close of case ... 32006
       Reading of ... 2324
       Rebuttal, for, presentation of ... 37445; 38134
       Use of, as exhibit or test. ... 2528-29
     Document:
       Authenticity of ... 11227
       Certificate, form of ... 11817
       Order of, presentation of ... 37895-96
       Presentation of ... 690; 693-94; 1158; 1316; 1322; 1914; 2264-67; 3514-17; 3575;

3603-04; 4672; 4860; 5898-99; 5901;
7346; 7666; 7713; 7900-01; 7908; 7914;
8914; 8940; 9497; 10139; 11408; 11786;
11820; 12128; 12381; 12893; 14907; 15186;
15428-29; 15604; 15609; 15644; 15756;
15815; 16080; 16082; 18505; 18509-10;
28620; 30400; 31390; 31497; 33796; 34116;
34118; 34246; 34293; 34309; 34372; 34426;
34707; 35361
 Presentation of, after close of case ...
  29814-16; 32421
 Presentation of, during interrogation of
  def. wit. ... 26331
 Reading excerpts from ... 24068; 24076-77
 Rebuttal, for presentation of ... 37236;
  37244; 37248; 37255; 37260; 37264; 37280;
  37284; 37315; 37322; 37324; 37339; 37350;
  37371-72; 37375; 37385; 37393; 37396;
  37408; 37417; 37422; 37432; 37548; 37557;
  37567; 37569; 37571; 37574; 37579; 37586;
  37589; 37598; 37603; 37605; 37609; 37618;
  37626-27; 37636; 37646; 37649; 37652;
  37665; 37668; 37672; 37674; 37686; 37689;
  37700; 37709; 37717; 37746; 37754; 37760;
  37766; 37770; 37772; 37778; 37781; 37788;
  37804; 37807; 37811; 37814; 37822; 37828;
  37831; 37836; 37838; 37905; 37910; 37915;
  37919; 37923; 37931; 37936; 37938; 37941;
  37948; 37958; 37960; 37966; 37971; 37980;
  37983; 37986; 37991; 37993; 37999; 38015;
  38030; 38065; 38070; 38073; 38085; 38098;
  38106; 38110; 38115; 38126; 38165; 38173;
  38180; 38185; 38188; 38190
 Service of ... 6045-46; 15997-98
Evidence:
 Conspiracy to commit conventional war
  crimes, presentation of ... 11408
 Cumulative, presentation of ... 2652
 Defendants, positions held by, presentation
  of ... 5901
 Harada-Saionji memoirs, presentation of
  ... 37545; 37548; 37557; 37567; 37569;
  37571; 37574; 37579; 37586; 37589; 37598;
  37603; 37605; 37609; 37618; 37626-27;
  37636; 37646; 37649; 37652; 37665; 37668;
  37672; 37674; 37686; 37689-700; 37709;
  37717; 37746; 37754; 37760; 37766; 37770;
  37772; 37778; 37781; 37788; 37804; 37807;
  37811; 37814; 37822; 37828; 37831; 37856;
  37841; 37845; 37857; 37864; 37874; 37880
 Interrogation of defendants, reading of excerpts from ... 3435; 5912-13; 5917
 Maps ... 3469
 Maps during interrogation of def. wit.
  ... 23701; 23717
 Oshima (Defendant) ... 5898-99; 5912-13;
  5917; 11408
 Panay Incident, presentation of ... 3514-16
 Russo-Japanese Non-Aggression Pact,
  Japanese refusal to sign ... 7713
 Tokyo Gazette, excerpt from ... 6732
 Tripartite Pact, USSR case ... 7908; 7914
French prosecution:
 Document:

  Presentation of, after close of case
   ... 15291
  Rebuttal, for, presentation of ... 38183;
   38188; 38190; 38580
 Interrogation, Tojo (Defendant) ... 10705
 Interrogatories, events prior to 1928 ... 888
 Opening statement, additional, admission
  of ... 1918
 Opening statement, theory of law ... 477
 Re-direct ex. of pros. wit. ... 37510-11; 37516
 Shintoism, truth of, test. ... 4009
 Summing up, during interrogation ... 27268
 Translation, Mongolian doc. ... 38351
 Witnesses:
  Answer of ... 4004; 4013
  Interrogation of def. wit., method of ...
   17812; 17829-30; 17832; 17934-35;
   17941; 17943; 17946-47; 17949; 17952;
   17967; 17971-73; 17975; 17982; 17984;
   18038-39; 18055; 18058-59; 18159-60;
   18476; 18478-80; 18493; 18564; 18570;
   18864; 18870; 19088; 19361; 19448;
   19455; 19607-08; 19610; 19642; 19650;
   19807; 19905-06; 19911; 19927; 19942;
   19948; 20128; 20639; 20645; 20649; 20651;
   20712; 20947; 21217; 21223; 21666; 21945;
   22019-20; 22030; 22050; 22064; 22192;
   22748-49; 22785; 22788; 22964; 23216;
   23244; 23408; 23681-82; 23895; 24009;
   24011; 24023; 24027; 24061-62; 24082;
   24090; 24101-02; 24104; 24107-08; 24493;
   26136; 26141; 26638; 26644; 26685; 26697;
   27441; 27549; 27711; 27770; 27871; 28323-
   24; 28330; 28335; 28342; 28347-48; 28351;
   28388; 28390-91; 28393; 28402; 28467;
   28494-95; 28662; 28719; 28732; 28948-
   49; 28958; 28973; 28990; 29092; 29281;
   20286; 29299; 29511; 29547-48; 29796;
   29804; 29984; 31304; 31377; 31469; 31491;
   31524; 31560; 31604; 32297; 32349; 32398;
   32404; 32901; 32903; 32909; 33030; 33035;
   33266; 33311; 33317; 33328; 33331; 33454;
   33519; 33591; 33593; 33637; 33646; 33647;
   33971; 34108; 34163; 34229; 34264; 34413;
   34434-35; 34457; 34459; 34577; 34581;
   34583; 34619; 34640; 34704; 34721; 34742;
   34753; 34915-16; 34978; 34980; 34982;
   34994; 35025; 35066; 35111; 35125; 35300;
   35400; 35402; 35526; 35887; 35902; 35911;
   36090; 36956; 37041; 37070-72
  Interrogation of pros. wit., method of ...
   824; 835; 888; 890-91; 895; 1387; 1965;
   2018-20; 2531; 2533-34; 2545; 2562-63;
   2570; 2646; 2681-82; 3232; 3257; 3284;
   3506; 3739; 3740; 3867; 3895; 3961; 4007;
   4030; 4422; 4428; 4433; 5357; 5367; 7776;
   10926; 10981; 11172; 14285; 14841; 14924;
   14936; 15225-26; 15288; 15860; 15862;
   15869
  Reading of note by ... 2657; 2639-40; 2657
  Recalling of ... 15852
  Re-cross ex. of def. wit., method of ...
   26344-34; 26602
  Re-direct ex. of pros. wit., method of ...
   14965; 31922; 32137; 32145

Tribunal Ruling *(Cont.)*

   Overruled, def. objections to USSR pros.:
      Affidavit:
         Presentation of ... 8086
         Rebuttal, for, presentation of ... 38237; 38288; 38420; 38531
      Document, rebuttal, for, presentation of ... 38227; 38250; 38271; 38514; 38518
      Evidence:
         Map of Nomonhan, authenticity of ... 38344; 38352
         USSR attack on Japan, 1945 ... 7539-44; 7666

   Overruled, pros. objections to def.:
      Affidavit:
         Presentation of ... 22893; 22992; 23092; 23577; 23636; 23655; 23868; 23934; 26243; 26984; 27953; 29321; 30536; 31688; 32524; 32801; 32946; 34535; 37000; 37005
         Presentation of part of ... 22105-06; 22259; 23504; 24286; 24395; 25911-12; 26709; 26744; 26880; 27487; 29041; 29407; 29648; 30031; 30080; 32803; 32873; 32891-92; 32941; 35595
         Service of ... 24380-81
         Surrebuttal, for, presentation of ... 38616; 38709; 38714; 38722; 38728; 38808
      Document:
         Authenticity of ... 20220-21; 24832; 26844
         Official, admissibility of ... 6897-6908
         Presentation of ... 17275; 17283; 17305-06; 17339; 17396; 17411; 17422; 17432; 17647; 17685; 17868; 18426; 18428; 18432; 18440; 18697; 18775; 18777; 19144; 19160; 19199; 19204; 19218; 19521; 19598; 19665; 19688; 19720; 20804; 20829; 20873; 20890; 20922; 20965; 20967; 21007; 21023; 21040; 21043; 21104; 21345; 21358; 21360; 21406; 21410; 21423; 21496; 21549; 21729; 21734-35; 22373-74; 22467; 22474; 22513; 22694; 22823; 22839; 22868; 22877; 22922; 22975; 23085; 23146; 23148; 23483; 23549; 23587; 23723; 24202; 24276; 24286; 24351; 24357; 24369; 24374; 24556; 24737; 24749; 24907; 24948; 24965; 25153; 25227; 25303; 25315-16; 25319; 25334-35; 25375; 25394; 25408; 25440; 25446; 25494; 25531; 25536; 25546; 25560; 25578; 25584; 25604; 25607; 25615; 25620; 25624; 25738; 26228; 26253; 26618; 27238; 28436; 28698; 29435; 29452; 29569; 29578; 29591; 29608; 29611; 29625; 29629; 29632; 29949; 29954; 29963; 29967; 30035; 30616; 32807; 33059; 34351; 34492; 34493; 34505; 34682; 34857; 34860; 34885; 35360; 36887; 36980
         Surrebuttal, for, presentation of ... 38598; 38620; 38638; 38645; 38650; 38653; 38658; 38669; 38674; 38685; 38750
      Evidence:
         Harada-Saionji memoirs, presentation of ... 38638; 38643; 38645; 38647; 38650; 38653; 38658; 38669; 38674; 38677

         Map of Nomonhan, presentation of, during interrogation of def. wit. ... 23842
      Opening statement, presentation of part of ... 22414
      Witnesses:
         Interrogation of def. wit., method of ... 17722; 17766; 17896-97; 18505; 18550; 18808; 18817; 18828; 18878; 18918; 19358; 20084; 20736-37; 24451; 24457-58; 24460; 24464; 26157-58; 26899; 27716; 28255; 29247; 31224; 31845; 31868; 31878; 31881; 31891; 31936; 31938; 31949; 31975; 31983; 31988; 32030; 32080; 32129; 32173; 32186; 33151; 34387; 34857; 34860; 34885; 34972; 35832
         Interrogation of pros. wit., method of ... 1109; 1143; 1269; 1271; 1307; 1353; 1366; 1375; 1378-79; 1470-71; 1649; 2482; 2546; 2812; 3104; 3138; 3143; 3379; 3385; 4065; 4134; 4324; 4330; 4445; 7519; 11293-94; 12279; 12771; 14398-99; 14879; 15457-58; 15461; 15860; 15862; 15869
         Re-direct ex. of def. wit., method of ... 22757; 22967; 23140; 23257; 30137; 33799; 33808; 34621; 35140; 36829

   Overruled, USSR pros. objections to def.:
      Affidavit:
         Presentation of part of ... 36843; 37116; 37129
         Rebuttal, for, presentation of ... 38849; 38853; 38856
      Document, presentation of ... 36887
      Witnesses, interrogation of USSR pros. wit. for rebuttal, method of ... 38444-46; 38449; 38464; 38472; 38496

Procedure, rules of:
   Affidavit, service of, exemption from compliance with ... 1860-61
   Interrogation ... 3205
   Modification of ... 806-07
   Rebuttal ... 19372; 34317; 37205; 37330-31
   Rule 6 b (1):
      Amendment of ... 1291-1303
      Exemption from compliance with ... 1846-47; 1869-71
   Summation ... 38590-92; 38743-44
   Surrebuttal ... 38589-90; 38596
   Witness, answer of, to strike out ... 865; 1229; 1231-32

Probative value:
   Cross-ex., admissibility of ... 1954; 4013
   Document of ... 1406; 3605; 20810; 20812-14; 21343-44; 22505-08; 22928-30; 23027-28; 24243-49

Prosecution *(See also:* President of Tribunal, Rebukes and warnings; President of Tribunal, Statements):
   Document, certificate of, should be supplied by ... 6897-908
   Objection of, not to be heard twice ... 3832-33

INDEX TO MILITARY TRIBUNAL PROCEEDINGS 85

Opening statement (*See:* Tribunal Ruling,
 Opening Statement)
 Rules of cross-ex., pros. may alter ... 3820
 Translation question, right to refer directly
  to language section ... 31231; 32551

Pu Y'i:
 Custody of, in Tokyo for further ex. ... 4351-53
 Handwriting of ... 15553
 Note by, inspection of ... 4225-49

Rebuttal:
 Document, presentation of ... 34317
 Evidence, nature of ... 19372; 37205;
  37330-31; 38222
 Prosecution doc., order of list for ... 37895-96

Recesses:
 Defense ... 13892-93; 13924; 16998; 19045-46;
  23968-69; 38443; 38745 (*See also:*
  Applications and Motions, Defense)
 IBM difficulty ... 2204
 Independence day ... 1622
 Power, restoration of ... 1836; 3583

Shidehara, speech:
 Rebuttal, not admissible for ... 38222
 USSR application and motion re ... 38217

Shimada (Defendant):
 Recalling of ... 37024
 Togo (Defendant) test., permitted to take
  stand again for ... 36964

Shiratori (Defendant), book by ... 6406

Siberian Intervention evidence, admissibility
 of ... 38211-13; 38215-22

Summation:
 Araki (Defendant), suspension of ... 45714-16
 Evidence in, limitation of ... 43222-23; 43228;
  43263; 43282; 43813; 44799; 44820; 45182;
  45253; 45473; 45564; 45670-71; 45711-13;
  46040-42; 46049
 Procedure ... 38590-92; 38743-44

Surrebuttal, evidence in ... 38589-90; 38596

Telegrams and other communications ... 6093

Testimony (*See also:* Tribunal Ruling, Cross-
  examination; Tribunal Ruling, Interrogation; Tribunal Ruling, Witness):
 Admissibility of, by aff. ... 10067; 10088-89;
  10620-21
 Admissibility of hearsay ... 1954

Translation ... 1066; 1073-74; 1174; 2303-04;
 3573; 4257; 7765-66; 10474-75; 31231;
 32551; 36052-53

Tribunal:
 Gen. Cramer, eligibility to participate ... 2361

Sir William F. Webb, eligibility to
 participate ... 98

Upheld, def. objections to pros.:
 Affidavit, Murakami, by, presentation of
  ... 7574-75
 Documents:
  Presentation of ... 6821; 7622; 7925; 13611;
   16175; 33202; 33473; 33504; 34242; 34317;
   34786; 36881; 36917
  Presentation of, in rebuttal ... 37272; 37305;
   37319; 37327-28; 37337; 37345; 37370;
   37378; 37382; 37401; 37411; 37415; 37426;
   37428; 37436; 37438; 37441; 37573; 37585;
   37591; 37594-96; 37639; 37644; 37658;
   37670; 37676-77; 37679; 37705; 37714;
   37735-36; 37745; 37759-60; 37762; 37764;
   37776; 37838; 37844; 37851; 37853; 37855;
   37860-61; 37878; 37969; 37988; 38077;
   38080; 38090; 38092
 Evidence:
  Cumulative, presentation of ... 9531
  Nomonhan maps, authenticity of ... 22636
  Panay Incident, presentation of ... 9481
 Leading question ... 3968
 Nomonhan maps, authenticity of ... 22638
 Witnesses:
  Interrogation of def. wit., method of ...
   17957; 17961; 17977; 17987; 18018-19;
   18500; 18866; 19820; 20541; 20664; 21316;
   21578; 21717; 22025; 22034; 22064; 22225;
   22777; 22965; 23212; 23529; 24081-82;
   24087; 24089; 25289; 27196; 27267; 27712;
   28343; 28367; 28612; 28623; 28900; 28955;
   31351; 31434; 32411; 33186; 33199; 33330;
   33374; 33493; 33517; 33520; 34101; 34216;
   34597; 34600; 34703; 34705; 34741; 34749;
   34764-66; 34768-69; 36536; 36572; 36804;
   36873; 36877; 36882; 36952-53
  Interrogation of pros. wit., method of ...
   3231; 3986; 7770; 10733; 10871; 11445;
   12649; 12682; 12751-52; 12771
  Note, use of ... 3965
  Re-direct ex. of pros. wit., method of ...
   31921; 31923; 31925; 31927; 32150;
   32194-95; 32197
  Re-direct ex. of pros. wit. in rebuttal ...
   37501

Upheld, def. objections to USSR pros.:
 Affidavit, presentation of part of ... 7622; 8164
 Documents:
  Excerpts from, without presentation of
   original ... 7748-49
  Presentation of ... 36881; 36917
  Presentation of, in rebuttal ... 38200; 38206;
   38211; 38213; 38243; 38258; 38262; 38265-
   66; 38269; 38409; 38412; 38511; 38521;
   38525-26
 Evidence, map of Nomonhan, authenticity of
  ... 38358
 Extra-comment ... 7650; 8136
 Witness, interrogation of USSR wit. in rebuttal,
  method of ... 38431; 38434

Tribunal Ruling *(Cont.)*

Upheld, pros. objections to def.:
  Affidavits:
    Presentation of ... 21748; 22090; 22441; 22555; 24269-70; 25249; 25418; 26465; 26550; 27894; 27950; 28052; 28478; 28481; 28483; 28520; 28544; 28562; 28564; 29237-39; 29376; 29405; 29676; 30140; 30143; 30543; 30546; 31662; 32978; 33059; 33069; 34549; 37002-03; 37005; 37008; 37011
    Presentation of part of ... 21158-59; 21561; 21697; 21764; 22715; 24392; 25269; 25907; 26510; 26553; 26614; 26780; 26870; 27103; 27132; 27251; 27271-72; 27619; 27763; 28019; 28075; 28536; 28556; 28675; 28866; 28869; 29037; 29138; 29232; 29258; 29425-26; 29480; 29658; 29682; 29901; 30004; 30024; 30054; 30076; 30100; 30149; 30215; 30568; 30575; 30583; 31631; 31654; 31746; 31750; 32482; 32488; 32501; 32546; 32620; 32873; 32891-92; 33304; 34399; 34401-02; 34833; 34952; 34954; 34994; 35181; 35376; 35460; 35590; 36851; 36892; 36934; 36993; 37016
    Surrebuttal, for, presentation of ... 38777; 38835; 38846; 38866; 38868
  Documents:
    Authenticity of ... 21806; 24803; 24809; 24814; 24824; 24826-27; 24837; 28591
    Presentation of ... 17280; 17302; 17453; 17455; 17460; 17463-64; 17689; 17691; 17902; 18024; 18028; 18173; 18385; 18387; 18414; 18418; 18419; 18422; 18424-25; 18428; 18430-31; 18433-34; 18437; 18587-88; 18593-95; 18598; 18628; 18765; 18790; 18793; 18795; 19138; 19615; 19620; 19694-95; 19700; 19716; 19722; 19727; 20217; 20219; 20266-67; 20457-58; 20510; 20514; 20516; 20550; 20592; 20607-08; 20796-98; 20802; 20807; 20809-10; 20816; 20825; 20826-27; 20860-61; 20866-67; 20872; 20882-84; 20886-87; 20940; 20961; 20963; 21012-14; 21016-20; 21022; 21037-38; 21046; 21048-51; 21054-55; 21057; 21065; 21068-69; 21085-91; 21093-95; 21098-101; 21103; 21107; 21109; 21115; 21117; 21118-20; 21122-24; 21126-29; 21131-33; 21139; 21141-42; 21144; 21342; 21349; 21362; 21370; 21378; 21388-89; 21393; 21395-96; 31403-05; 21409; 21418; 21420-23; 21427; 21429; 21432-34; 21494; 21496; 21545-47; 21806; 21813-16; 21819; 21822; 22377; 22379; 22381-82; 22457; 22461; 22463; 22477; 22498-99; 22504; 22511; 22535-36; 22538; 22557; 22839; 22848; 22850; 22865; 23182; 23188; 23647; 23649-50; 23732; 23734; 23736-37; 23739; 23741; 23744; 23746-47; 23752; 23754; 23756-59; 23761; 23763; 23781; 23954; 24221; 24223; 24226; 24271-74; 24311; 24575; 24600; 24657; 24671-72; 24675; 24678; 24680; 24687; 24690; 24736; 24803; 24809; 24814; 24824; 24826; 24944; 25089-90; 25108; 25117; 25119-22; 25126; 25128; 25130; 25132; 25134; 25136-40; 25145-47; 25149; 25151; 25163; 25170; 25197; 25219; 25221; 25224-25; 25232-33; 25235; 25240-41; 25250; 25301; 25330-32; 25351; 25367; 25390; 25401-02; 25438-39; 25457-61; 25465; 25467-68; 25473; 25475-78; 25480-93; 25500-05; 25509; 25514; 25516; 25520-21; 25524-30; 25535; 25555; 25559; 25570; 25572-73; 25575; 25578; 25581-82; 25588-89; 25591-601; 25603; 25606; 25614; 25627-30; 25632; 25634-37; 25641-44; 25646; 26359; 26361; 26382; 26385; 26432; 26451-52; 26606-07; 26780; 26964; 27082; 27845-46; 27961; 28026; 28045; 28047-49; 28243; 28250; 28253; 28416; 28422-23; 28426; 28431; 28445; 28472; 28474-75; 28513-16; 28521-22; 28539-40; 28551-52; 28571; 28575-76; 28579; 28588-89; 29380; 29386; 29447; 29465; 29468; 29472-73; 29568-69; 29606; 29609; 29620; 29638; 29643; 29655-56; 29666; 29895; 29897; 29933; 29948; 29962; 30048-50; 30057-58; 30060-61; 30073-74; 30146; 30544; 32550; 32703; 32772; 32838; 32857; 32918; 33958; 34033; 34336; 34350; 34540; 34858; 34868; 34870; 34872; 34881; 34883; 34890; 34897-98; 34996; 35137; 37018-19
    Certificate of ... 21961; 21965; 21967-68; 23014
    Service of ... 24334; 26609
    Surrebuttal, for, presentation of ... 38596; 38601-02; 38604; 38606; 38613-14; 38623; 38625; 38627; 38628-30; 38663-64; 38668; 38694; 38696; 38699; 38706; 38749-50; 38752; 38754; 38762
  Evidence:
    Harada-Saionji memoirs, presentation of ... 37573; 37585; 37591; 37594-96; 37639; 37644; 37658; 37670; 37676-77; 37705; 37714; 37735-36; 37745; 37759-60; 37762; 37764; 37838; 37844; 37851; 37853; 37855; 37860-61; 37878; 38637; 38663-64; 38668; 38694; 38696
  Harada-Saionji memoirs not accepted during pros. surrebuttal, presentation of ... 38637
  International law and ambassadorial immunity, facts of, presentation of ... 34355; 34358; 34362; 34364
  Interrogation of defendants:
    Interrogation of Matsuoka used in favor of other defendants ... 34350
  Matsuoka (Defendant), interrogation of, used in favor of other defendants ... 34350
  Opening statement, presentation of part of ... 20477; 20484
  Re-direct ex. of def. wit. ... 21580; 23140; 23848; 24147-48; 24659-60; 24662-63; 26906; 27226; 29564; 31799; 31823; 33803; 33806; 33810; 34621; 35152; 36117-18; 36119; 36832; 37159
  Witnesses:
    Answer of ... 24455-56; 26428

Interrogation of def. wit., method of ...
17736; 17800; 17861-62; 17877; 17882;
17926; 18017; 18068; 18078; 18084; 18302;
18316; 18334; 18339; 18533; 18558; 18605;
18609; 18624; 18626-27; 18806-07; 18900;
18902; 18987; 19067; 19539-41; 22151;
24459; 24462; 24469; 24473; 24487-88;
26584; 26897; 27330; 27332; 27462; 28246;
28281-82; 28850; 29025; 29249; 29663;
29744; 29913; 29996-97; 30134; 31222;
31225; 31234; 33157; 33167; 33750-51;
34392; 34836-37; 34858; 34868; 34870;
34872; 34881; 34883; 34890; 34897-98;
34969-70; 34972; 35010; 35846; 36531

Interrogation of pros. wit., method of ...
3064-65; 3083; 3092; 3095-97; 3099-100;
3103; 3105; 3110; 3113; 3115-17; 3119;
3133; 3384; 3414; 3825; 3840; 3845; 3852;
4139; 4145; 4146; 4198; 4205; 4212; 4304;
4306-08; 4318; 4324; 4326; 4328; 4336;
4347; 4349; 4892; 4957; 4974; 7470; 8693-
94; 8733; 8829-30; 11521; 11623; 12248;
12257; 12271; 12312; 12322; 12327-29;
12585; 12663; 14406-08; 14411; 14626;
14858-59; 14877-78; 14946-47; 15449

Upheld, USSR pros. objections to def.:
Affidavits, presentation of part of ... 36851;
36892; 36934
Documents:
Presentation of ... 36887
Rebuttal, for, presentation of ... 38891
Witnesses, interrogation of USSR pros. wit.
for rebuttal, method of ... 38451; 38453;
38465; 38468-69; 38477-79; 38485

Witnesses:
Affidavit, def. wit. test. must be in form of
... 21058-64
Answers of ... 2589; 2661; 4198; 14314; 15550;
31357-58; 36052-53
Behavior of ... 912; 2086; 2096; 2425; 2431;
2441; 3080; 3386; 4069; 4085; 4198; 4244;
4250; 4268; 4296; 4372-73; 4423; 11401;
15269
Calling of ... 1774-75; 2801; 4372-73; 4423;
7578; 27926-28; 28090
Evidence of, on commission ... 1726-28
Exclusion of, from courtroom ... 806-07
Hostile ... 20048-49
Interrogation of ... 883-85; 1593; 2484; 2640;
2657; 3871; 3878; 3896; 3947; 3952-54;
3965; 4074-75; 4149-50; 4185; 4263;
4623; 27654
Language of ... 15306
Qualification of ... 828; 830-32
Recalling of ... 1214; 8937; 14284; 26184; 34329
Subpoena of ... 1774

Tripartite Pact (See: Collaboration among
Germany, Italy and Japan)

"Tripartite Pact and the USA," Oshima (Defendant),
article by ... 34180-89

"The Tripartite Pact and the World of Tomorrow,"
Shiratori (Defendant), article by ...
5877-78; 6406-11

U

United Nations War Crimes Commission, Statement Prepared by ... 4608-09

US:

Aggression against (Pros. ... 9263-11628; Def.
... 24763-27116; 36964-78; Pros. summation ... 39519-735; Def. summation
... 43050-175) (See also: Preparation
for War)

Atrocities (See: Atrocities)

Ballantine, testimony by, 1931-41 relations
... 10712-61

Bataan Death March (See: Bataan Death March)

Captured air crews, Japanese treatment (See:
POW, Prisoners of war and civilian
internees)

Combined Fleet top secret operational order,
Japanese ... 11193-98; 11202; 11228-33
(See also: US, Pearl Harbor attack)

Doolittle fliers, disposition of (See: POW,
Prisoners of war and civilian internees)

Espionage, consular at Hawaii ... 11203-25;
11296-97 (See also: US, Pearl Harbor
attack), Togo (Defendant), test. ...
35938-41

Foreign policy (See also: US, US-Japanese
negotiations):
China:
Aid to ... 25308-10
Air craft, program for ... 25536-40
China Incident, during ... 9429-37; 9440-50;
9470-72; 9474-80; 9490-95; 9565-67;
9572-9601; 9614; 9628-29; 9635-42;
9707-11; 9717-18; 9723; 9767-70; 10068-
83; 10090-108; 10111-28
China Incident, prior to ... 9389-9428;
10068-128
FIC ... 6957-62; 6964-68; 9771-80; 9797; 10047-
50; 10235-40; 10402-09; 10418-19; 25753-
55; 25808; 36249-51; 36375-76
Germany and Italy ... 34238
Manchuria and Manchurian Incident ... 9340-
53; 9356-88; 9406-11; 9413-15; 9418-20;
9481-82; 10068-83; 10090-108; 10111-37
The Netherlands ... 9667-68; 10047-50; 10402-
06; 10418-19
Open Door policy ... 5209-22; 5233-46; 9867

US *(Cont.)*
  Foreign policy *(Cont.)*
    Pacific Ocean areas ... 9438-40; 9601-03; 9851-61; 9891-9903; 9906-07; 9937-46; 9951-53; 9974-78; 9982-83; 9988-95; 10005-19; 10047; 10235-40; 10402-06; 10418-19; 11702-13; 14189
      Warnings to ... 25620-21
    Philippine Islands ... 9851-61; 9937-46; 9951-53; 9979; 9988-95; 10005-19
      Defense of ... 25319-21
      Warnings to ... 25624-25
    Thailand *(See also:* US, Foreign policy, Pacific Ocean areas) ... 10418-19; aff. and test. ... 36249-51; 36375-76

  Grew, aff. ... 10090-108

  Hostilities, opening of *(See also:* US, US-Japanese negotiations) ... 10544-48; 10552-55; 10567-608; 10627-32; 10635-72; 10678-79; 10706-09

  Hull *(See also:* US, US-Japanese negotiations) aff. ... 10090-108

  Internal policies *(See also:* US, US-Japanese negotiations):
    Economic pressure on Japan ... 25308-10; 25312-13; 25319-21
      Commercial negotiations, rupture of ... 36250-51; 36338-44
      Discussion of ... 25360-66
      Embargo ... 25154-59; 25261-62
      Executive order *(See:* US, Roosevelt, Pres.)
      Freezing Japanese assets ... 25321-23; 25326-27; 33011-12
      Hull-Grew tel. 25168-69
      Japan, reaction to ... 25323-26
      Konoye request to President Roosevelt, Sept. 1940 ... 25368-73; 25376-88
      Muto (Defendant) ... 33011-12
      Shimada (Defendant), aff. and test. ... 25091-101
      Tojo (Defendant), aff. and test. ... 36248-51; 36272-73; 36277-78; 36319-20; 36338-40
    Lend Lease Act ... 25495-500
    National defense expenditures ... 25469-72; 25493
    National emergency, Hull, speech by ... 25560-61
    Neutrality Pact ... 25395-96
    Panama Canal closure ... 25303-05
    Pressure on Japan, effect ... 25585-87 *(See also:* US, US-Japanese negotiations)
    Shipping curtailment ... 25579
    War production controls, study of ... 25091-101
    World economy ... 24995-97

  Marshall, Gen., aff. by, Japan, neutral attitude toward USSR ships ... 46778-79

  Military preparation, Allied:
    Army strength prior to war ... 25435-37; 25441-44
    Military encirclement, ABD, Tojo (Defendant), aff. ... 36246-48; 36262-63; 36273-77; 36338-44; 36723-28
    Navy estimate of Japanese reaction to oil embargo ... 25336-50
    Pacific stronghold, strengthening of, June 1939 ... 25451-53
    Philippine Islands, defense of ... 25319-21; 25624-25
    Photographing Japanese Mandated Islands prior to war ... 25608-09
    Southeast Pacific ... 25408-12

  "Papers Relating to Foreign Relations of the United States-Japan 1931-1941" ... 5209-46; 9340-53; 9356-9411; 9413-43; 9456-60; 9463-64; 9470-72; 9474-83; 9490-95; 9497-99; 9501; 9503-04; 9534-41; 9554-71; 9590-9601; 9606-12; 9614-16; 9626-29; 9658-63; 9667-70; 9707-11; 9717-23; 9767-68; 9843-48; 9851-61; 9863-68; 9890-9909; 9914-17; 9934-78; 9982-83; 9988-97; 10005-19; 10037; 10040-42; 10047-50; 10766-74; 10782-94; 10825-29; 10831-44; 11679-80; 11702-07; 24209-15; 24328-31; 24335-39; 24717-21
    Pearl Harbor attack ... 10188-95; 10211-12; 10315; 10317; 10348-50; 10421; 10423; 10425; 10461-65; 10480-91; 10493-515; 10534-37; 10541-43; 10552-55; 10627-32; 11176-302; 26705-69
    German surprise at:
      Nuremberg, test. ... 24749-51
      Oshima (Defendant), test. ... 34351-54
    Kido (Defendant), knowledge of, aff. ... 35793-94
    Oka (Defendant), test. ... 33500-01
    Oshima (Defendant), aff. and test. ... 34035-36; 34351-54
    Shimada (Defendant), aff. and test. ... 10423-24; 34626-28; 34662-64; 34673-74; 34697-734; 34749-56; 34801-08; 34818; 34820 *(See also:* 10194; 10423-24; 10690; 31046)
    Shiratori (Defendant), test. ... 34827-28
    Suzuki (Defendant), aff. and test. ... 35226; 35312-18
    Togo (Defendant), aff. and test. ... 35700-03; 35729-35; 35911-12; 35939-49; 36077-100; 36134; 36140-41
    Tojo (Defendant), aff. and test. ... 36396-98; 36407-10; 36536-38; 36707; 36740-51; 36799-803; 36825 *(See also:* 10706-09; 26186-209; 27020)

  Preparation for war against *(See:* Preparation for War)

  POW *(See:* POW)

  Relations with Japan, 1931-40 ... 9275-80; 10712-46; 11029-35; 11052-84; 11092-114; 11127-49
    German, attitude toward ... 24721-29 *(See also:* Collaboration among Germany, Italy and Japan)

Hata (Defendant), avoiding war with US, aff.
and test. ... 29003-05; 29406-18
Hiranuma (Defendant), message to Pres.
Roosevelt, US reply to ... 29210-11;
29212-17
Hirota (Defendant), message to US, Hull
reply to ... 29469-70
Kido (Defendant), aff. ... 30897-917
Matsuoka, effort to improve ... 24717-21
(See also: 11686-87)
Shigemitsu (Defendant), peace feeler via
Sweden, aff. and test. ... 31076;
31114; 34531-34; 34559-64
Shimada (Defendant) ... 34604-25; 35469-78
Shiratori (Defendant), and ... 34872-74; 34878-
80 (See also: 6152-53; 6429-31)
Suzuki (Defendant), aff. ... 35190
Togo (Defendant) ... 10312; 10318-29; 10343-
48; 10381-88; 10399-406; 10418-20;
10442-43; 10450-51; 10524-41; 10544-48;
10552-55; 35349-50; 35413-14; 35487-90;
35665-736
Tojo (Defendant), aff. and test. ... 36185-86;
36632-34; 36648-55; 36688-94 (See
also: 31749-823)

Roosevelt, Pres.:
Konoye, proposal for interview with ...
10778; 25766-808
Message to Emperor ... 10825-29; 26166-206
Japan, reply to ... 25756-59; 32921-31
Kido (Defendant), aff. and test. ... 35598-
600; 35728-29; 35793-801; 35825-29;
35869-76; 35885-87; 35897-911; 36120-25
Togo (Defendant), aff. and test. ... 35727-31;
35792-99; 35828-29; 35869-73; 36120-25
Tojo (Defendant), aff. and test. ... 35728;
35825-29; 35879-81; 35889-901;
35910-11; 36410-11
Nomura, interview with ... 25750-52
Proclamation ... 25191-94; 25219-20; 25222-
23; 25227-30; 25240-41; 25251-55; 25258-
61; 25263; 25321-23; 25328
Speech, May 27, 1941, US position and right
of self-defense ... 25723-24
War, declaration of, receipt ... 26254-56

Stimson, aff. by ... 10068-83

Submarine warfare (See: Submarine warfare)

US-Japanese negotiations:
China, Japan, withdrawal from:
Hata (Defendant), aff. and test. ... 29003-18
Kido (Defendant), conversation with
Suzuki (Defendant) ... 35205-13; 35251-
54; 35304-06; 35311-13; 35325-32
Togo (Defendant), aff. and test. ... 35685-
89; 35699-700; 35999-36001
Collaboration with Great Britain and the
Netherlands against Japan ... 25532-34;
25547-50; 25565-68; 32644; 34678-82;
35690-92
First phase (January-June, 1941) ... 9268-
9326; 9643-46; 9652-57; 9667-70; 9797-800;
9804-06; 9833-34; 9841; 9843-48; 9851-
61; 9863-68; 9873-74; 9884-93; 9904-78;
9982-83; 9988-97; 10001-03; 10005-19;
10026-28; 10040-42; 10047-50; 10130-37;
25673-75; 25677-724
FIC (See also: US, Foreign policy):
Japan, advance into ... 7058; 7079; 25734-39;
25808-10; 25753-55
Japan, policy toward ... 11753
(See also: 6566)
Hoshino (Defendant), test. ... 33157-58
Hostilities, notification of opening of:
Imperial Conference, aff. ... 36371-83;
36721-28; 36744-50; 36779-803 (See
also: 26074; 26702) (See also: Japan,
Conferences)
Liaison Conference, aff. ... 36389-93 (See
also: 26186-209) (See also: Japan,
Conferences)
Shimada (Defendant), aff. and test. ... 35693-
94; 35714-17; 35830-60; 36116-19; 37025-46
Togo (Defendant), aff. and test. ... 35714-17;
35721-27; 35731-32; 35834-62; 36042-47;
36100-05; 36131-33; 36141-43; 37025-46
Tojo (Defendant), aff. and test. ... 36371-83;
36389-93; 36721-28; 36744-50; 36799-
803 (See also: 26186-206)
Hull, note, Nov. 26, 1941:
Kido (Defendant), aff. and test. ... 30934-36;
35707-08; 35819-25
Liaison Conference, Nov. 27, 1941 ...
36357-59; 36389 (See also: Japan,
Conferences)
Shimada (Defendant), aff. ... 35707; 35830-34
Togo (Defendant), aff. and test. ... 35703-08;
35710-11; 35719-21; 35802-07; 35818-25;
35830-34; 36077-97; 36108-09; 36127-28;
36135-38
Tojo (Defendant), aff. and test. ... 36355-59;
36389; 36781-97 (See also: 10815)
Hull, reaction to Japanese proposal to US
... 25765-66
Hull, remarks to Nomura ... 10848-49
Imperial Conference (See also: Japan,
Conferences):
Sept. 6, 1941 ... 25810-11
Dec. 1, 1941 ... 26072-93
Resolution ... 6567-69
Kaya (Defendant), aff. and test. ... 30704-06;
36047-57
Kido (Defendant), test. ... 30917-47; 31055-71;
31145-81; 31362-73; 31583-88; 31595-
96; 31604-11; 33162-68; 33344-50; 34600-
02; 34690-92; 34792-94
Koiso (Defendant), aff. ... 32248-50
Konoye:
Cabinet (3rd) ... 25743-49
Cabinet, fall of ... 24858-73 (See also:
36316-98; 36505-09; 36694-707; 36721-
28; 36737-40; 36744-50)
Proposal, interview with Roosevelt ...
10778; 25766-808 (See also: US,
Roosevelt, Pres.)
Kurusu, reason for mission to US ... 25957-58

US (Cont.)
  US-Japanese negotiations (Cont.)
    Last phase (July-December, 1941) ... 10145-48; 10162-68; 10176-78; 10202-03; 10224-27; 10235-40; 10251-79; 10282-88; 10309; 10312-13; 10316; 10318-29; 10343-46; 10351-54; 10356-61; 10376-79; 10383-86; 10389-90; 10399-409; 10411-14; 10418-21; 10429-37; 10442-45; 10450-54; 10468-72; 10475-78; 10482-91; 10493-517; 10523-29; 10532-37; 10541-48; 10552-55; 10567-608; 10627-32; 10635-72; 10690-700; 10761-849; 10887-994; 11008-29; 11035-52; 11085-91; 11115-25; 11149-64; 25724-33; 25740-41; 25743-873; 25907-26115; 26167-74; 26180-81; 26186-204; 26209-15; 26229-32; 26244-56; 26258-67; 26275-84; 26296-99; 26326; 26331; 26350-57; 26361-80
    Matsui (Defendant), test. ... 33910-17
    Muto (Defendant), aff. and test. ... 32933-35; 32979-90; 32992-33049; 33052-56; 33101-08; 33124-26; 33151-58; 33161-72; 33174-79; 33194-98; 33206; 33677-84; (See also: 15867-69; 15871; 33050-51)
  Neutrality Pact ... 25395-96
  Nomura:
    Kurusu, request for ... 25952-55
    Roosevelt, interviews with ... 25750-52
    (See also: US, Roosevelt, Pres.)
  Oka (Defendant), aff. and test. ... 33291-93; 33297-302; 33319-35; 33341-55; 33364-74; 33377-78; 33387-410; 33430-47; 33487-500; 33526-27
  Oshima (Defendant), aff. and test. ... 34027-42; 34231-47; 34284 (See also: 6638-50; 6654-56; 9918-34)
  Proposal A ... 25974-85
  Proposal B ... 26041-42
  Proposal, Japan, to US ... 25760-64
  Roosevelt, President (See: US, Roosevelt, Pres.)
  Shigemitsu (Defendant) ... 16253; 34528-34
  Shimada (Defendant) ... 33155-57; 33333-34; 33346-50; 33398-99; 34450-51; 34575-602; 34604-25; 34656-62; 34664-67; 34673-74; 34704-24; 34749-70; 34791-92; 34801-08; 34812-13; 37025-46; (See also: 10811)
  Shiratori (Defendant) ... 34886-89; 34961-62 (See also: 6662-65)
  Suzuki (Defendant), aff. and test. ... 35199-213; 35223-26; 35242-46; 35229-318; 35315-30 (See also: 16232; 16253)
  Togo (Defendant) ... 16197-98; 33323-24; 33401-02; 33430-47; 33526-27; 34575-602; aff. and test. ... 35524-31; 35542-44; 35546-47; 35550-53; 35559-67; 35569-70; 35666-67; 35670-72; 35674-737; 35792-807; 35818-949; 35978-88; 36001-12; 36026-27; 36042-109; 36116-28; 36131-33; 36135-38; 37025-40; 37164-68
  Tojo (Defendant):
    Formation of cabinet, aff. and test. ... 25874½-26164; 26285-347; 31583-96; 35215-20; 35224-25; 36814-15 (See also: 10452; 10815; 15986; 26186-209; 26702; 26825-27)
    Konoye cabinet (2nd) as War Minister, aff. and test. ... 36218-31
    Konoye cabinet (3rd) as War Minister, aff. and test. ... 36316-98; 36505-09; 36694-707; 36721-28; 36737-40; 36744-50
    Speech by, Nov. 30, 1941 ... 26375-78
    Tripartite Pact and ... 25820-22 (See also: Collaboration among Germany, Italy and Japan)
  Ultimatum, Japan, Nov. 20, US reply to ... 26361-73; 26378-80
  War, declaration of ... 10686-88 (See also: US, US-Japanese relations, Hostilities, notification of opening of):
    Distribution of decoded message ... 26252-53
    Emperor, advice to Tojo (Defendant), to deliver prior to attack, Tojo (Defendant), interrogation ... 10480-81
    Muto (Defendant), role in drafting ... 16124-28
    Oka (Defendant), aff. and test. ... 35561-67; 35569-70; 35721-23
    Recipients of message of ... 26238-51
    Suzuki (Defendant), aff. and test. ... 35246; 35312-18 (See also: 10685)
    Text of ... 10482-86 (See also: 10686-88)
    Time decoded ... 26231-32
    Togo (Defendant), interrogation ... 10505-12
    Tojo (Defendant), interrogation ... 10482-91; 10493-504
  War, termination of:
    Imperial Conference ... 35783 (See also: Japan, Conferences)
    Shigemitsu (Defendant), test. ... 35601-02 (See also: 34559-64)
    Supreme War Council ... 35783-88 (See also: Japan, Conferences)
    Togo (Defendant), aff. and test. ... 35545-46; 35591-97; 35603-10; 35776-90; 35801-16; 36110-12
    Tojo (Defendant), aff. ... 35807-16
    Umezu (Defendant), aff. ... 35778; 35782; 36937-39
  Yamamoto plan ... 10188-90; 10194-95 (See also: US, Pearl Harbor attack)

USSR:
  Aggression against (Pros. ... 7213-8182; 31824-32199; 38197-575; Def. 22400-24166; 24667-762; 28062-84; 37103-63; Pros. summation ... 39763-76; Def. summation ... 42697-850) (See also: Preparation for War; Collaboration among Germany, Italy and Japan; Prosecution, USSR)
  Araki (Defendant):
    Cabinet meeting (1932) ... 15843-45
    Manchurian Incident and USSR, speech by ... 31824-37; 31911-17
    USSR, attack on, five year plan ... 37614-17

Border incidents:
  Agreements and protocols:
    Japanese proposal, renewal of, to USSR
      for border demarcation ... 23008-09
    Manchuria-Mongolia Boundary Protocol
      (Togo-Molotov Agreement) ... 23151-52
    Sino-Japanese, Basic, Treaty of 1924
      ... 22975-76
    Sino-Mongolian border:
      Aff. and test. ... 22978-23005
      Japanese policy ... 23008; 23085-86
    Sino-Russian Border Treaty ... 22698-22700
  Burning of embassy documents, Moscow, aff.
    and test. ... 22759-800; 22844-46
  Changkufeng Incident (Lake Khasan) ... 7751;
    7753-57; 7760-63; 7767-7818; 7825-27;
    17079-80; 22417-19; 22804-19; 22824-
    36; 22839-40; 22852-62; 22868-70;
    22875-76; 22878; 22903-10; 22913-17;
    22922-27; 22931-42; 37755-58; 38284-340
    Aff. and test. ... 4202-05; 7767-7806; 7808-
      13; 7816-17; 22579-89; 22713-58; 22879-
      902; 22943-68; 23859-72; 23884-904;
      30303-04; 30331-32; 30471-77; 32232-33;
      32395-400; 32439-41; 32511-12; 34508-09
    Burning of doc., aff. and test. ... 22759-800
    Cabinet meeting ... 30854-55
    Maps of, test. ... 7840-43; 22724-28; 22732-
      41; 22943-68; 32086; 32088; 32152
    Report concerning ... 7571
  Hailar Sappa, map of ... 28062
  Nomonhan Incident (Lake Khalkin Gol) ...
    7829; 7846-49; 7851; 17079-80; 22419-21
    Aff. and test. ... 7854-56; 22575-78; 22594-
      66; 23010-22; 23025-83; 23087-114;
      30477-79; 31885-87; 32233; 33091-92;
      35637-38; 38359-93; 38527-75
    Maps of ... 7840-43; 22614; 22617; 22623;
      23073; 23690; 23694-95; 23697-98; 23702;
      23718; 23842; 23844; 23848; 28063; test.
      ... 22616-38; 22661-66; 23114-41; 23662-
      722; 23829-56; 38344-48; 38352
    Togo-Molotov Agreement, attached to,
      test. ... 23114-41
    USSR, maps, authenticity of:
      Def. objections to ... 38342-44; 38350-
        52; 38354-56; 38358
      Pros. statements concerning ...
        38343-44; 38349-54
      Tribunal rulings ... 38344; 38352;
        38358
      Tribunal statements concerning ...
        38348-49; 38351; 38354; 38356-57
  Truce negotiations:
    Text of settlement ... 7851
    Togo-Molotov Agreement, Togo, letter
      certifying ... 23147
    Togo-Molotov negotiation ... 35377-78
    Truce agreement ... 23141-43
  Non-availability of documents, certificates:
    Non-availability of doc. ... 23184-85;
      23351; 23543
    Provenance of ex. 2713 ... 28063
    Status of affiant not produced for def.
      cross-ex. ... 23154-65

Chinese Eastern Railway:
  Sale of:
    Admissibility of evidence, tribunal
      ruling ... 29441-45
    Affidavit and test. ... 29319-33; 29387-90;
      35417-23; 35485-86; 35490; 35630-33;
      35949-69; 35973-75; 36129-30; 36139-40
    Agreement, signing of ... 29616-19
    Hirota-Litvinov message ... 29614-15
    Negotiation ... 29474; 29614-19
    Togo-Molotov negotiation, settlement of
      payment of, aff. ... 35378-80
    Subversive activities vs. ... 38250-54 (See
      also: 29427; 29429; 35418; 35484; 35967)
  Trouble in:
    Karakhan-Ota statement ... 35961
    Litvinov-Ota statement ... 35963

Collaboration (See: Collaboration among
  Germany, Italy and Japan)

Communism, menace of, in China ... 22432;
  22470-73

Dohihara (Defendant) (See also: Manchuria):
  Mukden Army Special Service Organ and,
    aff. and test. ... 28602-26
  Nomonhan Incident and, aff. ... 28710-21

General Staff:
  Attitude toward USSR ... 23298
  Operational plans against USSR, aff. and
    test. ... 23302-89
  Proposals by, Russian-Japanese fishing
    problems ... 7457-58
  Soviet F. E. troops strength, estimate by
    ... 23549-53

Germany (See: Collaboration among Germany,
  Italy and Japan)

Hirota (Defendant):
  Chinese Eastern Railway, sale of ... 29387-90;
    29419-33; 29436-40; 29474; 29614-19
  Conversation with Harada (Maj. Gen.),
    Moscow, 1931 ... 7452-53
  Non-Aggression Pact with USSR, attitude
    toward ... 29381-84
  Relations with USSR, aff. ... 29387-90; 29419-
    33 (See also: 7241; 7246; 7254)

Hoshino (Defendant) (See also: Manchuria):
  Manchukuo govt., appointment of ... 29099-104
  Manchuria, industrialization of ... 29127-31;
    29137-60
  New economic structure ... 29164-65
  Non-Aggression Pact with USSR ... 29166-67
  Scientific Research Institute for Total War
    ... 29181
  Strategic bombing survey ... 29072-94

Hsuchow campaign ... 22579-86

Itagaki (Defendant) (See also: Manchuria,
  Kwantung Army):

USSR *(Cont.)*
  Itagaki (Defendant) *(Cont.)*
    Aggression against USSR, 1939, aff. ... 30877
    Changkufeng Incident ... 30303-04; 30331-32; 30471-77
    Mongolia, problem of ... 7830-34
    Nomonhan Incident ... 30315; 30477-79

  Japan *(See also:* Collaboration among Germany, Italy and Japan; Manchuria, Kwantung Army):
    Attack, possibility of, on Moscow ... 7347
    Attitude toward German-Russian war and neutrality ... 7417; 7937-40; 7956-59; 23290; 36254-65; 36807-08
    Attitude toward USSR ... 7878; 7937-40; 23181
    Maritime province, Japan, attack on, study concerning ... 7438-44
    Military bases, establishment of, against USSR ... 7587-94; 7544-62; 7565-66; aff. ... 7571; 7576; 7579-80; 7582-87
    Military preparation for war against USSR ... 7330; 7411-12; 7438-44; 7452-53; 7508-10; 7515-19; 7524; 7527-28; 7530-34; 7565-66; 7568-70; 7618-20; 7624-30; 7647-71; 7929; 7962; 8128-34; 8139-46; 8167-74; 8176-77; 23456-77; aff. and test. ... 7516-19; 7527-28; 8077-80; 8093-126; 23189; 23276-77; 23282; 23302
    Non-Aggression Pact with USSR, question of ... 7714-15; 7719-20; 7722-23; 7729; 22682-90
    Offer of mediation between Germany and USSR ... 7992
    Order of battle estimate, USSR and Japan ... 23428-55; 37103-07
    Peace proposal to US through USSR ... 31164-72
    Peace with USSR ... 24681-82
    Policy toward USSR ... 7326; 7419; 7452-53; 7884-87; 7911; 7960-62; 7975; 7989; test. ... 7459-99; 7618-38
    Proposed entry of, into war against USSR ... 8014-20
    Protest to Germany, Non-Aggression Pact with USSR ... 7911-12; 7915-16
    Relations with USSR after Tripartite Pact *(See also:* Collaboration among Germany, Italy and Japan) ... 6323-43; 6396-99; 6450-79; 7981-82; 8014-20; 23303-45; 23359-60; 24280; 24290-307; 24667-775
    Ships, USSR ... 8026-39; 8041-47; 8051-54; aff. ... 8049-50; 23492-545
    Siberian expedition ... 7309-10
    Soviet Far East, attempt to include GEACPS ... 7348-50; 7419-20; 7422-24
    Soviet-Japanese incident ... 3685-86
    USSR entry into war against, aff. ... 23564-611
    USSR, mediation, tel. ... 23590-611
    USSR, military strategy, aff. ... 23637-41
    USSR, ships, Hong Kong ... 27513-27
      (See also: 8041-47)
    USSR, Yalta Conference ... 23643-44
    White Russians, use of, aff. ... 7603-04

Kido (Defendant):
  Aggression against USSR, 1939, aff. ... 30877
    (See also: 7249)
  German-Russian Non-Aggression Pact, attitude toward ... 30882-84

Korea:
  Army operational plans against USSR, aff. ... 23287-89
  Military bases in, establishment of ... 7578-94
  Military, Japanese strength, 1931-45 ... 23555-56
  Military strength of ... 23651-59
  Order of battle, 1943-45, test. ... 23425-55

Kwantung Army:
  Army interpreters, education of, in Russian language ... 8081-82
  Attitude toward USSR, test. ... 31885-87
  Military preparation vs. USSR ... 8093-126; 8138-54; 8167-74
  Military strength of, 1945 ... 23651-59
  Organization of divisions of ... 7536-37
  Special Maneuver of, (Kantokuen) ... 7581-86; 7598-600; 7730; 8078-80; 8082-84; 23183-84; 23189-263; 23270-79; 23282-86; 23302-88; 23390-424; 31824-931; 31959-62; 37128-34
  Table of increase, military strength, 1932-45 ... 7531-35
  Table of increase, technical equipment, 1932-45 ... 7537-38
  White Russians, use of against USSR, test. ... 36575-60

Kyowakai ... 7596-616; 18798-881; 19968-71

Manchuria:
  Anti-Soviet activities of white guards in ... 7603-04; 7694-709
  Colonization policy in ... 7557-59
  Economic policies of, against USSR ... 37119-24
  Industry, war, aff. ... 37124-28
  Japanese military strength, 1931-45 ... 23555-56
  Military base ... 7501-02; 7544-62; 7565-66; 7571; 7576; 7579-80; 7582-87
  Military training in, aff. ... 7596-600
  Military service of troops in, extension of ... 7562-65
  Occupation of, war plan against USSR, aff. ... 7501-02
  Order of battle, 1943-45, test. ... 23425-55
  Protocol, Mongolia-Manchukuo boundary ... 23151-52
  Puppet troops in ... 7541-43
  South Manchurian Railway Co., role of, against USSR ... 7566-68
  Table of Soviet-Manchukuo border violations, 1932-45 ... 7744-45

Mongolia:
  Meteorological organs, establishment of ... 7561-62

INDEX TO MILITARY TRIBUNAL PROCEEDINGS

Military preparation against USSR, aff.
... 8087-90
Problem of ... 7830-34
Puppet troops in ... 7541-43
Sino-Mongolian border, aff. and test. ...
22978-23005; 23008; 23085-86

Muto (Defendant), Nomonhan Incident and, aff.
... 33091-92

Oshima (Defendant):
  Anti-Comintern Pact, interrogation ...
    7870-72; 7891-92
  Collaboration with Germany against USSR ...
    7879-82; 7884; 16925; 34828; 34831-44
  German-Russian Non-Aggression Pact, aff.
    and test. ... 34014-16; 34150-68; 34325
  Matsuoka, relations with, aff. and test. ...
    34023-25; 34170-73; 34216-22; 34231-
    47; 34284
  Relations with USSR, aff. ... 6026-28; 6562-
    65; 7994-98; 10031-36; 33764-67; 33770-
    72; 33991-97; 34026-27; 34216-22;
    34269-84; 34331

Otsu operational plan, 1935, aff. ... 23264-69

Scientific Research Institute for Total War, and
... 7575; 8816; 27066; 31996-32013;
32041-58

Semyonov, aff. ... 23484-92

Shigemitsu (Defendant):
  Changkufeng Incident ... 22826-36; 34508-09
  Litvinov, conversation with:
    Border violation ... 7760-63; 7818; 7825-27
    Changkufeng Incident ... 22826-36
  Relations with USSR, as Foreign Minister
    ... 34551-58

Shiratori (Defendant):
  Changkufeng Incident ... 22826-36; 23859-72;
    23884-904; 34508-09
  German-Russian Non-Aggression Pact ...
    34854-58; 34874-75 (See also: 6175-77)
  Litvinov, conversation with, concerning border
    violation ... 7760-63; 7818; 7825-27

Soviet Far East, strength of, estimate of ...
23549-53

Suzuki (Defendant):
  Attitude toward USSR, aff. ... 35188-90
  Non-Aggression Pact with USSR ... 16216;
    16232-33; 16253; 35231-32

Togo (Defendant):
  Chinese Eastern Railway, sale of, aff. and
    test. ... 35417-23; 35485-86; 35490;
    35630-33; 35949-69; 35973-75; 36129-
    30; 36139-40
  Manchukuo-Outer Mongolia boundaries,
    test. ... 35970-73

  Manchukuo-USSR boundaries, aff. ...
    35630-34; 35742
  Molotov, negotiations with ... 35374-84;
    Manchukuo-Outer Mongolia border
    map ... 35973
  Moscow, recall from ... 35385-87
  Non-Aggression Pact with USSR, aff. ... 35374-
    85; 35395-96; 35422-23; 35638-40
  Nomonhan Incident, aff. ... 35637-38
  USSR ships, restriction on, aff. ... 35743-44
  USSR, war with, refusal to participate in, aff.
    ... 35740-42; 35745-46

Tojo (Defendant):
  Fortified districts, USSR frontier, establish-
    ment of ... 7565-66
  German-Russian war, policies ... 36254-65;
    36807-08
  Manchurian military bases, establishment
    of ... 7560-61
  Meteorological organs, establishment of
    ... 7561-62
  Mongolia, Inner, special investigation
    ... 3675-86
  Non-Aggression Pact with USSR ... 36213-18;
    36261-62
  Scientific Research Institute for Total War
    and USSR ... 7575; 8816; 27066; 31996-
    32013; 32041-58
  South Manchurian Railway Co., role of,
    against USSR ... 7566-68

Treaties and Agreements:
  Manchurian-Mongolian Boundary Treaty
    ... 23151-52
  Russo-Japanese, Basic, Treaty of 1925
    ... 17347-54
  Secret, Russo-Japanese, Convention of 1925
    ... 17347-54; 17357-58
  Sino-Japanese, Basic, Treaty of 1924
    ... 22975-76
  Sino-Mongolian Border Treaty ... 22978-23005
  Sino-Russian, Basic, Border Treaty of 1860
    ... 22696-98
  Sino-Russian Border Treaty ... 22698-700

Tripartite Pact (See: Collaboration among
Germany, Italy and Japan)

Umezu (Defendant) (See: Manchuria, Kwantung
Army)

Witnesses (See also: Defense; Prosecution;
Tribunal Ruling):
  Production of, def. application concerning
    ... 6301-06; 7581; 7710; 8135; 8162; 9087-
    89; 10556; 10558-60; 10612; 10617-18;
    10633; 10677; 11338-39; 11731-34; 12042-
    43; 12053; 13850; 13857; 13863; 13865;
    14228; 32776-95; 38350; 38355-56
  Status of, presentation of, def. application
    concerning ... 7578; 7581-82; 7710;
    8091; 8135; 8162; 8173

USSR *(Cont.)*

    Wuchang-Hankow campaign ... 22589-94

    Yalta Agreement ... 23643-44

V

Versailles Treaty ... *(See:* Treaties and Agreements)

Vice Minister ... 578 *(See also:* Japan, Constitutional organization)

"Voice of Japanese Democracy," Ozaki by ... 576

W

Wanpaoshan Incident ... 4208-10

War *(See:* Aggressions; Preparation for War)

War Crimes *(See:* Tribunal, Law)

War Crimes, Japanese, in China ... 2268-70; 2697-2712; 4540-4580

War Minister *(See:* Japan, Constitutional organization)

War Ministry *(See:* Japan, Constitutional organization)

Wartime Changes in Government Administration ... 618-37 *(See also:* Japan, Constitutional organization)

Wartime Economic Council ... 623 *(See also:* Japan, Constitutional organization)

Wartime Imperial Headquarters ... 593-94 *(See also:* Japan, Constitutional organization)

Wartime Legislation ... 632-33 *(See also:* Japan, Legislation)

Washington Naval Treaty *(See:* Treaties and Agreements)

"The Way of Japan and the Japanese," Okawa, book by ... 15610-11

"The Way of a Subject," translation ... 1047-65

"The World War and New World," Shiratori (Defendant), article by ... 35128-31

Y

Yamamoto Plan ... 10188-90; 10194-95 *(See also:* Japan, Operational Plans; US, Pearl Harbor attack)

Yearly Budget of Japanese Government for the War and Navy Minister, doc. ... 8539-41

Yokohama Specie Bank ... 8201

Z

Zaibatsu ... 8393

    Kokusaku Kenkyu Kai and ... 7400-01

    Manchukuo, industrialization of ... 29130-31